Advance praise for *Crazy Little Thing*

"Each day science teaches us more and more about love and attraction. In highlighting some of the most unusual love stories around, Langley shows us brain chemistry and neuroscience in action, providing insight into why, how, and who we love."

—Sarah Forbes, curator of The Museum of Sex

"If you've ever uttered the words 'what the hell was she thinking,' read this book. Liberally spiced with Liz Langley's trademark humor and curiosity about the human condition, *Crazy Little Thing* is a tour de force of scientific info (this is your brain on love) and real-world examples of how our brains trick us into landing on the evening news, if not *The Jerry Springer Show*. Plus it's proof that truth is, indeed, stranger than fiction."

—Lara Dien, author of *Heat Index*

"Liz Langley balances along the tightrope between love and sex with considerable thoughtfulness, compassion, and wit. Applying the precision of a skillful surgeon, she probes the mysteries and myths of mating and marriage alike. But who knew that reading about the role of brain chemistry in romantic relationships would give me an intellectual hard-on?"

—Paul Krassner, author of *In Praise of Indecency*

"Like Mary Roach in *Bonk*, Langley takes you behind the scenes of the Lov~ ~~ ~~ ~~ ~~ ~y mad scientists mixing up bitter~~ ~~ ~~ ~~ ~~ ~t will leave you thirsting ~ morgue rats, *Crazy Little*

Thing takes you on a fascinating leaky loveboat adventure that will leave you feeling incredibly and refreshingly sane. Langley affectionately pulls no stops in her quest to uncover the bewitching reasons why love drives even the best of us batty. Buckle your life vest and join her in this madcap journey that will have you sipping dopamine tea with Romeo and Juliet at Heartbreak Hotel under the twinkling lights of the Eiffel Tower."

—Kendra Holliday,
writer and editor of The Beautiful Kind

"Like a hearty cabernet sauvignon, Liz Langley's writing is a pleasingly complex combination of earthy flavors accented by subtle notes of humor and piquant insights. Whether paired with meaty discourse or just desserts, her work is the perfect complement to both sweet and savory, and delivers a full-bodied 'mindfeel' that will leave readers with a long, rewarding finish."

—Judy Cole,
editor emeritus, *Playgirl* and *SexIs* magazines

"In the decade that Liz Langley has been writing for AlterNet, she's developed a cult following. Her work is smart, witty, and wild. She's piqued our curiosity, opened our hearts, and vigorously stirred the pot of ideas when it comes to love, relationships, and sexuality."

—Tara Lohan, senior editor, AlterNet

"*Crazy Little Thing* author Langley has applied the burgeoning field of neuroscience to romantic love. She has done it with cutting-edge science, insight, and—most importantly—a sense of humor. The science is backed up with real research studies, referenced in 14 pages of endnotes, but Langley describes it all with phrases like 'big new brain,' 'love is a pain-killer,' 'love drugs whizzing through our veins,' 'the cuddle hormone,' and 'Gandhi neurons.' The book is creative, very readable, comforting, and a standout in an e-detached world which is trying to replace human contact with electronic networking. It will not only make readers who are struggling with the symptoms of unrequited love feel more in control of their lives, it will also encourage everyone to take a new look at old-fashioned, in-person socializing."

—Anna Jedrziewski, *New Age Retailer*

"In *Crazy Little Thing,* Liz Langley takes one of our most complicated emotions, love, and explains it in a way that is factual, entertaining, and sometimes downright funny. We may never ultimately solve the puzzle of who we choose to love but now we understand how and why—and Liz reminds us that even though the low points make our stomach feel funny, the thrill of the roller coaster ride called love will keep us coming back for more."

—Deborah C. Beidel, PhD, ABPP,
author of *Abnormal Psychology*

"This book is simply irresistible! With wit like a machete, Liz Langley clears a path through the jungle of neurological research investigating why we fall in love and what happens to our brains when we do. Hilariously funny, Langley goes beyond neurologists to talk to lovers of all kinds, mingling science and unexpected sexual scenery. Insightful, compelling, beautifully written, filled with eye-opening facts and extraordinary people, Langley's *Crazy Little Thing* will make you appreciate the truth of Bryan Ferry's song 'Love is the Drug' in whole new ways."

—Lev Raphael, author of *Rosedale in Love*

"Liz Langley says she's written a book about crazy love (is there any other kind?) you can read on a flight across the country, and she's done it. A fun, freaky survey—with a dash of science, a soupçon of nuttiness, and best of all, Langley's charming voice that can make necrophilia sound like a prom date."

—Brian Alexander,
author of *America Unzipped: In Search of Sex and Satisfaction*

"When it comes to love and sex, everyone seems to be trying to find answers to the eternal questions. But in *Crazy Little Thing*, Liz Langley instead decides to question all of the answers, and it's a heck of a lot more satisfying. Let's face it, the 'He's just not that into you, you complete me' stuff is only making all things love and sex more confusing. So Langley skips the easy road and the clichés and gets to the heart of things. From incestual love and necrophilia to freaks and the divine, Langley dives in and goes straight to the source, not to finish the conversation, but to further it. She talks to the experts. She talks to the people who have been there. (As well as those who have done that...) And she talks to her readers like the intelligent knowledge seekers that we are, looking for a little help when it comes to better understanding this crazy little thing called love."

—Jenny Block,
author of *Open: Love, Sex, and Life in an Open Marriage*

"If Baudelaire and Tina Fey had a kid, they might give birth to Liz Langley. In *Crazy Little Thing*, she combines a journalist's eye and knack for pointing out naked emperors with prose packed with more zingers than an express lane at Walmart—the whole time with tongue planted firmly in cheek."

—Curtis X Meyer, poet, author, and essayist

CRAZY little THING

CRAZY little THING

WHY LOVE AND
SEX DRIVE US
MAD

BY LIZ LANGLEY

ViVa
EDITIONS

Published in the United States by Viva Editions,
an imprint of Cleis Press, Inc.,
2246 Sixth Street, Berkeley, California 94710.

Printed in the United States.
Cover design: Scott Idleman/Blink
Cover photograph: iStockphoto
Text design: Frank Wiedemann
First Edition.
10 9 8 7 6 5 4 3 2 1

Trade paper ISBN: 978-1-936740-03-1
E-book ISBN: 978-1-936740-08-6

Library of Congress Cataloging-in-Publication Data

Langley, Liz.
Crazy little thing : how love and sex drive us mad / by Liz Langley.
p. cm.
ISBN 978-1-936740-03-1 (pbk. : alk. paper)
1. Love. 2. Sex (Psychology) 3. Lust. 4. Man-woman relationships--
Psychological aspects. I. Title.
BF575.L8L267 2011
155.3'1--dc23
2011040197

To my friend Doug Rhodehamel
for putting up with (fill in the blank)…
and to anyone who has a broken heart right this minute.

Acknowledgments

Special thanks to Sam Singhaus, Elizabeth Levensohn, Charles Martin, Lu Chekowsky, the Rhodehamel and Sisk families, Queen, Richard Torres, Jeff Truesdell, the pharmacy staff (especially Raj and Sofie) at Target on E. Colonial Drive, Orlando, for being so nice when I was so sick, and everyone who allowed me to interview them for this book.

Table of Contents

Preface

> As long as the world is turning and spinning we're gonna be dizzy and we're gonna make mistakes.
>
> —MEL BROOKS, IN *THE 2000 YEAR OLD MAN*

When I was a kid in the '70s Engelbert Humperdinck had a huge hit with a song called "After the Lovin'." It was the cheesiest thing you could find outside of an actual cheese shop, the kind of industrial-strength '70s smarm that would make people deny that the '70s ever happened until the '90s, when it was far enough away to feel safe.

In fairness to Engelbert this was also the era that gave us Debby Boone's "You Light Up My Life," the Captain and Tennille's "Muskrat Love," and Morris Albert's "Feelings." It was a fabulous decade but when it came to schmaltz we never said when. You want to know why people embraced the Sex Pistols? "Muskrat Love." That's why.

At 11 years old I had no idea what Engelbert was talking about. The lovin' was a pretty blurry concept to me. I was about 10 years away from knowing exactly how romantic love could make you literally crazy and 11 years from understanding the devastation the end of a romance could wreak. After the lovin'—the fights, the therapist, the cynicism.

My mother was a very vocal woman—in fact the only place you'll see a bigger mouth is on Mount Rushmore—yet she was conspicuously economical on the subjects of sex and relationships. She'd occasionally offer something like "You're going to have to marry someone who makes you laugh," or the simpler "Don't get stuck," but it wasn't ever something she wanted to talk about at length. My parents were married for thousands of years and never managed to make it look appealing. Between this and my natural autonomy it was easy never to get stuck. Even now I rent, I freelance, and I'm agnostic about everything from religion to romance.

This didn't mean I was immune to love, and when it did pop up, like a brain aneurysm or a winning lotto ticket, I was as unprepared for its consuming power as Carrie White was for her period. If you had told the self-contained 18-year-old me that there would be men in the future who would make me want to sideline my ambitions just to lie in bed with them all day long—who might make me *want* to get stuck—I'd have checked for your lobotomy scar, but it happened and I had no idea how to handle it.

I think a lot of us judge ourselves terribly harshly when love doesn't work out. When we're hurt or confused in love, or love outside convention, we feel like the only person who failed to memorize the script. This is *primal,* we think. *Penguins* can do this—how hard can it be? And our culture is no help whatsoever. There are 3,000 cover versions of the Beatles' *Yesterday* but only one culturally approved type of relationship: straight, married, monogamous, and forever. Love offers itself to us in a giddy, dizzying burst of variety, as everything in nature does, and we often don't have the imagination to accept. It's like making Sálvador Dalí a housepainter and asking him to please stick to beige and oatmeal.

This is starting to change, but the long-standing model of Happy, Hetero, and Monogamously Hitched (all by a certain age or you're doomed. Doomed! DOOOOMED!) is pretty dug in, despite the fact that it makes an awful lot of people feel weird and wobbly. Living modern lives on antique rules is like shoving oats and hay into your gas tank and being surprised when you don't get anywhere.

And people judge each other's romantic lives and allow theirs to be judged pretty casually. I've had people I barely knew ask me why I didn't marry my then boyfriend and offer their opinions about my personal life *as though I'd asked.* Our love lives are as sacred a thing as there is, yet we allow them to be eyeballed and judged like some garage-sale butter churn on *Antiques Roadshow,* with way too many people openly doubting that what you feel in your heart is worth anything. You'd never hear anyone say to a religious person, "Maybe God's just not that into you."

Love is more mysterious than death. Death you will at least probably understand once you have done it. Not so, love. The more times you do it, the more confused you get. Even Agatha Christie needed more than one try to figure it out.[1]

So if you feel alone in your problems with love, please believe me: you're not. You are not the only one who is confused, frustrated, nervous, or once traded a cow for magic beans and has no idea why you did it. You can look back on thousand-year-old poems and on this week's *Desperate Housewives* and see how problems in love haven't changed and how normal you are to feel nuts. It's a powerfully alluring madness. Love is the mental illness we all want to have. It *does* make us crazy.

Now scientists are showing us how.

Psychologists, academics, and analysts of culture continue to offer us better understanding of ourselves in love and other areas, but neurologists and other specialists have taken the game to a higher level. They are holding a new mirror up to us—the brain scan—that shows what chemicals and structures are active when we feel different things, and like Narcissus, we can't stop staring. I think that neuroscience—the study of the brain, its mechanics, and how its chemistry affects our behavior—is poised to alter, indeed is already altering, the way we think about ourselves as profoundly as Darwinian thinking did. We no longer see depression or addiction simply as character flaws, but as biological and behavioral. What else do we now judge as bad character that will later be found to be the function of wiring or chemistry? How can we judge ourselves for being unable to get over an ex if we know that our brain chemistry is creating an addiction similar to that of a drug user?[2] What if we discover that someone we thought was cold and indifferent to us simply has the neurological disorder known as Asperger's syndrome and just can't engage socially in certain ways?[3] How much of our behavior is really our choice?

This stuff is opening a Pandora's box the size of a cruise ship, and I'm thrilled. We may have to reassess how much we really should judge ourselves and others, which won't come easy. Judging is a lot of people's only hobby and they're not going to let go of it that quickly. And so, like the study of evolution, neurology may change the way we see ourselves, but only if we let it.

This book isn't a how-to. It's more of a "guess-what!" I have included some pearls of wisdom from interview subjects, and I hope this book will be a rich narrative journey and a source of increased perspective on some of the ways your brain might be screwing with your emotional GPS, setting your destination for Crazy Town when you meant to go home and get a good night's sleep. The brain is so complex, and research on it is so massive, I don't expect to be comprehensive just by offering some ideas for why you're not the only one who's lost it in love. I interviewed 23 people, some of them specialists in various fields of study who provided depth of understanding in the ways of love and our universal predicaments in it. Others gave me their personal stories about loves they have known or survived. I chose them because their stories were variously amazing, affecting, amusing, or appalling—often a combination. Some stories are pretty dark, but I hope you are able to empathize with all of them at least partially. "Nothing human is alien to me," Terence said, and while I'm not quite that elastic, it's an admirable statement. To understand is not necessarily to condone, and to condemn anyone's actions without attempting to understand their feelings and motives is unfair. We all have a dark side, and we understand more than we let on; pretending that we don't is like ignoring a bill we don't want to pay. The problem is just going to get bigger.

Finally, I wanted to write a book a person could read on a cross-country flight without getting bored and picking up the *Sky Mall* catalog. That's only happened to me once. The author was mystery writer M.C. Beaton and my gratitude was immense. If I can get you from, say, Orlando to Vancouver without buying a pair of night-vision goggles or an automatic cat feeder—and in the process make you feel better about the love you're in, were in, or will be in—then we'll both be in good shape. That's enough to wish for today.

Liz Langley

Chapter 1

Brainiac

YOU ARE HERE: THE LAYOUT OF THE BRAIN

Why you're reading this book is your business, but chances are you liked the cover, identified with the subject matter, and decided to investigate further.

How you're reading this book is a much more difficult proposition. The brain is incredibly complicated. There are a lot of things you've found murky in your life, like algebra and David Lynch movies, but these are simple compared to the three pounds of material that has enabled you to pick up, open, and read what you're reading.[1]

Yep, that's all that keeps you going: three pounds of neurons, synapses, glia, and various other squishy oddments housed in a protective skull. A gallon of milk weighs more than everything that enabled Handel to write *Messiah*.

And I'm sure I'm not the first person to observe that the only thing the brain can't seem to figure out is itself; hence the inevitable "What was I thinking?" when it comes to love and other endeavors.

One of the people helping to figure out why we do the things we do is Dr. Joseph Shrand, an instructor in psychiatry at Harvard Medical School and medical director of CASTLE (Clean and Sober Teens Living Empowered) at the High

Point Treatment Center in Brockton, Massachusetts. I originally wanted to interview Dr. Shrand about the adolescent brain, but he took the time to describe the basic layout of this intricate organ in plain terms, which was pretty beneficial for a tourist like myself. Like the old announcements that told people where they were arriving on the elevator ("Fourth Floor: women's apparel, camping gear, pets"), Dr. Shrand explained the brain to me from the bottom up.[2]

"The brain is a very clunky organ that has evolved over hundreds of millions of years—and humans, we never threw anything away. We just built one chunk of brain on top of another," he says. I can't help thinking of *Hoarders* and my brain insisting, "No! I'm keeping my prehistoric ability to kill a rabbit with a rock. It's perfectly good and I might need it one day!"

The first level of the brain is the brain stem, which is, Dr. Shrand says, "the most ancient part of the brain, responsible for heart rate and breathing and sweating and all those things that happen automatically that we're not aware of. The brain stem really has to be ready to go at birth."

The brain is made up of neurons, which have long offshoots called axons, and the insulation around these axons is called myelin—Dr. Shrand compares it to the insulation around an electrical wire. The reason babies don't walk but "squiggle around" is because the motor part of their brain is not fully myelinated, "so even though parts of the brain are functioning, they may not be functioning at a fully mature level." The brain develops with us.

In fact, check out this beautiful finding from Pilyoung Kim of the National Institute of Mental Health in Bethesda, Maryland: The brains of new mothers grow, not greatly but significantly, in the areas responsible for "motivation, reward behavior, and emotion regulation," reports Emily Sohn on Discovery News. The brain is reconfiguring itself to respond to its new role, and on top of that, the mothers who are the most gooey and gushy about their babies have the biggest growth. "These are the areas that motivate a mother to take care of her baby, feel rewarded when the baby smiles at her, and fill her with positive emotions from simple interactions with her infant."[3]

The second layer of the evolutionary hoard is the limbic system, sometimes called the reptilian or lizard brain. "This is a very complex set of structures that are involved in emotions, memory, pleasure, addictions, impulses," Dr. Shrand says. Hundreds of millions of years old, the limbic system was crucial to human survival. It houses responses like anger and the fight-or-flight instinct. "Animals that have the ability to recognize danger and fight that danger or get away from there survive to have babies, and those babies continue to develop the limbic system," Dr. Shrand says. It's filled with cool-sounding stuff like the amygdala and the hippocampus and the ventral tegmental area—"this really complex interplay of structures that's evolved over millions of years."

And because the limbic system involves very primal urges like pleasure and romantic elements like emotion, there's a whole lotta love taking place in here. To me it sounds like the physical embodiment of the id, that element of our psyche Freud referred to as "a cauldron full of seething excitations…" that strives only "to bring about the satisfaction of the instinctual needs subject to the observance of the pleasure principal."[4] Sounds like a good time waiting to be had, right? We'll see.

★ ★ ★

OK, if you think of the brain as TV, this is how I see it so far:

First level, brain stem: basic functions. If your brain were a TV this would be rabbit ears.

Second floor, limbic system: fear, fun, anger, addiction, fight-or-flight. Far more intriguing stuff, but not quite all the way there yet. This would be Basic Cable.

Third floor: This is where you get all the pay channels, a really broad range of depth and intrigue.

Dr. Shrand has a sweeter simile. "Then, glommed on top of that like the third scoop of an ice cream cone is this really large part of brain, the new brain or the neocortex, and this is the part that really distinguishes mammals."

New brain.

Wow, right? I love this. It sounds so shiny and current, like something you want to buy. Better than the daunting "neocortex" though they are exactly the same thing. "New brain" seems to imply "*our* brain." This is not some dusty old hand-me-down alligator brain. It's *new*. It's ours. It's cranial couture.

"And human beings have evolved this size in proportion to other animals that's enormous," Dr. Shrand says.

Even better: BIG new brain!

"In particular," Dr. Shrand says "there's this one part of the neocortex or new brain right behind your forehead. It's the part of the brain called the *prefrontal cortex*. This is the part that really distinguishes us as human beings, because located in the prefrontal cortex is what we call "executive functioning," a way to describe our ability to solve problems, integrate information, do our thinking, make decisions, and anticipate the consequences of those decisions."

These are the qualities that allowed human beings to

work together as a group, with one bonus: "Housed there is also the ability to appreciate somebody else's point of view—what are they thinking and what are they are feeling. This has a name. It's called Theory of Mind. Theory of mind is a critical developmental process that happens very young; it can happen as early as eighteen months, two years old."

The ability to read other people's feelings and thoughts from their behavior or facial expression is not just good for the reader, because they know what they're dealing with—happiness, anger, uncertainty; it's also good for the person being read, because they know they're understood by the reader; they can relax because the reader gets them. Or worse: "If you're not interested in what I'm thinking or feeling, does that mean you're looking at me like lunch?" Dr. Shrand says.

Here are some more basics it's helpful to know, with help from MedicineNet.com:

First there are *neurons*, which send electrical impulses to different parts of the body and receive them from sensory and other neurons.[5]

Then there are *neurotransmitters*, chemicals that act as the body's messengers, sending information from one nerve cell to another.[6]

Hormones are another important component—as you know, because they're associated with sex. Estrogen and testosterone are hormones, but they have other jobs too, like metabolism growth, stress reactions, producing parts of the blood, and keeping other hormones regulated.[7]

GLIA CLUB

"You remember that theory that says you only use ten percent of your brain?" Dr. Shrand asks.

I do.

"The reason that theory came about—and it's described wonderfully in a book by Andrew Koob titled *The Root of Thought: Unlocking Glia*[8]—is that ten percent of the brain is neurons and ninety percent is glial cells. People felt for a hundred years that the glial cells were really a garbage group of cells to collect the waste products of neurons, but it's absolutely the opposite," he says. Now it's thought that the real action is probably in the glial cells. "Neurons are probably the sensory cells that bring information in from the outside to the internal world. The glial cells interpret them and then tell the neurons what to do. Over the next twenty years or so people like me are going to be much more in interested in doing things to glial cells than directly to neurons."

We're not going to explore glia here, but when you hear about glia in the future you can throw the term around as cocktail chat, and you'll look like you're using 100 percent of your brain—because you are.

We'll temporarily take our leave of Dr. Shrand here, but not before telling you that, in 1972, he was Joey on the children's TV program *Zoom*. You can see him on YouTube.[9]

"How much mileage do you get out of that?"

"More than I realized," he laughs.

I completely believe it, because when I tell people this nearly everyone has the same reaction. "Oh, *Zoom*! I loved *Zoom*!" and then they sing the theme song—even remembering, with emphasis, the zip code of the mailing address from the closing credits (Boston 02134).

Interestingly, a new study by McGill University in January 2011 says that music can stimulate the release of dopamine—the neurotransmitter associated with sexual attraction, pleasure, and addiction.[10]

Being associated with a song people love to sing, then, would seem a very fortunate thing. This might be a good time to hum the title of this book.

MIRROR, MIRROR

Within the neurons there is a subset called *mirror neurons* that fire when we see someone else doing something, as though we were doing that thing ourselves. They were discovered in the early '90s by Giacomo Rizzolatti and his team at the University of Parma, who found that the same neurons would fire in the brains of a monkey that saw or just *heard* someone open a peanut as would fire when the monkey itself opened a peanut.[11] In a TED talk on YouTube titled "The Neurons That Shaped Civilization," Professor V.S. Ramachandran of the University of California, San Diego, calls these "Gandhi neurons," because they help us empathize with others and show just how interconnected we really are.[12]

These Gandhi neurons could go a long way to explain a lot of things—like our constant hunger for entertainment. Obviously we need the escape of movies and TV sometimes, but if the same neurons are firing in our brains when we see Ryan Gosling kiss Rachel McAdams in *The Notebook* as if it were happening to us, well, no wonder we never get tired of being stuck to the screen. (You can draw your own conclusions about the popularity of porn right about now.)

SHE FOCUSED ME WITH SCIENCE

A few years ago I would never have associated the brain with love. The two simply didn't mix as far as I was concerned. Brains made you smart and love made you dumb. They went together like leopard print and plaid: no.

Then in 2004 a book came out that would help change the way I thought about love by showing where it is in the brain, by talking about the chemicals in it that activated my behaviors, and yours, too. It was a tipping point in my ability to comprehend behavior in love as having a basis in chemistry, not just character. The book was *Why We Love: The Nature and Chemistry of Romantic Love*, by Dr. Helen Fisher. It is about what happens when we fall under the influence of this bewitching drive, what actually occurs in your brain when you see your own personal Jake Ryan. Having a new way to see it gave me a new way to handle it.

Guess what? You're not a hopeless feeb because your brain continually returns to the kisses of a certain someone, you're not an idiot because she's the wasabi in your sushi and her not returning your calls just makes you want her more, you're not hopeless because your heart is making your eyes cry over someone your head knows is an ass, you're not a fool or a tool because you've realized that Copernicus was wrong and it *is* your beloved around which the universe revolves. When love happens there are chemical releases going on that can to turn you from Ren into Stimpy. It's up to you to find a balance in between.

"Romantic Love is an addictive drug," Dr. Fisher writes,[13] comparing it to cocaine, but it's one we need for the survival, health, and happiness of the species. Dr. Fisher details how she and her team came to the conclusion that love was an addictive chemical. They got volunteers—first, people who were wildly in love, then people who were brokenhearted by love—to be scanned in an fMRI machine, which records blood flow within the brain and shows which areas are activated at particular times. They showed the subjects photos of their beloved and then neutral photos, and looked for the differences in the functioning of the brain.

Dr. Fisher wanted to test whether the neurotransmitters dopamine, norepinephrine, and serotonin were components of romantic love, since they inspire all the behaviors we think of in someone who's been hit by Cupid, including addiction, anxiety, exhilaration, loss of appetite, and obsession. She was right. When the subjects looked at photos of their beloved, specific parts of their brains lit up like pinball machines.

Or better, like an Indian summer evening sky.

"When I first looked at those brain scans, with the active brain regions lit up in bright yellow and deep orange, I felt the way I feel on a summer night when I gaze at the sparkling universe: overwhelming awe," she writes.

This is beautiful not just because we can empathize with her feelings (with our intact Theory of Mind) but because it shows how alienated people are from their own bodies.

Our bodies perform so many functions we never see; we are fascinated by them and want to see them. That's why museum shows like *Bodies: The Exhibition* are so popular.[14] We *are* Narcissus. We want to see ourselves. We want to know. Now fMRI scans are able to show us more about the mystery we carry around in our heads. Awe is the perfect word for it.

What surprised Dr. Fisher when viewing the smitten brain was the regions that were involved. The first was the *caudate nucleus* in the limbic system.[15] The second was the ventral tegmental area, or VTA, a tiny little bead right in the middle of the brain that is the great repository of the neurotransmitter dopamine, which is concerned with motivation toward reward—and mania.[16] When you're smitten, when just the thought of your sweetheart makes everything OK, when it makes you feel, as my friend Paige used to say, as if you're a little magnet and they're a great big refrigerator, dopamine is afoot. It's the breakout star of the neurotransmitter set.

If love continues and matures, the obsessive thinking does stop and we move into the calmer romantic and attachment phases, thanks to the hormones vasopressin and oxytocin, which promote bonding, emotional security, and attachment in mammals. Dr. Shrand says it's hugely important, this oxytocin, because it binds people together and we need that sense of attachment.

"I think you can argue that above all a human being wants to feel valued by someone else," he says. "If you think about this from an evolutionary point of view, this is critical"—because we weren't so strong or fast, but "what we were really good at was hanging out together and being able to protect each other and to develop social networks whereby we could use the combined resources of our brains to forage, get food, find shelter. And to use tools as well as have sex and have more babies with fully myelinated brain stems, ready to go. If you were not valuable, you ran the risk of being excluded from this social network and being incredibly vulnerable and probably being lunch for some other animals."[17]

This bonding agent is even being looked at by neuro-economists in regard to questions of cooperation. Ten years after finding that countries with lower levels of trust had slower economies, Dr. Paul Zak is studying how oxytocin can work in day-to-day business. His research using oxytocin administered through a pump-action inhaler has shown that it does indeed appear to play a part in trust, trustworthiness, and reciprocation.[18] Oxytocin is popularly called "the cuddle hormone"; women release it during orgasm, childbirth, and lactation, while men release vasopressin during orgasm.[19]

And that's not the only thing men release. Amazingly, but somehow not surprisingly, semen has antidepressant properties. Writing on the *Psychology Today* blog, David J. Ley PhD noted the research of anthropologists Gordon Gallup and Rebecca Burch:

When analyzed, men's semen is shown to contain high levels (higher than mere accident) of numerous psycho-active hormones and substances. These include testosterone (which increases a woman's libido and interest in having more sex), as well as neurochemicals. Epinephrine, norepinephrine, oxytocin, vasopressin, melatonin and other opioids are all present in semen, and all have detectable impact upon mood, cognition and memory. Gallup and Burch have shown that women who use condoms during sex have higher levels of depression. As the chemicals in semen are absorbed, vaginally, anally or orally, the woman experiences a real antidepressant effect.[20]

See? Just jerk the handle and you'll win a prize!

All these love drugs whizzing through our veins and brains should just make us all cooperative love-happy cuddle bunnies, right? I wish. There's an interplay of chemicals that—of course—means things aren't that easy. Dr. Fisher writes, for example, that testosterone can reduce attachment, while oxytocin can also decrease the impact of dopamine and norepinephrine.

In his 2007 book *Sex on the Brain: 12 Lessons to Enhance Your Love Life*, Dr. Daniel Amen divides the brain chemicals associated with love into categories: chemicals of attraction (testosterone, estrogen, nitric oxide, and pheromones), infatuation (epinephrine, norepinephrine, dopamine, serotonin, and phenylethylamine), commitment (oxytocin and vasopressin), and detachment (serotonin and pheromones). "The brain is a chemical factory looking for love," he writes.[21]

Dr. Fisher also addresses what happens when our beloved releases us back into the wild and we don't want to go. At this point a number of chemical reactions can occur, including the fact that "these dopamine-producing neurons prolong their activities—increasing brain levels of this natural stimulant" if the lover is frustrated,[22] making their determination even greater. Separation anxiety can cause the "stress system"[23] to activate—long story short, the adrenal gland releases the hormone *cortisol*, which can trigger "production of dopamine and norepinephrine and suppresses serotonin activity—the combination of elixirs associated with romantic love." So rather than back off and give us a break, the chemicals of love *increase when we are rejected*, causing us not to say, "Oh, well, easy come, easy go" and move along, but to hunger for our love object even more. It's like putting a nice warm heating pad on a blistering sunburn. Or like having your soul pulled out through your pores.

Or, as David Bowie said it in *Cat People (Putting Out Fire):* "putting out fire with gasoline."

The dopamine finally backs the hell off when you put on Hall & Oates's "She's Gone" and resign yourself to the fact that it's over. Curtain. The end. This leads to the dopamine drop, which leads to despair, which can lead to serious depression.[24] Awesome. Whoever coined the phrase *intelligent design*—a billion broken hearts would like a word with you.

No wonder the ancients saw the mentally ill, perhaps depressives or addicts, as "having demons." They weren't so far wrong, only it's a chemical, not a little horned beast, that's gotten into you.

And the chemicals hang in there instead of going away. "When a reward is delayed coming, reward-expecting neurons in the reward system prolong their activity," Dr. Fisher writes in her latest study, in May 2010, conducted with Lucy L. Brown, Arthur Aron, Greg Strong, and Debra Mashek.[25] It's like someone getting fired from a job and not going home. Fisher's team looked further at the torment of the brain of a rejected lover and found that the brain areas associated with cocaine and nicotine addiction became active when subjects looked at pictures of their ex, as did areas associated with pain and distress.

Allow me to underscore that. You have been rejected but you are still in love, so you now have an addiction that's as bad as a coke problem, plus you're in physical pain. This is serious stuff. One person in the Fisher study said, "I was scared I would die of my feelings."[26]

But do you get a patch or a rehab stay? No you do not. You get a glass of wine (alcohol is a depressant) and the advice "You just need to move on."

Molly Edmonds, who hosts the *Stuff Mom Never Told You* podcast with Cristen Conger, noted when commenting on Fisher's study, "Just as you wouldn't say to a person who was an addict, 'Oh, it's been two weeks, you shouldn't really still be craving cocaine'—you would never say that to a person!—you can't say it to someone who's going through a breakup, because it's the same thing."[27] She makes a perfect case for having more compassion and empathy for the brokenhearted and for ourselves when we have a tough time letting go. Separation can be essential, but there's no need to be hard-ass about it, especially not to yourself.

But—in that later study by Dr. Fisher and her colleagues, subjects also showed greater activity in regions that process both gains and losses. So, the team thought, they might have been engaging in a learning process: looking at the picture, assessing the reward, and "adjusting their behavior accordingly."[28]

Hallelujah! Finally! "Calculating gains and losses" Dr. Fisher calls this, which sounds like the light of reason trying to shine through, even though what you need it to do is knock down the door and say "Somebody clean up these reward-expecting neurons. What am I, the maid?" But it's a beginning, the first stop on the road to everything feeling better.

So you can go out and do it all over again.

But as much as it can put us into high loony mode, love can also heal us. A *New York Times* story by Tara Parker-Pope reports that researchers at Stanford University have discovered that love is a painkiller. Having scanned the brains of a group of college students, they found that "looking at a picture of a loved one reduced moderate pain by about 40 percent and eased severe pain by about 10 to 15 percent, compared to viewing the picture of an acquaintance."[29]

"A little kindness ... and putting her hair in papers ... would do wonders for her," the Red Queen says of the White Queen in Lewis Carroll's *Through the Looking Glass*. In real life, a little kindness can be enough.[30]

Understanding that part of love is literally chemistry was a huge game-changer for me in 2004. I had been a writer for many years, but a few of my choices in love had made me feel like a world-class dumbbell, and I started wondering if my thoughts on anything were worth broadcasting. My confidence plummeted. (There were other reasons, but my emotional state had a big hand in it.) Why would anyone listen to a person who wasn't *smarter* than I had been?

Why We Love made me see that falling in love is not a matter of smart or dumb: it was dopamine, not dopiness, that had gotten me. With that understanding I was able to see that *I* was not fundamentally flawed, I just had some out-of-whack chemicals to corral.

This would be like a 14th-century peasant finding out he got the Black Plague not because Got hated him, but because of fleas. Fleas! It's still plague and it sucks, but at least *you* don't suck, not any more than anyone else, and certainly not as much as the fleas. Love, like hideous, black, pus-oozing lumps, just happens. As with getting rained on or winning money, it's how you handle it that counts. "Freedom is what you do with what's been done to you," Jean-Paul Sartre said.[31]

Being able to drop the defensiveness I had when I was

looking through the lens of ego was incredibly freeing, and I had this new understanding of chemistry to thank for it.

Leap forward to October 2010. Stephanie Ortigue, assistant professor of psychology and adjunct assistant professor of neurology at Syracuse University, has published a study in the *Journal of Sexual Medicine* stating that there are 12 identifiable areas of the brain that release the aforementioned chemicals and that different kinds of love take place in different parts of the brain: passionate love happens in the reward and cognitive centers, while unconditional love (parent–child love, for example) takes place in the midbrain. Also—and this is the most dumbfounding part—falling in love only takes about a fifth of a second.[32]

A fifth of a second? What else takes a fifth of a second? A bullet? A pickpocket? What kind of defenses do you have against anything that fast? In *Blink,* Malcolm Gladwell's brilliant book about rapid cognition, he tells us that many of the decisions we make are made in two seconds.[33] I thought that was quick. But love has one and four-fifths seconds to sit around and drum its fingers on the table waiting for "snap judgment" to show up. Rapid cognition is fast. Love is like Clark Griswold's specially treated sled in *Christmas Vacation.*

That may be why someone came up with the phrase "fall in love" in the 15th century rather than "have a cup of coffee, give it a little thought, and then get up and walk into love." Any more than a fifth of a second and it wouldn't probably seem as romantic.

There's only one problem with the idea that all these impulses initially get triggered in certain parts of the brain so it's not actually your fault: what about personal responsibility? If someone drugs you, you're generally exonerated from your behavior under the influence; love is Mother Nature slipping you a roofie. How much do you get to blame on chemistry and how much do you, hapless pawn of biology, have to account for on your own?

Sometimes we give love's victims greater leeway than we do other people, hence the "crime of passion."

The crime of passion, or "temporary insanity defense" (which you can read all about on the websites of the National Museum of Crime & Punishment and the American Law Library), was first used successfully in America in 1895[34] when a promising Democratic congressman, Daniel Sickles, discovered his young wife was having an affair with Barton Key (son of Francis Scott Key). When Sickles saw Key trying to signal the lady from a park across the street, he stormed out with his pistol and shot at Key several times, eventually killing him. (Not to add insult to murder by noting this, but, by way of self-defense and probably not knowing what else to do, Key threw his opera glasses at his assailant.)[35]

It was quite a trial, and the jury ended up acquitting Sickles of a murder he had committed in broad daylight in a public place after chasing the victim literally into the gutter to shoot him one last time. So before we really even knew the chemistry occurring in our brains we were making allowances for those chemical floods. And we still are.

When Clara Harris discovered her husband, David, was having an affair in 2002, she had him detail the reasons why he preferred the other woman. He did, citing Clara's weight, her conversational dominance, and the fact that the mistress was a "perfect fit" to sleep with his arms around all night. "I couldn't believe he could sleep holding her all night, because we had never slept like that—never," she testified, according to CBS News.[36]

Clara Harris ran David over with her Mercedes-Benz after catching him with his mistress at the hotel where the Harrises had had their wedding. She claimed to be aiming for his car, but their teenage daughter, Lindsey, who was Clara's passenger, testified that Clara aimed for David and he could not get away.

Clara Harris might have been sentenced to life, but the jury saw it as an act of "sudden passion," and under that label the most she could get was 20 years in prison, which was what she got. And this was in Texas.

So our society sometimes recognizes passion as a mitigating factor, especially when love is at the root of it. But how many people get cheated on every day and manage not to resort to murder? We can still make sound judgment calls, even under chemical bombardment. When we're stinking drunk, for example, we can choose to get in a cab instead of the driver's seat of our own car. The point is, chemical impairment isn't always an excuse.

"Being a biologist who studies behavior, everything's a combination of your biology and your upbringing," says Dr. Marlene Zuk,[37] author and professor of biology at UC Davis, whom we'll talk to about animal passions later on. As for our responsibility to stay in control of ourselves while under the influence of love, she says, "There's a chemical change in your brain if you pick up a donut. There's always a chemical change in your brain. That's how we work—we're physical beings. I've always thought this idea of 'If you can demonstrate there's brain change'—à la PMS—'you're not responsible' is not understanding what you mean by responsible."

It's comforting to feel that reason can bust through that dopamine flood like the Kool-Aid man through a Styrofoam wall. It means we don't always have to be the puppet of biology. Even when idiocy is foisted on us by nature we still have that reasoning prefrontal cortex to handle it. There's power in that knowledge and there's knowledge in that neocortex.

Helen and Me on the Ancient Imaginary Plains of Africa

So, *Why We Love* made me feel a million times better.

"Oh, that's a blessing to hear," Dr. Fisher says to me during our phone interview, which is brief, but that's OK. It's a little heady to get to speak to someone who has been so influential on you, and I'm pretty sure my dopamine is circulating like a schmoozer at a cocktail party right now.

My reason for studying love is that I never cease to be amazed by its power to elevate or destroy people, including me. When we're handed love's lemons, why do some of us make lemonade, some of us make vodka tonics with lemon, and some of us throw the lemons through the mirror and make boiled bunny soup? Those questions are my motivation, and I'm curious to know if Helen's was the same.

"Well, we all suffer from romantic love," she says. "I've often wondered why it is that we've evolved such a strong system. At times it just seems so unproductive to waste years of your life pining over somebody who's walked out on you. I mean, certainly, I've been dumped. I'm very much like everybody else.

"But I don't think that's the reason I have done this. People ask me why I study this and I always wish I had a sexier answer, but probably the real answer is because I'm an identical twin. Long before I knew there was a nature/nurture controversy—I mean, as a small child everybody asks you, if you're identical twins, "Do you like the same foods? Do you have the same friends? Do you get the same grades? Do you have the same cavities in your teeth?" It's just constant. And I grew up measuring how much of my behavior came from my biology and how much of my behavior came from an experiential origin." Dr. Fisher's twin sister, Lorna, is an oil painter and hot-air balloon pilot; both are Explorer/Negotiator personalities, as detailed in her latest book, *Why Him? Why Her? Finding Real Love by Understanding Your Personality Type.*[38]

Helen decided in grad school to study the evolution of female sexuality, "because women are really very unusual in terms of other primates in that they've lost all signs of estrus periodicity (regular periods of 'heat'). Not only can they copulate throughout the monthly cycle, but at midcycle, when other creatures ovulate and show clear physical expressions of estrus, we do not. And so I started my career with my PhD in why the human female lost estrus periodicity and the evolution of pair bonding, why we form pair bonds. You know, ninety-seven percent of mammals do not pair up to rear their young, but people do. Well, why do they?"

Helen thought that we may have evolved three distinctly different brain systems from mating and reproduction—sex drive, romantic love, and deep feelings of attachment—and maybe the sex drive evolved to get you out there looking for a whole range of partners. She says, "I think romantic love evolved to enable you to focus your mating energy on just one person at a time, and I think this third brain system for attachment evolved for you to be able to tolerate this person and stay together long enough to rear at least a single child together as a team."

That was when she began to study the brain circuitry of love.

★ ★ ★

At the root of every "Behind the Music" or "E! True Hollywood Story" about a star who plummeted into the gutter there seems to be a cocaine addiction that involves snorting the cost of a house every month. This is the chemical addiction to which Dr. Fisher compares love. So, if love is a hard drug you don't voluntarily take, are you then less responsible for your actions with this unbidden guest in your bloodstream? And out of empathy, do we more easily forgive people who commit crazy acts for love?

"We probably do, but rather foolishly," Helen says. "There's basically three very broadly sketched parts of the brain: the cortex, with which you do your thinking, the limbic, which is sort of more in the middle of the head where a lot of your emotions are generated, and way at the bottom of the brain are brain regions associated with drive, with wanting, with obsession, with craving, with focus, with attention, and with motivation. And it's that brain system—the dopamine system, the wanting system—that really generates the feelings of intense romantic love.

"But we *do* have a cerebral cortex with which we make decisions, and you *can decide* not to kill her because she walked out on you. Now, some people have poorer impulse control than others and their emotions overcome them, but basically just because we have all these feelings doesn't mean we should be totally out of control. There's no question about it, though: when you are addicted to something your craving for the drug—the person or the cocaine or the alcohol—overcomes your thinking cortical processes and you do things that are stupid. Real stupid."

What we're talking about here, she says, is more than an emotion: it's a drive.

"Even an emotion is hard to overcome," Dr Fisher says, but the cortex helps you control it. You can be very angry at someone and "even though you're absolutely furious and you feel the emotion, you don't act on that feeling, in the same way that people who crave alcohol or drugs don't act on it or go get the drugs. Same thing with the craving for food. Now, a great many people can't seem to control that impulse, and we've got a nation that's way too fat. In the same way, romantic love is a primitive, profoundly powerful mating drive which evolved millions of years ago to allow us to focus on an individual and start the mating process. And anybody who's ever felt it—which is just about everybody on the planet—has probably had times when it overtook their rational mind and they went to call somebody when they shouldn't have, or drove by their house when they shouldn't have, or sent too many emails when they shouldn't have. This can overpower the brain center for impulse control and you do stupid things," she says.[39]

I have long theorized that computers should come equipped with breathalyzers that lock up the Send key if the user's blood alcohol level is over the legal limit for driving. Think about how much humiliation the senders of drunken "I love you" emails would be spared. Is there an app for that?

Dr. Fisher also mentioned the mating drive as part of the reason we react so strongly when we've lost out in love. We invest our time in a person, thinking, consciously or not, that they'll help catapult our DNA into the future. Now we've lost that reproductive time, we have to start the search over again, with older eggs or sperm than we had before, possibly with less desirability and confidence. The anger at these losses can be huge.

But what if you're not going to reproduce? What if you have looked at the prospect of pushing someone's head through your vagina—outward—and thought you'd rather not? That's not the only reason I didn't want kids, of course. There were many reasons, and by the time I was 45 I knew the decision was final. I evidently just fall in love and have sex to pass the time. So why do I have to go through the same agonies as those for whom it has far-flung consequences? Must it be so damned dramatic even if I'm just auditing the course?

"I never wanted to have children either," Dr. Fisher says. "I once read that about one percent of women really never wanted to have children. I am definitely one of them. And I haven't for five minutes of my life been sorry I didn't have children." But that doesn't mean people like us are off the hook.

"These systems are so intricately woven into the brain that they don't die out. For example, even though cortically you and I have made decisions not to have children because we want to do other things with our lives, we still have all that brain circuitry for romantic love and attachment. I imagine you've attached to various men and had relationships that were two, three, five years long. Have you?"

I have.

"And you just didn't want to have children. So one could ask the same question, Why do we continue to fall in love after our reproductive years? You know very small children fall in love way before their reproductive years, and I think what they're doing is practicing, practicing one of the most important things we do on this planet, which is to form pair bonds in order to have baby."

And just as with our ecstasy and rage in love, our body

has a reason for being tired and worn-out but still getting butterflies over some wrinkly old Casanova or Jezebel.

"As people get older what would the advantage of romantic love be?" Helen asks. "Well, let's dial back to the grasslands of Africa. We're traveling around, you and I are traveling around with a little band, and suddenly, you're age forty-five and I'm older, and we both fall in love with somebody. Well, that gives you energy, vitality, optimism, enthusiasm—these are good qualities in a band! Other individuals could use an older person who's happy and energetic and optimistic, and also, if you fall in love with somebody when you're older, you've got a companion in old age, maybe somebody to help you into your grave, so that you're not a pest around everybody else, you're busy doing something. So a brain system can really evolve for one purpose and then be commandeered for many other purposes. For example, the eye did not evolve to read books. The eye evolved to swing from trees and pick ripe fruits, and of course in the modern world we evolved writing and reading. We no longer swing through the trees—we don't need our eyes for that—but these brain systems are so woven into the matrix of the mind that they are not ever selected against."

It makes me feel like really big stuff to get to hang out with Helen Fisher on the imaginary ancient grasslands of Africa, picking up guys and helping the young people take care of their kids since we didn't want to have any. Even this fanciful adventure of friendship makes me feel all warm and fuzzy; compare that to the wild enchantments of worldly, real, reciprocal romantic love and it's easy to see why becoming smitten, even with all its travails, was never selected against. Like having kids—enough people must have felt it was worth it to keep it going.

In my research I've met with some people who were poster children for dopamine-and-pals, both as a tether to hell and a conduit to the muses. I tell Dr. Fisher about Burt and Linda Pugach, a couple who met in the 1950s. She dumped him and he paid to have her assaulted, an attack that eventually blinded her, yet when he got out of prison she married him. Helen is taken aback. I thought she'd have heard it all by now, but love can still spring some surprises even on someone who has scanned it in an fMRI machine.

And that's probably why love never jumps the shark: its capacity to come up with riveting new plots is endless.

Chapter 2

Love, Birds, and the Lesbian Albatrosses

We are all animals, my lady.

SATAN, IN THE FILM *LEGEND*

To enjoy walking in central Florida you have to leave the house before the weather gets oppressive. The wet heat here in America's flaccid wang is humbling. Walk smack into a wave of humidity and it reminds you that while you might feel all sassy with your iPhone and your Bluetooth, Mother Nature actually has you on a short chain and she's not shy about jerking it.

As spring turns to summer I get up progressively earlier every day and walk down the brick streets of downtown Orlando's residential neighborhood while it's cool enough to stand it. Cascades of jasmine make thick patches of perfume as they vine down from huge gray oaks. The mallards have their ducklings and the moorhen has six fuzzy black chicks so cute I'm sure they were designed in Japan. There's a pit bull that barks ceaselessly from behind a white picket fence, which he is slowly but very surely tunneling under, just like Andy Dufresne in *The Shawshank Redemption*. A little sand every day, and soon he'll be off to Mexico.

The only birds I can hear over my iPod are the peacocks.

Sometimes their call begins with a honk that sounds like a goose getting sucked into a truck horn, but usually it's a series of mournful, earsplitting wails that could scare the entrails out of you if you heard it at night and didn't know what it was. The sound is so sad and spooky it's hard to believe it comes from one of the most beautiful creatures on earth. The tail feathers of the males can be bigger than a headboard when fanned.

A group of peacocks is fittingly called an *ostentation*. An ostentation of peacocks lives about eight blocks from my house. At 9:00 a.m. I pass one of the males, which is preoccupied with a black car parked in someone's driveway. Seeing his own reflection in the shiny paint, he's mistaken it for another male, a rival for the affection of the ladies (or so says a neighbor who has watched this happen). He won't budge, not even for food, while he's fixated on his imaginary enemy.

An hour from now he'll still be there and I'll pass just in time to see him lunge at his perceived rival, possibly scratching and bloodying the car a bit. (I've seen cars scarred from this before.) Eight hours later, when I drive by, he'll still be there, having put in a full day of being neurotic, sexually possessive, and nearsighted.

Been there.

I've considered moving closer to the peacocks so I could see them every day, but I think that would ruin them for me. If I were to move closer, they'd become mundane. They'd scream all night long, poop on my car, and block the driveway. They might go from being a prize to a pest, from peacocks to albatrosses. In order to keep them as a joy I have to keep them at arm's length, but to be without them is more than I can bear.

If you can hear the earsplitting thud of groundwork being laid for a romantic analogy, good for you. I've often had the same feeling about the men in my life: if grand creatures become routine, then what would we have left that's grand?

I tell Dr. Marlene Zuk about my peacocks because she's told me about her chickens. Marlene is an author and professor of biology at UC Davis; her book *Sex on Six Legs* is about the amazing world of insect erotica that is going on, probably right under our chairs, without our knowing it. In her book *Riddled with Life: Friendly Worms, Ladybug Sex, and the Parasites That Make Us Who We Are*, Marlene writes about studying jungle fowl to see whether females preferred males that didn't carry parasites. The visible differences between males were subtle, but the females picked the uninfected males by a 2:1 margin.[1] Marlene got results and an affinity for chickens.

It's easy to assign human feelings to animals. It's easy to imagine affection, spite, or a desire for clothing in chimps or cats. It's also easy to be wrong. Chickens aren't human-like or cuddly, so you can't look at them and imagine them being loving, pensive, or cautiously optimistic. You never think they'd look cute in a little sweater. Marlene likes that in a creature.

This is one reason she likes studying insects. "They're so much harder to anthropomorphize! And yet they do all this incredibly cool stuff," she says. They have individual personalities. Honeybees can recognize different human faces. "So you wonder, what does it take to have an emotion? Do you have to have a cerebrum? I don't know. Do you have to have hormones? Well, they have hormones, just not testosterone and oxytocin. I don't know. I just really like that they make you ask a lot of questions about what *does* it take to make you do things."

Besides a little smile and a big cocktail.

Since we are animals too, I wanted to know if Marlene sees in the animal world any crazy-love behavior like what we display—the equivalent of some cow obsessively checking some bull's Facebook page. Birdsong is meant to attract mates. How do we know a bird singing is not the sparrow equivalent of bad teenage poetry, or "Sexual Healing" by Marvin Gaye, or musical stalking?

When it comes to animals, Marlene says, it's difficult to tell whether they're feeling anything like human emotions, "so it's not like they're going to do crazy things that aren't going to get their genes passed on." If a person acts jealously, "that's not going to get them anywhere. But with animals the jealousy, if you want to call it that, or the protection of your mate does make sense biologically, especially if you're going to put a bunch of work into raising the offspring. If somebody else has fathered the offspring in your nest, then that's a really bad thing in terms of you passing on your genes, so being protective of your mate is a good thing."

This jealousy (whether motivated by mate protection or just ego) is not found in all societies. In *Sex at Dawn: The Prehistoric Origins of Modern Sexuality*, authors Christopher Ryan and Cacilda Jethá handily illustrate many cultures worldwide that make a joke of the notion of happy, het, and hitched. In these cultures possessiveness is not practiced; partners and even paternity are shared. The Ache of Paraguay, for example, distinguish four types of fathers:

Mirare: the father who puts it in;

Peroare: the father who mixed it;

Momboare: those who spilled it out; and

Bykuare: the fathers who provided the child's essence.[2]

The children of these many fathers benefit from having more than one person looking out for their welfare, and the fathers benefit from knowing that more than one person will care for their progeny—a far cry from the me-and-mine view of Western culture.

ARE WE MORE FAITHFUL THAN WE THINK?

Speaking of protecting your genetic investment, Marlene has recently been looking at our perceptions of misassigned paternity: cases in which the man who is supposed to be the father is not the father. When asked to guess the percentage of misassigned paternities in the US most people guess 10 percent and some, like me, guess as high as 30 percent. (In my defense, the question threw me. It was like on *Family Feud* when they say, "Name things you bring to the beach" and some idiot says "Jell-O!" That was me.)

Marlene writes, "According to the most unbiased research, the real incidence of misassigned paternity in Western countries hovers around 1%, with a few studies pushing that number to 3% or nearly 4%."[3]

"There are lots of cases in animals where there's a male and female with a nest, and there will be another male that's fathered some of the chicks in that nest. It's apparently more common than it is in humans, yet people always think if any species is screwing around it's going to be people," Marlene says.

(In fairness to my cynically high 30 percent guess, it's true that we might be more faithful than we think, but we might also just be more adept at birth control. This study after all, doesn't say who is sleeping with whom, just who is breeding with whom.)

It might often be difficult to tell what animals are feeling, but there certainly seems to be evidence—evidence that's warm and fuzzy to look at—that they do feel.

Koko, the gorilla that famously learned sign language, certainly seemed to sign feelings like "love" and "obnoxious" frequently, or at least she did in a web chat on AOL in 1998.[4] And chimpanzees seem to mourn death. The death of a 50-year-old chimp named Pansy caused a stir when researchers at the UK safari park where she lived watched how the other chimps behaved as she was dying.[5] A few days beforehand, they became quiet and hovered around her. As she died, they tested her for signs of life. After her death, they wouldn't sleep where she died and they ate less for some time afterward. A PBS *Nature* episode showed that elephants exhibit joy, grief, and compassion, and calves even experience posttraumatic stress—waking up screaming after seeing a family member fall to a poacher.[6] Anyone who has ever found their personal belongings peed on can at least guess that cats feel spite. If animals can feel fear, why not love?

In animals that have pair-bonded, Marlene says, you do see behaviors that you could call love if you wanted to. "The two members of the pair recognize each other, they hang out together, they have little things they do together— special vocalizations or gestures that are only between the two of them. I'm hesitant to call it love because I don't know if what's going on in their heads and hearts is what's going on with ours. You look at them and say, How is this behavior going to help them pass on their genes? Because if it's not selection, it should have been removed."

I want to know about these special vocalizations. Does she mean, like, pet names?

Not exactly.

Sea birds in large colonies, for example, where mates have to find each other among thousands of birds after one has gone to get food, use special vocalizations. "To find each other they often have vocal signatures, these special vocalizations that mean 'This is me and I'm calling to you.' Sometimes mothers and offspring have these too."

For a long time, Marlene says, people mistakenly thought that birds would just plunk down to help whatever bird was there, because it was about survival of the species. It's not. It's about survival of your genes, which means finding your specific mate.

"It is a funny question," Marlene says. "If it looks like love and they're doing it and it's beneficial, why isn't it love? What is it that makes it love?"

Which brings us to the lesbian albatrosses.

"There's one kind of albatross called the Laysen albatross that occurs in Hawaii. A new colony has been established on Oahu just in the last twenty or thirty years or so. It's very close to Waikiki, and it's the most successful albatross colony in the world. Usually what happens is a male and a female stay paired, not for life, but certainly for a long time. They raise one chick together because a female can only lay one egg per year.

"My friend Lindsay Young was studying this species and started noticing that a bunch of the nests had two eggs. She couldn't figure out what was going on, because this is a very new thing in albatross nests or—albatrossity.

"The male and female albatross look exactly alike; you cannot tell them apart just by looking at them. So she genetically tested them and found out that thirty percent of the pairs in the colony were two females rearing an egg together. It looks like the two females get together and one or both of them mate with a mated male in the colony—which is kind of amazing; no one knew they did that. Then, if they both lay an egg, one of the eggs gets pushed aside and dies, but for the egg that remains, the two adults are like two mommies. They rear the chick and feed it. The females are pair-bonded; they do all the little things that males and females do. They do what looks like mating, though Lindsay's only seen that once—but you don't see sex between males and females very often either. And for all the world they're just two females together, and the chicks do just as well as the chicks of heterosexual albatrosses."

Marlene says there are more females than males in the colony, so it seems to make sense that the females would get together to do the very demanding job of raising an albatross chick, which requires two adults—one to stay with the chick, the other to go get food. But their behavior is as pair-bonded as a heterosexual couple's.

And from my nonacademic perspective it's far more intriguing, because though it may not be about love or any of its spinoffs (affection, kinship, keeping company), it can't be about just passing on genes: only one of the pair's genes is going anywhere.

Marlene says that usually when people see same-sex coupling in animals they regard it as an aberration, something animals do because they're in zoos. But the albatrosses are doing this same-sex bonding in the wild, which makes it all the more interesting.

"I think this behavior is way more common than people think," Marlene says. "Animals are flexible about what they do. They do whatever works, and it's not that big a deal."

If only everyone could be this bird-brained. Kind of hard to keep cramming humans into the hetero-and-hitched model, believing it's the only "natural" thing, when nature seems to have other ideas.

But the question was—Is it love? Plenty of human couples take care of their kids like these same-sex albatrosses, and plenty of them are in love, while others may not have been in love for years. We all know what the phrase "We're staying together for the sake of the children" means. I would say we can't communicate with animals well enough to know if that's what they're doing but, frankly, you won't get a straight answer about such matters from many humans either.

So what about human animals? How do *you* know whether what you're feeling is love?

Unfortunately, there is no quick and easy test you can take to be sure, no magic stick you can pee on and watch for a plus sign to tell yes or no. And even if you're sure it's love, love evolves. Dr. Fisher describes the love morphing in three stages: sexual attraction, romantic love, and attachment—and even within these we find that our feelings evolve. No wonder we can't say with certainty what love is: if you have it, it probably changes every day.

But look at some of the other things you *can* find out if you have with one quick test: A dead car battery. Most STDs. No pulse. Maybe it's better that love is more compli-cated.

IT'S IN HIS KISS

Kissing someone doesn't necessarily mean you love them, but being in love with someone certainly means you want to kiss them. Bonobo chimps—the Pepe Le Pews of the animal kingdom and some of our closest relatives—kiss frequently, regardless of sex, to ease tension, or for no reason.[7] Other animals seem to engage in kissing behavior that can mean different things, including grooming and bonding.

We humans think we kiss just for fun, but other animal instincts are at work here that we don't even realize. (Anyway, who can think during a good kiss?) Betsy Mason, reporting for *Wired* in 2009, says that what's in our saliva may be yet another way we chemically assess a mate. Mason wrote that neuroscientist Wendy Hill tested blood and saliva samples taken from couples after 15-minute kissing sessions and found that cortisol, the hormone that responds to stress, was down (kissing is relaxing), and in men oxytocin, the cuddle hormone, was up. (Interestingly, oxytocin was down in women, perhaps, Hill says, because the study was done in a school infirmary—not a place you usually associate with cuddling.) Dr. Fisher, who was also at the conference, said that there's evidence of testosterone in saliva— which men may be trying to pass on to women through kissing to goose up their sex drive.[8]

Over and over again we see how writers, musicians, artists, and poets have, for centuries, intuitively expressed the things science is now finding evidence for. A perfect example of this is "The Shoop Shoop Song

(It's in His Kiss)," written by Rudy Clark and recorded by Betty Everett in 1964 and covered by Cher in 1991: "If you wanna know if he loves you so, it's in his kiss … that's where it is."

My cortisol fell through the floor just thinking about it.

Chapter 3

What You See in Them:
Ideas on Attraction

IS SHE REALLY GOING OUT WITH HIM?

Usually I walk to my peacocks alone, but today my friend Sam has come with me. A former Broadway dancer from the original cast of *La Cage Aux Folles,* Sam at 51 still has a body that a 20-year-old would envy: lean, tan, and blond, with eyes the color of newly minted dollar bills. While we walk I pitch him the idea of making a little road trip.

"Where are we going?" he asks.

"We're going to Gibsonton," I say. Gibsonton, sometimes called Gibtown, is a little place outside Tampa where the people who work the carnival circuit come to stay for the winter. They used to call it "Freaktown," because people like the World's Tallest Man and the Lobster Boy and the Human Blockhead used to live there. "We're going to hear the story of what happened when the Alligator-Skinned Man wanted to marry the Monkey Girl," I tell him.

Sam thinks about this as we walk past an oak tree that has grown up so bent you can sit on the trunk like a bench.

"That makes me feel like something's wrong with me," he says with a tinge of sadness. "The Alligator-Skinned Man can find somebody, but I can't get somebody to text me back? Is there something the matter with us?"

We're both having confounding times with our respective romances this week, so it probably feels that way. It often feels like something's the matter with us when your love life is a bitch and you hear of someone else's that's just goddamn peachy. It's the feeling of indignant disbelief in the Joe Jackson song: "Is she really going out with him? Cuz if my eyes don't deceive me there's something going wrong around here." Confess: how often have you heard someone gushing about their fabulous love life when yours wasn't doing so well and you just wanted to shut them up with a right hook? Well, since we found out (in chapter 1) that love is a painkiller, it must mean that they're anesthetized by love when they're gushing like that, so it's the perfect time to bop them in the puss.

So why is it that the Alligator-Skinned Man and the Monkey Girl found romantic bliss while many others don't? What do we see in some people and not in others? More importantly, why can't everyone see how great we are and fall for us passionately right this minute?

THE EYES OF LOVE

"Do you see what I mean?" "Look at it from my perspective," "I see what you're saying,"—kind of interesting how our culture uses vision as a metaphor for deep comprehension. It confirms that the way we perceive things through the senses counts emotionally. Dr. Daniel Amen writes, in *Sex on the Brain: 12 Lessons to Enhance Your Love Life*, "Fifty percent of the brain is dedicated to vision, so how people look, how they move, how they smile and how their eyes appear are critical to the process of attraction."[1]

That would mean that *half* of everyone's brain—not just men's brains, but everyone's brain—is devoted to visual stimulus. It would make sense that we use half of our brain on looks, leaving half left over for *everything else*. And not just because we often judge people on their looks. We usually get a look before we get close enough to sniff for genetics (more about that below) or lean in for a telling kiss. It would make sense that those of our forebears who had sharper eyesight and could spot the good berries and tell them from the poisoned berries lived to procreate another day, while the ones who said "What tiger? I don't see any ti—" got scooped right out of the gene pool.

In 2006 the *New York Times* reported on what is thought to be the oldest love poem in the world—a 4,000-year-old Sumerian cuneiform tablet found in the 1880s.[2] These words of a priestess addressed to a king may have been used for the ceremonial recreation of the liaison between the love goddess Inanna and Dumuzi, god of shepherds:

"Bridegroom, dear to my heart, Goodly is your beauty, honeysweet," she says. "You have captivated me, let me stand trembling before you. Bridegroom, I would be taken to the bedchamber."

Appearance counts. Tuck your shirt in.

To get some advice about what draws one person to another—what it is that grabs us in one-fifth of a second—I've enlisted the help of Sheri Winston, who isn't just a genius, she's a vagenius. A wonderful sex educator and author of the award-winning *Women's Anatomy of Arousal: Secret Maps to Buried Pleasure*, Sheri is former nurse-practitioner, and she is good at knowing what makes people happy, body and soul.[3] We've talked about attraction before and it's a subject she clearly enjoys—she has one of those full, wicked, coming-up-from-the-toes laughs you just have to hear—so I asked her to name a few of the reasons for attraction that go beyond perfectly aligned eyes. She has quite a few.

"I don't think it's random," she says. "Our attractions tend to be very specific, and while everyone might have an ideal physical type, it's not just about 'I like tall men with dark hair.' There's way more to it. I guess it's a holistic perspective, but there are multiple lenses through which we can look at it."

One way, Sheri says, is the Dr. Harville Hendrix way. Hendrix's 1988 book *Getting the Love You Want* is a classic of the relationship advice genre. His theory is that people have an unconscious template he calls the Imago. Sheri says we're attracted to people who fulfill the Imago, which is formed of many things, one of them being the qualities of our primary caregivers, "more commonly the negative ones, depending on how much work we've done on ourselves."[4]

Sheri refers to the Hendrix model as "the Flavor of Love model." She says, "This is my take on it. When we're an infant, whatever flavor love comes to us as, that's the flavor we think love is. If love feels cold and critical to us as an infant, we feel loved when someone is cold and critical to us as an adult, even though we hate it and we're miserable and we're so mad because they're cold and critical!" She laughs. But on a very deep level, our environment in the first two years of life "is what the milieu of love feels like to us, so we get attracted to that."

There's two sides to the Imago coin: we initially don't see that unconscious attraction. "We see how great the person is and what a fine, incisive mind they have—we see all the good stuff—but then, when the glamour and the in-loveness wears off, we go, Wow, this person is really critical and judgmental! I might be attracted to somebody who is really easygoing and then realize, Gosh, they have no ambition, right? And then realize, Wow, that's kind of just like my father!"

(I don't want to interrupt her by piping up to say there used to be a show on TV called "The Flavor of Love," in which a surprisingly large number of women were competing for the affections of musician Flavor Flav. One girl got so excited during Flav's equivalent of the rose ceremony that she defecated on the staircase of the mansion. Perhaps in her infantile template love meant that someone would still care for you even if you couldn't control your poop reflex. And she was right—for at least one more episode, I think.)[5]

Another Hendrixism Sheri notes is that "any part of ourselves we've lost or disowned or are really ashamed of, that we really keep in the shadow" can also be something that attracts us. "There's the part we've completely disowned and we've vowed, I am never going to be like that. So, take the critical mother, for example. We hated being criticized and we vowed, I will never be like that, but we really are—not only are we critical of other people but we're critical and judgmental of ourselves. And so we're often attracted to someone who holds those qualities."

The more work we do on ourselves, Sheri says, "the

more we are attracted to people who hold the positive of the love that we got, the positive qualities of our caregivers and our families." By this work on ourselves Sheri means becoming aware of the traits that are causing difficulty in our relationships and doing something to address them. In other words, not masking the problem with another girls' night out or expensive purchase or one-night stand. These all have their place, but you don't want to just paint over rotten wood so you can comfortably ignore it.

Another possible root of attraction has to do with yin/yang energy. We all have polarities within us; one way to consider them is through the Daoist framework of yin and yang, light and dark, feminine and masculine.

"Everyone's got both polarities," Sheri says, but in most of us one predominates. "For most women, in our erotic relationships we tend to be attracted to people who hold the opposite polarity; most women are core yin—except the ones who are not."

I can't help but laugh at this, not because it's funny but because it's so wonderfully simple: it's this way or it isn't. I know everything can't be like this—most things in life are full of gray areas—but I wish they could. I've decided, thanks to this moment with Sheri, to adopt a new life philosophy: Things happen for a reason, and the reason is that they didn't happen some other way.

"It's important to recognize that!" she says, catching my giggle, almost like a teacher who gets the joke but has to maintain order in the classroom. "Most women are core yin, except the ones who aren't. Most men are core yang, except the ones who aren't." Some people are 50–50, but Sheri thinks 90 percent of us have a stronger core of one type or the other and that for "most women it's the yin energy, and we're attracted to somebody who holds core yang energy."

That typically means men, but not necessarily. In same-sex relationships, one partner is likely to have more yin and the other more yang energy, thus their ability to complement each other. If you look at the yin/yang symbol, Sheri says, you also see that within each type of energy is the seed of the other; everything contains it's opposite. This can be seen in the Hendrix model, where a relaxed attitude can betoken laziness, and a sharp mind can quickly turn critical. Every trait is a sword that can cut both ways.

"Let's say I'm a woman and I'm core yin—and I am," Sheri says. "In order to function in the world, especially the world of work, I have to manifest a lot of yang energy: yang initiates and focuses, it has a goal, it gets things done. I have to do a lot of that if I'm going to be successful." This develops the yang energy but ignores the core yin, which is the greater part of her, so when she's done with the competitive grind of the workplace, she says, "I don't know how to take off the yang hat. I don't know how to receive very well. I want to be in control, active, doing. So, who am I going to be attracted to?—I'm going to be attracted to someone who's core yang but who hasn't strengthened their yang energy. It's like a compensation. So if I'm a really ball-busting woman I might be attracted to a really wimpy guy. Rather than engaging in a healthy relationship, I'm attracted to someone whose weakness fits my weakness." This way, she can be the dominant one at home and at work and she never has to develop a balance. "This is where we get terms like *ball-buster* and *pussy-whipped*," she says.

"These sensitive New Age guys have developed their complementary yin energy. They're really good listeners and nurturers, but they don't have that yang fire and they never get laid and they don't know why. Everybody wants to be their friend but nobody wants to fuck 'em! What do we say to them? We say, 'You're too nice!' And they say, 'But you…you…you wanted nice! Don't you want nice?' Yes, we want nice but we still want strength, we want fire. So there's a lot of unhappy people out there because they don't understand their own wiring: where they're strong, where they're weak, what they need to work on. So we get attracted to someone whose dysfunction works with our dysfunction.

"If I have a really weak, wimpy partner, I don't need to work on my yin—I don't need to learn how to put my yang down, I can just keep being a ball-busting bitch at work and at home. And then I get pissed off at my husband because he's a wimp and he won't stand up to me. This is what I mean by compensation—we get attracted to people who can compensate for those areas where we're not healthy and developed. The more developed and balanced we are, the more we are going to be attracted to other healthy, well-balanced, well-developed people."

So is this the truth behind the old saw "opposites attract"?

"It's superficially true," Sheri says, but it doesn't go very deep, which is why the yin/yang model is so good. "By having this more complex understanding it helps us see where we want to go, where we need to go, and where we can go."

What happens if we *don't* look at it and work on it? "We're going to keep being attracted to the same dynamic and we won't even think it's the same," Sheri says. "We'll think, Oh, this one is so much better than the last one! And then six months or a year later, we'll realize that fundamentally, underneath, the dynamic is the same." When you keep ending up in the same dysfunctional pattern, "you know you've got some work to do."

I tell Sheri about my own ricochet pattern: I go from sweet, stable guys who make me feel claustrophobic to less-sweet-and-stable guys with whom I feel free but eventually empty.

"And that's a common thing," she says, "where we ricochet between two extremes: somebody who feels really safe, who feels like a sibling, and somebody we have a lot more polarity with but later realize there's too much and it's not good.

"We struggle with autonomy versus intimacy—this is part of the game, too. Right? I want to but I don't want to. I want to be free but I want to be loved. I want fire and spark—but not too much."

She laughs that Sheri laugh.

See how good it is to talk to a therapist?

So there is some emotional truth to "opposites attract," and some biological truth too, if mice have anything to say about it (and don't they always?)

Early in the "humans rule, other animals drool," phase of our species' development it was believed that we humans didn't use scent to attract mates the way animals do, or so writes F. Bryant Furlow in *Psychology Today*. Superficially, it certainly seems as if dogs, rodents, and other animals rely more on scent than we do. For humans, the expression "sniffing around" is a pejorative for getting information in a sneaky way or getting ready to hit on someone. Furlow says that it was once thought that humans didn't have vomeronasal organs (VNOs), which other species use to detect those all-important chemical signals, pheromones. Come to find out, we do have a VNO, "it's just so enveloped by the massive frontal cortex that it's difficult to find."[6] Moreover, Furlow writes, we have a tiny pair of pits inside the nose that react when presented with certain odors. The owner of the nose doesn't smell a thing; he or she only reports a sense of well-being.

What this has to do with mice is something called *major histocompatibility* (MHC). Sheri Winston points out research showing that mice can detect by scent other mice that are genetically dissimilar and therefore more likely to produce healthy offspring. But it gets even more specific than that. Furlow writes that female mice can detect the odor of MHC genes in a male mouse's urine and will choose the genetically dissimilar mouse, not only preventing incest, but to add his immunities to hers and so create more disease-resistant babies. Even cooler? Humans could also sniff the *mice* and tell which ones had different MHC genes. A 2010 study at the University of Cambridge found that mandrills can tell members of their own family by scent, thus avoiding inbreeding by finding mates with different MHC genes; researchers also found a link between the composition of a mandrill's individual odor and its MHC gene pattern.[7]

Fat lot of good mice and mandrills do us, right? Actually, they do. In scent tests, ovulating women also tend to prefer the scent of men whose MHC is different from theirs. Ovulating—that is, fertile—women have a better sense of smell than they do at other times of the month, by the way.

Sheri points out another element of attraction: women are more attracted to more masculine men—those with higher testosterone—when they are ovulating; when they aren't, they're attracted to men with lower testosterone.[8] Women on the pill, which suppresses ovulation, tend to choose men with more similar genetics to themselves.[9] Couples who have difficulty conceiving also share more similar MHC. In addition, men prefer, sight unseen, by their *scent*, women who are ovulating—this from a study where men smelled T-shirts worn by ovulating and nonovulating women.[10] Ovulating women who work in strip clubs make much better tips than nonovulating women, menstruating women, or women on the pill: they hit the primal spot in the male brain that says "fertility goddess."[11]

But Sheri also notes that humans are rare among animals in that we can and do have sex anytime we want, not just when we're ready to breed—the curious trait that drove Helen Fisher's initial interest. "Most other animals only mate when the female is fertile," Sheri says, "so sex for us has evolved way beyond reproduction to include all kinds of bonding and attachment and tribal things. We have sex for fun and pleasure—we can have sex for profit. We can have sex for revenge or out of boredom. We can have sex for pretty much any reason you can imagine, so it's really interesting to look at the biology, the animal mating template that's still there, which is about finding the best possible reproductive stock that will be most successful in reproducing with. Then it makes sense that all the other stuff that sex means to us is mixed in together.

"For humans, our sexual template evolved beyond reproduction. That's the part that people need to get: our template includes nonreproductive reasons to have sex."

Most animals, in fact, only have sex during the limited time that the female is ovulating; the constant ability to do it—the "ability to copulate throughout the monthly cycle" that triggered Helen Fisher's study of female sexuality— is pretty rare among animals. In fact only bonobos and humans use sex for all the reasons Sheri described above.

In *Sex at Dawn: The Prehistoric Origins of Modern Sexuality*, Christopher Ryan and Cacilda Jethá shrewdly posit that the idea of an oversexed person "acting like an animal" has it backward: "An excessively horny monkey is acting 'human,' while a man or woman uninterested in sex more than once or twice a year would be, strictly speaking 'acting like an animal.' "[12]

Let's look at bonobos for a moment. Bonobos are notorious among apes for constantly screwing around. They use sex playfully, for comfort, to make points, to get food, to resolve conflict. They do it in all kinds of combinations all day long: boy–girl, boy–boy, girl–girl. They kiss. Sex has come to define these smaller, more delicate apes that, like chimps, share a remarkably high percentage of our DNA. Ryan and Jethá write that our DNA differs from theirs by only "roughly 1.6 percent" and that we are closer to them than an Indian elephant is to an African elephant.[13]

In 1998, for a column in the *Orlando Weekly*, I wrote an article titled "Monkey See, Monkey Screw," positing that in the great potluck of evolution some of us must have inherited more bonobo and some of us more chimpanzee.[14] Chimps, the more butch of the two species, make tools and have male-dominated societies. "They reign supremely and often brutally," writes the primatologist Frans de Waal in *Scientific American*. They are mechanically inclined and omnivorous, sometimes eating small monkeys. The males make great shows of their strength. Chimpanzee groups don't mix, "but males of different chimpanzee communities engage in lethal battles."[15]

Bonobos, by contrast, are smaller, quieter, don't make the big shows of strength, and aren't as handy with tools. Their society is female-dominated; the females mix with other groups, bonding with other high-ranking females and assimilating, nonviolently. The males are deferential to the females. Bonobos are all about bonding, sympathy, empathy, playing, and sex. They're imaginative and sensitive. De Waal writes, "During the World War Two bombing of Hellabrun, Germany, the bonobos in a nearby zoo all died of fright from the noise; the chimpanzees were unaffected."

If bonobos tossed their lot into the genetic grab bag of evolution, I got away with more bonobo DNA than chimp, as did most of the people I pal around with. I think some people got a nearly even mix—it's my theory that bonobos might be, typically, the artists, chimps might be the agents, and the perfect chimp/bonobo split would be the sensitive musician who can still shrewdly sell himself. It's not scientific, but it would explain a *lot*—about the human use of sex for everything from selling hamburgers to providing comfort to *really* crazy things like making babies.

So those are just a few of the myriad reasons we become attracted to one another. When you can't figure out why you've been thrown over for someone you think of as the green potato chip ("She could have anyone and she chose *him?*") look at all the possible reasons you now know why it's probably not something you did or anything you are. You don't remind her enough of her father. He's looking for a wimpy woman so he never has to balance his masculine energy. She can smell that you're not MHC compatible. And none of it matters, because as humans we can screw around as much as we want, so it might just be a matter of waiting.

And what about your receptivity to the right person? Love is chance, Dr. Fisher writes in *Why Him? Why Her?* "The perfect partner can sit next to you at a party and you might not notice him or her if you are exceptionally busy at work or school, enmeshed in another relationship or otherwise emotionally preoccupied."[16]

If, however, you are a little rocky, the appeal of others—like a virus to a weakened immune system—has more of an opening. States of agitation, Dr. Fisher writes, lead to the release of dopamine. So the more riled up you are over anything, the more dopamine is released and the more ready you are to be smitten.

And the someone with whom you are presented—well, it could be Prince William or Flavor Flav and there's probably not much you can do about it. Think of the love potion in *Midsummer Night's Dream*. Your agitated heart is as a plowed and fertile field in which dumb ideas—or lovely ones—can take root in one-fifth of a second.

So, to Sam's knitted brow over the fact that the Alligator Man was happily paired while he and I, respectively, are having rocky romantic times, there are numerous potential answers, none of which make it suck less. And when you're having a sucky time there's nothing as nice as a road trip to the Gulf Coast to hear about what happened with the Alligator Man and the Monkey Girl.

GIBSONTON

In truth, when I first realized I was going to be writing a book on strange love and wanted to go looking for it Gibsonton was my first thought, not because it's known for love, but because it's known for being strange. I have a sentimental attachment to it from being in a bar near there once into which someone tried to bring a horse. I thought there had to be some intriguing stories there. It looks no different from anywhere else in rural Florida: lots of mobile homes and guys at the gas station you think you might have seen being arrested on *Cops*. If it weren't for the fact that there are things like Tilt-a-Whirls and funnel cake stands parked in so many backyards, it would be just another "no-collar town."

But Gibsonton was once the home of numerous "human oddities," or sideshow acts, and the reason the town is littered with carnival rides is because it has historically been the chosen spot for so many carnival, circus, and fair folk to winter. It might be the evidence of its luminous sideshow heritage or just my awareness of it, but there are some different-looking people here, like a man sauntering out of the Showtown Bar who is so thin he looks like he's made out of rice paper. Inside the Showtown, a classic Gibtown haunt, there are paintings of various circus acts: a man with two eyes and four eyeballs, a lady dressed as Cleopatra, and, curiously, a demonic bartender with metallic bloodred eyes who looks like he's glad you finally showed up so he can eat your esophagus. Around the bar from this painting a woman is sitting on a barstool. She has long, lustrous red hair and a hairline that goes back to her ears—picture a serene Queen Elizabeth I nursing a beer. At 5:00 p.m. on a sunny afternoon there are a good 10 people sitting in this dark, smoky den in silence. There is no music and little talk. It's like Jack Daniel's put everyone in time-out.

Finally someone fires up the jukebox and the crowd comes to life as if connected to it by an invisible cord. (There's the dopamine power of music for you.) They start talking, even to us. One couple recommends an al fresco restaurant where we can watch the sunset over the bay, and it's about time for that. Sam and I have just spent a very intriguing afternoon with Ward Hall, the greatest friend the sideshow ever had, hearing tales of romances past.

"It was my first job. A circus had an ad for a magician and a fire-eater and I wanted to go to the circus so bad," Ward says, and you can still hear the pang of love in his voice after 67 years in the business.[17] He got his first circus job at 14 and since then he's been everything from a magician to a fire-eater to a ticket seller to a sideshow owner and promoter. Now 81, Ward is preparing to take a waxworks show of famous circus acts on the road, but he has agreed to take a little time to tell Sam and me stories of love among the—

"Freaks! F-R-E-A-K-S. That's what they call themselves," Ward tells me of the sideshow folk who used to populate the town, dismissing my search for a more politically correct term. We meet him in his front yard, where he's rolling up tarps beside a sparkling swimming pool flanked by cherub statues and a big red-and-yellow sign leaning up against a bus that announces "World Wonders! Strangest Show on Earth."

"My life on the wall," Ward says as we enter a very long, very close oblong porch filled with sideshow memorabilia. On our right is his wall of press clippings and advertising posters from shows he's been in or put on all over the world, including at the Smithsonian. Across from these is something with a sheet thrown over it. Two squat, hairy legs stick out from underneath. It looks like a gorilla trying not to be seen. I decide not to ask.

In a Plexiglas case next to this there is a 10-foot stuffed python with the snakeskin head of a woman wearing a turban. She's the kind of attraction Ward likes because they don't come around looking for a paycheck every week.

He says this, but Ward's great affection for the performers he's worked with is apparent. He begins his stories of love among the freaks with a tale that's nothing short of the Capulets and the Montagues, had they lived under the Big Top. These stories are entirely Ward's recollections, which I have supplemented with additional reading about some of the characters we discuss.

"The young man's name was Emmett Bejano," Ward says, settling into a chair in the backyard. He gives his narration the timing, drama, and phrasing befitting a carnival barker of nearly seven decades. "Emmett had a skin condition called extreme ichthyosis." This a very rare ailment that's often fatal. The body overproduces skin cells and the skin doesn't shed properly, becoming dry and scaly; *ichthys* is Greek for "fish."[18] There are many different kinds of ichthyosis; some of its dangerous symptoms include dehydration, the inability to perspire, cracking of the skin (which causes pain and exposes the body to infection), and skin growing over the eyes and ears. It's treated with creams to moisturize the skin and make it pliable.

"We've had several alligator-skinned people—oh gosh, they really suffer in hot weather because they can't perspire. They perspire through their eyes, which damages their eyes, and they get blind or suffer loss of sight. They have to put oils on their face to take away the scales," Ward says.

"Emmett was born in Naples, Florida," Ward says. "And at the time"—through the 1930s—"it wasn't unusual for sideshow owners to actually adopt human oddities." A sideshow operator by the name of Johnny Bejano adopted Emmett, who was then about 12. Johnny also had another adopted son, Paul, who was a dwarf. By the time Emmett was 17 or 18 he wanted to do something different, so he went to another sideshow, run by Carl Lauther, who had also adopted a child: Percilla (pronounced Per-SILL-a).

"She was a little living doll," Ward says, "and always had a great personality. She also had two sets of teeth and black silky hair growing over her face, and her body had a complexion that was kind of a brownish-green in color." He remembers her as a marvelous dancer.

Percilla was 17 or 18 when Emmett came along, and a spark ignited between the Alligator Man and the Monkey Girl. Carl Lauther didn't approve, but luckily 20th-century youth were a bit more bold and canny than their mopey medieval counterparts, Romeo and Juliet.

"The family had all gone to sleep in their house trailers, and late at night Percilla and Emmett eloped," Ward says. The Lauthers were frantic, but the young couple eventually returned. They became staples with the Lauther sideshow and even worked together one season for Ringling Bros. and Barnum & Bailey. So they had a much happier ending than those silly Italian kids.

Ward and his partner Harry got to know Emmett and Percilla in the 1960s when they were all living in the same area. Everyone belonged to the Showmen's Club. "Percilla loved to dance, but Emmett didn't. In those years I would rather dance than eat, so many, many an hour we spent on the dance floor. We just had great times together. They had their own show, billed as 'The World's Strangest Married Couple! Percilla the Monkey Girl! Emmett the Alligator-Skinned Man!'" They did well, Ward says, and retired comfortably.

Eventually Percilla's teeth began to cause her pain and she had one set removed, Ward says. In one of the documentaries the couple appeared in, Percilla relates that she wanted to shave all her hair off, but Emmett wouldn't have it. "He said, 'If you do, I'll leave you, because I love you just like you are,'" Ward relates. "And then she laughed. But after he died she had the facial hair removed. Percilla lived for several years after that. So that's the story of Emmett and Percilla Bejano."

Ward knew another Alligator, Mildred, who was a 5 on a scale of 1 to 10 for ichthyosis. (Emmett, he says, was a 9.) She ended up with a man named Bill Durks who became part of the sideshow, as Ward says many people do. Bill went to the fair and thought, My god, I'm stranger than anything they've got in here. This looks like an easy way to make a living.

And it was.

Bill Durks met Mildred the Alligator-Skinned Woman. "Companionship became love, and they got married, and they were married for quite some time"—until Mildred's death. Bill worked on Ward's show, but only for one season, because "there was nobody for him really to buddy around with." Only one guy in the show was interested in going out and seeing the world like Bill Durks, "a little black man," Ward says. "His name was Bill Coles. He had been run over as a young adult, got drunk and lay down on the railroad tracks and the train got him, and so he lost both legs and lived in Buffalo, New York." Like Bill Durks, Bill Coles attended the fair in Toronto and was spotted by someone who said he'd be a great attraction: the half-boy. He eventually went to work for Ward.

Just when I'm wondering if the heat or the day has gotten to me or if I just can't remember Bill Durks's claim to fame as a human oddity, Ward comes out with it.

"Bill Durks looked like somebody took an ax and hit him right on the end of his nose, because his nose split like that." Ward makes a gesture to illustrate a nose splayed out across an awfully wide area of face. "He had two eyes, but also another indentation like an eye socket in his head. He would take a cosmetic pencil and draw in an eye, so he was billed as 'The Man with Three Eyes and Two Noses,' or sometimes 'The Two-Faced Man.' He only stayed with us one year because he was, after all, a Southern white gentleman from Alabama and Bill Coles was a northern Yankee black man. They were not unfriendly with each other, but they did not feel comfortable running around Memphis, Tennessee, or Savannah, Georgia, or Birmingham, Alabama, together. They were the best of friends on the show. But Bill Durks didn't have anybody to buddy around with, really. And he missed that, I think."

What does this have to do with love?

Nothing. But I thought you'd want to hear the story of a nice, shy, curious man with two noses and three eyes who couldn't hang out with his African-American friend from work because it looked peculiar.

THE MELANCHOLY STORY OF THE LOBSTER BOY

In general, Ward Hall says, sideshow people tend to stay together once they fall in love. Like Percilla and Emmett, like Bill and Mildred. The reason the relationships do so well, Ward says, is the fact that these circus people have one thing in common, and it's not their unique physical traits.

"They're ham actors! Would you expect to see the Penguin Girl performing the part of Gloria Swanson in *Sunset Boulevard*? Would you expect to see Mildred the

Alligator Woman performing with Fred Astaire instead of Ginger Rogers? No."

"But I'd kind of like to," I confess.

What Ward is trying to tell me is that it is their jobs as entertainers that make human oddities prefer each other's company. Because they can't always be in mainstream performances, they end up together and have the kind of camaraderie that often springs up in the workplace. Theater people, like all people with common interests and desires, tend to group together. They understand each other. They love the sound of applause, a sound that Ward says means "You're receiving love."

No matter how unconventional your job is, it's a good place to meet a love interest. CBS Moneywatch says the frequency of workplace romances is increasing, and though the carnival is probably not what they had in mind, the same factors apply there as in other workplaces: common interests, common colleagues, and time spent in proximity.[19] All the examples of love that Ward cites are couples who were working the same gig.

Grady Stiles, in the opinion of Ward Hall, was not so happy to be part of the sideshow crowd.

"His wife was a very sweet lady," Ward begins when the subject of the Lobster Boy comes up. "And Grady is a sad story."

According to Joe Nickell's *Secrets of the Sideshow*, Grady Stiles was actually the fifth generation of Stileses, going back to the mid-19th century, to have the condition known as *ectrodactylism*, meaning "monstrous fingers," also called "split hand/foot malformation."[20] It is not as uncommon as other syndromes; 6 in 10,000 people are born with it. It's characterized by a deep split between the fingers or toes and often the fusing together of remaining digits so they look more like a lobster claw than a 5-fingered appendage.[21] In western Zimbabwe one in four members of the Vadoma tribe are born with this mutation of the seventh chromosome in their feet. The "ostrich people," as they are called, are proud of this unique feature.[22]

"I knew Grady's father," Ward says. "His father was an attraction in Dick Best's sideshow: the Lobster Man. He had legs. He could walk. Grady was born with the condition not only in his hands but also in his legs, and he could not walk. He was wheelchair bound."

Not everyone who has unique traits like the ones we've been talking about should be in a show, Ward says. They have to be comfortable with their condition and want to make a living; and the best, he says, are proud of their bodies.

"Grady was one of those people who was born and put on exhibition when he was not much more than a baby, which was certainly not correct. And in a way I know he was bitter about his condition but he also realized that it was that condition which, in effect, made him a wealthy man." He also had a drinking problem, which Ward says got worse every year.

"When Grady was young, if you didn't see his legs or his hands you would have to class him as being a very handsome young man. I'm not sure where he and Teresa met, but obviously they were very much in love."

According to *Murder in the Tropics,* by Stuart B. McIver, they met in 1959, when Mary Teresa was a ticket seller at the carnival; she had just left an abusive husband.[23]

Grady Stiles and Mary Teresa had two children, one of whom inherited ectrodactylism. One daughter, Donna, worked for Ward. The Stileses were living in Pittsburgh when Donna found a boyfriend. "They fell in love. They wanted to get married, but Grady said, "I want to meet this boy. Bring him to the house." The boy came and, Ward says, he and Grady had words. As the boy turned to leave, Grady shot and killed him.

"He was convicted of murder in the state of Pennsylvania and was sentenced to the penitentiary. He never spent one day there. They said they did not have the facilities to take care of a person with his physical condition, so he got off scot-free. He got away with murder."

Grady actually got 15 years' probation for his crime but it was tantamount to getting away with murder.[24] Ward is right about the fact that he wasn't incarcerated because no prison had the facilities to accommodate his condition. To hear Ward tell it, Grady's knowledge that he could get away with murder gave him a feeling he could get away with anything.

Following the trial, the Stileses moved down to Gibsonton and their second daughter, Cathy, was born—with the ectrodactylism in her hands and legs. Grady was moving up. In 1967 he was on the board of directors at the Showman's Club, where Ward was also a board member.

"He would get drunk at the club," Ward recounts. "He could move fast, and he'd pick an argument with some guy and then kinda slide out of his wheelchair and come up to the guy real fast and reach up with those claws. He had as much power in those as a wrestler would have in his whole body, and he'd reach up and grab the guy by the testicles. In my vague recollection it seems like he even pulled a gun on somebody at the club. Anyway, he was voted off the board of directors."

Teresa eventually left Grady for Harry Glenn Newman,

a little person billed as "The Smallest Man in the World," and Grady married another woman, Barbara Browning, who gave birth to a son, Grady III, who also had ectrodactylism.

So here's Grady getting convicted for murder, and he's on his second wife while some guys, guys who don't do bad things, who don't Kung Fu–grip their colleagues' family jewels at a meeting, who aren't abusive drunks, can barely get a kiss on New Year's Eve? Why? Why do we fall for some people and not others?

Well, we have all those subconscious reasons Sheri Winston touched on: we're drawn to people who remind us of our parents, who balance us, with whom we have a workplace attraction. Grady, Ward says, would have been considered an attractive guy in his earlier years, and Teresa was a carnival worker who understood life on the fair circuit. Then we have Dr. Fisher's notion about being more vulnerable when you're in a volatile state. Grady could be charming, so the many ways we have of falling for people and our inexplicable attractions begin to become at least a little more explicable.

Anyway, Grady married Barbara but later reunited with Teresa, and his drinking and abuse got worse. According to Joe Nickell, Grady struck his daughter Cathy during her pregnancy, causing her to require a Caesarian. (She delivered a daughter with ectrodactylism.)[25]

After a while, enough was enough. On November 29, 1992, while Grady was watching TV in his home, he was shot in the head by Christopher Wyant, a neighbor, who had been hired by Teresa's son, Glenn Jr., and paid $1,500. Glenn was average-sized and was billed as "The Human

Blockhead" for his performing skill: driving nails into his nostrils onstage. He was convicted of first-degree murder and sentenced to 25 years to life without the possibility of parole for his role in the murder.[26] Teresa, claiming battered spouse syndrome, was convicted of manslaughter and sentenced to 12 years.[27] Francine Hornberger, author of *Carny Folk: The World's Weirdest Carnival Acts*, writes that Teresa was railroaded. She pleaded with the court, explaining, "My husband was going to kill my family. I believe that from the bottom of my heart. I'm sorry this happened but my family is safe now. At least I know they're alive and I thank God for that."[28] Christopher Wyant was convicted of second-degree murder and sentenced to 27 years.[29]

As Ward said, it's a sad, sad story.

There's no arguing that the setting and the characters in this tale make it a colorful one, but the deterioration of love into violence and murder happens in more mundane settings all too often. Meanwhile, it has been a long, hot afternoon in Gibsonton, and I ask Ward if we can end on happier note. He obliges.

Jeanie (Bernice Evelyn Smith) was born without legs and with one twisted arm. According to Ward, she was adopted from an orphanage by a woman who immediately put the little girl on exhibition. He doesn't know whether she was abused, but "she certainly was an unhappy little girl." Eventually the woman booked Jeannie to be in the Ringling Bros. and Barnum & Bailey Circus.

"Now, also on that show was a young Italian gentleman who was over eight feet tall," Ward says, and love in the workplace bloomed between Al Tomaini, the Giant, and Jeanie the Half-Girl. Al went to Jeanie's adoptive mother and announced to her, "You are no longer Jeanie's manager. From now on I'm her manager." The woman resisted, but as Jeanie said, "You know how demanding those Italians can be," so shortly afterward they were married, adopted two girls, and moved to Gibsonton.

Eddie and Grace LeMay were a carny couple who ran concessions and were in the habit of camping and fishing on the nearby Alafia River. This was in the 1940s, Ward says, and as more and more of their friends started joining them on their annual trips they built some cabins and started a little cookhouse, Eddie's Hut. The Tomainis bought 10 acres alongside them and set up the Giant's Camp, a restaurant that became the social center of Gibsonton.

"Starting in the early fifties there were anywhere from seventy-five to eighty-five professional human oddities who made their homes in Gibsonton, and so it became the Sideshow Capital of the World," Ward says.

"We had the Tomainis, and show owner Mickey Mansion had a place with all his people. Slim Kelly had a place with all his people, the Fat Lady had a place on the corner over there, and oh gosh, the Bull Dog Girl and her husband was Jakey Altman, a little Jewish man who had hands growing out of his shoulders, he was the Seal Boy—so there was a lot of them."

So for one brief, shining moment there was a happy little wonderland in sunny Florida where, for the Giant and the Half-Lady, the Alligator Man and the Monkey Girl, the Seal Boy and the Bull Dog Girl, love bloomed, and they lived if not forever after, then at least happily.

"Love doesn't recognize those kinds of things," Ward says about Percilla and Emmett and their forbidden love. And he's right. Love doesn't recognize its obstacles. It doesn't recognize the advice earnestly given by cadres of dating coaches, doesn't recognize wedding rings or age, doesn't recognize alligator skin or two noses. And it often doesn't know how to quit. Love doesn't recognize a thing besides what it loves.

Chapter 4

"The Ballad of Burt and Linda"

IF YOU BREAK UP WITH NEW YORK, CAN YOU STILL BE FRIENDS?

In 2009 I got sick. Really sick. I was in and out of various medical offices almost every week with a yeast infection that would not go away, and no one could pinpoint why my body couldn't fight it. (It turned out to be stress.) Well-meaning friends tried to tell me I could visualize my way out of it and I tried. Let me tell you something about bacteria. When it realizes that the only weapon you have on your side is the power of intention, it laughs till its belly jiggles and then invites its friends over for drinks and colonization.

The one thing I *had* to visualize was another way to do my job—I was a sex and relationships writer, heavy on the sex, who couldn't even stand to think about the subject. I faked it for a while (who hasn't?) but eventually focused on the relationships side of the category and started researching love stories, the more unusual the better. Eventually I came across one of the most celebrated couples in the popular history of crazy love. They even have a documentary about them, *Crazy Love*, directed by Dan Klores (where much of my knowledge of them comes from).[1] No pair better illustrates how complex human relationships can be than the couple you'll read about here.

★ ★ ★

Autumn in New York is extraordinarily beautiful, ener-
gizing, colorful, and soft, an energy that could facilitate
anyone falling in love. It was in the autumn of 1957 that
Burton Pugach, then 30 years old, a successful lawyer
specializing in negligence cases (and a successful woman-
izer), first saw 20-year-old Linda Riss in Joyce Kilmer Park
in the Bronx and fell like a brick for her. Linda would have
been easy to fall for. It wasn't just her doll-like face and
pinup figure: she had an aura about her, an allure you can
see even in still photographs. A presence. She would still
have that presence 50 years later.

Burt and Linda started dating. He had the money and
status to show her a lavish good time in the way younger,
less affluent suitors couldn't. He showed her a jet-set style
of living: he had his own plane, he owned a nightclub, she
got to meet stars, including Johnny Mathis. Burt sometimes became wildly jealous if he thought Linda was dating
other men, so much so that she agreed to have her doctor
confirm for Burt that she was still a virgin. And there was
another problem: Burt's wife. Linda was devastated to
discover that this man, who seemed so promising a catch
and had pursued her so doggedly, had been married all this
time. She wanted him to get a divorce. Burt agreed, and
he claimed to have done so, but Linda's suspicious mother
discovered that the papers were fraudulent. Linda finally
broke it off with Burt after his wife called her and said she
would never give him a divorce. Linda became engaged
to Larry Schwartz, a handsome heartthrob she met while
vacationing in Florida with her girlfriends.

Burt completely came apart at the seams. He was hopelessly in love with Linda, but he had a wife who didn't
want a divorce and a young daughter who was severely

mentally handicapped. The Bronx DA was coincidentally investigating Burt's law practice, and Burt's firm was charged with illegal conduct for fee-splitting—a practice wherein professionals such as doctors and lawyers share fees with colleagues for referred business. Burt denied it. He was hitting the bottle pretty heavily and still pining over Linda. At one point in *Crazy Love* he talks about having been committed to a mental hospital at that time and a friend getting him out, which was "the worst thing that could have been." Linda complained to the police that he was harassing her—phone calls, rocks thrown through her window—but no one did anything. Burt asked one of his clients if he knew someone who could beat up a girl, and he gave him Linda's name. He was hoping to scare her into running back to him for protection. A man named Heard Harden went to the Riss home on June 15, 1959, pretending to deliver a package, and threw lye in Linda's face. To this day Burt insists that he never asked for that to happen—he would tell me he didn't even know what lye was. Linda was in the hospital for three months recovering from the damage done to her skin and her eyes.[2]

Larry Schwartz stuck by Linda, but after she got out of the hospital he eventually left.[3] In *Crazy Love* Linda says that she encouraged him to leave right after the attack. She got a job and her own apartment, and, with her limited vision, she even took up painting and proved to be quite a talented artist. In the early '90s Linda's vision seriously deteriorated. Now she can see light but cannot discern forms. When I ask if things are generally pretty good she says, "Well, I guess it's okay. I'm not thrilled by not being able to see—that's something I've been trying to handle for years. I guess you learn to live with it—that's the way it's gonna be."

Burt and Heard Harden went to trial. (Two other defendants pleaded guilty.) Feeding the media frenzy over the story were delays including Burt's attempt to get rid of his lawyer, Henry Lowenberg, who was epileptic and who Burt claimed had seizures during the trial. Burt asked to defend himself instead. At one point he set out to cut his wrists to try to get a mistrial. He was sent to the hospital but later returned to court. Linda, appearing in court, was led to the witness stand—she could see, but her vision was limited.

In 1961 both Burt and Harden were found guilty on three counts of maiming and two counts each of second-degree assault, conspiracy, and second-degree burglary (because the jury believed Harden had gone into Linda's home). Burt was sentenced to 15 to 30 years in prison.

After the trial, Linda went to Europe with friends for a while, but she never married or even seriously dated; she was, in her own words, "damaged merchandise." Marianne MacDonald reported in the London Observer, "A Southern boy had proposed marriage but cried off when she took off her glasses."[4]

Burt was released after 14 years. He had been sending money to Linda while he was in prison, and when the parole board asked him if he would continue to give her money upon release, he said, "If I make it." Interviewed on TV after his release, he took advantage of the moment to propose to Linda—on camera—since he wasn't allowed to see her in person. Friends set up a date, and eventually Linda accepted. They've been together ever since.

I would soon hear about their happily-ever-after from the couple themselves.

I have to leave my peacocks behind and travel to New York to meet with Burt and Linda. It's a city with which I have a past. I was born in Brooklyn but my family moved to Florida when I was a kid, so I fetishized New York the way one fetishizes a lover with whom one has no closure. As I got on with freelancing I fantasized about having a job that would allow me to travel between the comforts of Florida and the thrill of Manhattan, and this I eventually managed to do. New York and I had this casual relationship for years.

Then, like a fool, I moved in. I left Orlando in 2003 and took a sublet in Brooklyn. Seeing New York every day almost immediately put the big Monty Python foot down on any romance we had between us. Thanks to overfamiliarity, financial stress, and other circumstances, the passion was gone and the romance came to an end.

Now I was coming back to meet Burt and Linda. The May afternoon I arrived was glorious—the most beautiful day I've ever seen in the city. Everyone was outside. Bodies that had been suffocating all winter in warm coats, tights, and boots were getting a chance to breathe in short sleeves and breezy cotton skirts. Flowers were blooming in flower boxes and everyone had a gelato, an iced coffee, or a cold Chardonnay. I had the afternoon to acclimate, plan, and wander around the streets off Riverside Park.

If love is an addiction and I had, at one time, a bubbly-wubbly, infatuated, twitterpated romance with New York, this would be the part where I fell off the wagon and considered jumping back in, as people often do with an ex. She's so beautiful! She's so…big! I'm so glad to be back inside her!

The great thing about ex-lovers is that when you start falling into the mire of getting reattracted to them they will do something that reminds you why you left, hopefully before you open your big stupid mouth and suggest reuniting.

The next morning, New York reminds me of her less-attractive qualities—cold and frantic. Getting to Queens from Manhattan for an 8:00 a.m. meeting is the nicest thing I've done for anyone since I was in the Brownies, and I'm doing it for Burt, who requests that time. We'll have breakfast at their local diner and then I'll meet Linda, who has enough sway in the world not to have to get up too early.

Burt pulls up to the train station to meet me in a Cadillac the size of a Carnival cruise ship and bids me to get in. There's a fur coat in the backseat that looks like you'd be snug wearing it in Alaska and which, given Burt and Linda's ages, I'm sure is real fur. Burt is wearing a tan suit. He's impressively on the ball at 83. He went on a health kick in prison, he says, when he started lifting weights and became a vegetarian. It gave him something to do.

After a little polite chat, Burt tells me what a crock it was that he got arrested for harassment in the 1990s. Evangeline Borja, then 42, and Burt, then 70, had a five-year affair. Burt was convicted by a six-person jury, evenly divided by sex, of one count of harassment, which is a violation and thus less serious than a misdemeanor. The *Times* reported that after several attempts to get her to reconcile with him, Burt became jealous that Evangeline had met another man, and when she still refused to come back "despite Mr. Pugach's offers of a mink coat and $1 million, he threatened to have her killed, she testified." It was his repeated phone calls to Evangeline that got him convicted of the one violation.[5]

En route to the Shalimar Diner on Austin Street in

Flushing, Queens, Burt says that he's the one who broke up with Evangeline because he didn't want to leave Linda. Evangeline had come to see him in his office.[6]

"You had a fight," I say.

"An argument!" Burt says, extremely conscious of such subtle differences. "Not this!" He holds up his fists like a boxer.

"Right, well—verbal," I acknowledge.

"What happened was, she threw my old legal case in my face. She said, 'You're just a criminal.' And I responded... crudely. I said, 'This didn't stop you from fucking me for five years,' and she started crying and left my office. One of her fellow employees saw her in tears and called the hundred-and-twelfth precinct, which sent over two officers. Evangeline told them what happened. They're *haimishe*, you know, ordinary guys, so they told her, 'Stay out of his office.'"

Burt says that Evangeline was coerced into pressing charges. He was arrested that night and told that they were going to ask that he be held without bail, which Burt knew was illegal: the charges were misdemeanors, and with a misdemeanor you had to fix bail.

I ask him to list the charges.

"Harassment. Menacing. Menacing requires you to have a weapon. I had no weapon. Like if I opened up my jacket"—he does, showing the way people let you know they have a gun—"hey, you see? Sexual abuse. The big sexual abuse was I was supposed to have touched her tit. We were screwing for five years. I did not touch her tit."

The judge finally fixed bail at $50,000. Burt spent the night in jail. The next morning, Linda arrived at the courthouse dressed in black leather from head to toe and carrying a suitcase filled with $50,000 in cash for Burt's bail.

"That's her pin money," Burt says. She didn't want to waste time going to a broker. "I give her an allowance every week and she's a miser and she saves it, so that's her pin money."

"Is that where she got the coat?" I ask, gesturing to the fur in the backseat.

"That's mine," Burt says. "It's coyote."

We've barely taken up residence in a booth before a waitress comes up and starts talking to Burt. She's probably in her forties and everything about her is soft: her blonde hair, her blue eyes, her voice, a feathery whisper, like angel food cake. Even when she isn't whispering there is a cushion to her speech, possibly characteristic of someone who has had to do a lot of soothing of others. Burt has given her legal advice and she can't say enough nice things about the most notorious couple in Queens.

"I've been working here twenty-one years, so I've known them twenty-one years," she tells me. "He's an amazing man."

How long have you and Linda been married? I ask Burt.

"Linda and I? We're newlyweds! Thirty-six years. I always ask her, "Are you still my girlfriend? I don't care about this wife stuff. I need a girlfriend."

Burt isn't shy about what was once a rapacious appetite for women. "Wilt Chamberlain wrote his book that he had three thousand women. I was talking to one of the guys in my building and I said, 'That's impossible!' He said, 'What are you, like, a hundred behind him?' "

"So you were a big Don Juan before and after jail. Did you calm down when you got married?"

"No."

"Linda—"

"She didn't know. I was very discreet."

He's done with all that now, he says. He's 83 years old.

"You're done?" I ask.

"Yep."

"Forever."

"Yep."

I remind him that I have this on tape.

He has only one regret in terms of women.

"Fourteen years in prison—of course I have regrets."

I ask if Burt sent that money to Linda while he was in jail out of guilt, wanting to make up for his actions as much as he could.

"Of course! 'Cause I indirectly caused what happened to her. Not directly."

It is Burt's contention that while he did hire men to beat Linda up, the maiming—the throwing of lye—was not something he ever intended. He had no idea this was what they had planned.

"Has Linda always been the only one?"

"No."

"Well, there's a difference between sex and love," I say. "She may not have been the only one you were attracted to but was she the only one you ever loved?"

"I guess so."

"I mean, there's a difference—right?"

"Yeah. Yeah, I guess so."

Burt's a smart guy—in fact *Crazy Love* shows a picture of a document attesting that he has an I.Q. of 133—so it's genuinely surprising to me that he doesn't seem to have much considered the differences between love and sex, nuances that I could spend eternity flipping over with a stick and examining.

★ ★ ★

The reason Burt asked to meet with me alone is that he wanted to discuss a book he's writing about his prison time and about the crookedness of the justice system, a passionate topic of conversation. He sees himself as a victim of many injustices and feels that many others don't get a fair shake in the courtroom either. (He's no fan of Dan Klores, the maker of *Crazy Love,* by the way; he sued Klores and HBO for $15 million, saying they falsely enticed Linda and him to sign over the rights to their story.[7]) He gives me the book to read later. Between the intricacies of his own cases and his having been an inmate at Attica during the 1971 riot, it's very interesting stuff. While he was in jail a woman named Lenore wrote to him and swore she would wait for him until he got out. Burt says her letters were withheld from him. Upon his release, he discovered that Lenore had committed suicide. One of the reforms that resulted from the Attica uprising was fewer restrictions on mail.[8]

"Okay," he says as we wrap up our breakfast meeting. "Let me call my girlfriend." And with that we're out the door and en route to the Pugaches' apartment, where I will get to meet Linda. For some reason, I find Linda a bit more intimidating than Burt.

LINDA

Linda is waiting at the apartment, drinking her morning coffee, looking elegant in a black crepe blouse, long black skirt, large black glasses, black choker, and white pearl-finish nail polish on nicely manicured midlength nails. She's tiny-tiny, as fragile as a baby bird. Not only has her eyesight been totally gone for the last twenty years, she has arteriosclerosis. An operation for it was proposed, but it was determined that it would do more harm than good. She quit smoking just last year—no help, no pills, no patches. She's very strong-willed, Burt says. Her charisma is as evident in person as it was on screen.

The first thing she does is bitch at Burt for getting phone calls from Japan.

Linda: I just got a call for you, Burt; I'm not handling it. Japan called you.

Burt: Japan?

Linda: Japan.

Burt: What do they want?

Linda: What do they want. Probably an interview.

Burt: Tell them I don't speak Japanese.

Linda: Gimme a break! How did I get involved here?

Burt: Did you get the number?

Linda: No. I'm not calling Japan. I told her to call you back in an hour. [To me:] So you've got an hour.

Burt: And Japan wants me? Hey, maybe we'll get a free vacation to Japan.

What I see of their apartment is nicely furnished and comfortable, but I don't stray far into it. Linda has given me an hour and I get the impression she's not a person to fool with, so I get on with it.

"So, when you first met Burt, did it take a little while or did you fall for him quickly?"

Burt comes in with the coffee Linda has been asking for and says, "She hasn't fallen for me yet," which gets a very big laugh out of Linda.

"Is that true?" I ask.

"I don't know how true it is, but, no, I didn't flip out for Burt when I first met him."

"Everybody else did," Burt says. I wonder if her self-possession, the fact that she *didn't* fall right away, is what made her the one he wanted. As we discussed earlier: desire doubling when it's thwarted.

"I thought he was a geek," Linda says. She gets a girlish kind of pleasure from this word, a new word she knows will get a reaction.

"You thought I was a what?"

"A geek!"

"They didn't even have that word in the vocabulary then!"

"Right," she says, "But now it's in the vocabulary. I mean—I was not terribly impressed." But Linda's grandmother *was* impressed because Burt was a lawyer.

Burt adjourns to do some computer work and I get to ask Linda about the day it happened.

"Well, it's something I really hate rehashing over and over again, but needless to say I opened the door and I thought it was maybe flowers or a present from Larry and I got a face full of liquid, and that's all that happened. After that I was taken to the hospital and a lot of the rest is sort of blurry, except I said it was Burt who did it."

We go over the fact that it wasn't Burt himself who did it but people he hired, and when I ask what he hired them to do, she says I would have to ask him. "But I think he hired them to beat me up or something of that nature. I certainly don't think he ever had this intention."

She's surprised when I ask how she came to want to marry him right after his release from prison.

"You're talking a hundred years later!"

Fourteen years later, I remind her.

"Yeah," Linda says, "but that's a long time between drinks."

This cracks me up.

"I think it was probably a very boring time in my life and I wanted a little excitement." At the time Linda still had enough of her eyesight to work. "I was a receptionist for a large company. I didn't do very much of anything except smile when people came in, which is very nice. I had a nice job and it went day to day. There we go."

"You wanted a little excitement and he proposed to you on television," I say.

"Yeah," she says, her voice suddenly so soft it doesn't sound like the same woman. Still softly, but a little more determined, she goes on, "I figured, you know, what the heck? Let's see where it goes and that's it but I didn't expect it to go anywhere. I really didn't."

She wanted to date awhile and get to know each other, but "he was always in a rush and he got a ring and blah, blah, blah," she says.

Here Burt, promising he won't interrupt again, interrupts, evidently having been eavesdropping and wanting to correct something for the record.

"Listen to this baloney. Here—read this letter," he says, giving me a handwritten note from a friend of Linda's dated June 8, 2007. I begin to read aloud:

"Your name was still Linda Riss when you and I were friends more than three decades ago … Burt was still in prison and you kept talking about marrying him when he got out."

Burt laughs.

"Is that true?" I ask Linda. "How did you feel about him when he was on the inside?"

"How did I feel when he was in there? I felt safe."

Burt points to the letter and says that Linda can snow me all she wants, but the letter is proof of her real thoughts. I continue to read.

"I so disagreed with that decision that I backed away from our

friendship. I couldn't bear to be a witness to his hurting you again or possibly even killing you. I want you to know how sorry I am that I was such a lousy friend when you needed one so badly. But I'm glad I was wrong and that you have a pretty decent marriage. You made the right decision, with good wishes."

"Can I have a tissue?" Linda says. "I'm dripping."

Linda recently had a cornea operation and her eyes tend to tear. The operation was supposed to restore some of her sight. "I think it's dubious," she says gently. "But we live in hope."

Eventually she asks Burt, "Am I bloody?"

"No, I don't think we're going to have that anymore."

"It's just tears?"

"Just tears."

On TV, news anchors are always so cool when they're interviewing people. When they open their mouths you can almost feel a cool draft of air, as you do when you walk into Barnes & Noble. But interviewers can sometimes sweat it as much as their subjects. There are some nosy questions I like asking and some I don't, but with Burt about to leave the room, I ask him if he had hired someone to beat Linda up.

"That's right," he says.

"Tell me what would you have done differently."

"I never would have done that."

In an email subsequent to our interview Burt noted a pertinent detail. He says he asked his client, Al Newkirk, "if he could find anyone to beat up a girl, telling him who. He never got back to me." Burt says he had a change of heart and called Linda to try to warn her, but she hung up on him. Burt didn't remember making that call at the time; it wasn't until 1969 when he got the transcript of the grand jury that he found out about it. "The jury never had the opportunity to consider that I had abandoned my criminal intent," he says.

"Would you have tried to pursue her in a different way?" I ask.

"Maybe, or I would have gone for someone else. This [the attack] really was not a reaction to her, it was a reaction to a frame-up for something else"—a shakedown by the District Attorney's office. His threat to expose the frame-up, he says, is what got him arrested, not the plan to have Linda harmed, though he never denies that he did ask for that to happen.

It's impossible not to note that Burt has a million mitigating factors to present. It's also impossible for them not to be overshadowed by Linda's big dark glasses.

LOVE AND ANGER

Burt's emotional turmoil when he feared he had lost Linda was probably a combination of a great many factors, but one thing all lovers feel when spurned is anger. No one can make us feel more insane than the person who is supposed to ground us. It's an irony that can be played both comically and tragically.

In the Tony-award-winning musical *Avenue Q* a Korean character named Christmas Eve explains to her friend in broken English:

"The more you ruv someone, you the more you want to kill them / The more you ruv someone, the more he make you cry / Though you are try for making peace with them and loving / That's why you love so strong you like to make him die!"[9]

Othello, after strangling Desdemona because his jealousy makes her imagined betrayal of him unbearable, asks to be thought of as "one who loved not wisely, but too well." In the song "Everyone's in Love with you" David Byrne sings, "I want to kill and kiss you, too." And Oscar Wilde famously wrote in *The Ballad of Reading Gaol*, "Yet each man kills the thing he loves, By each let this be heard, Some do it with a bitter look, Some with a flattering word, The coward does it with a kiss, The brave man with a sword!"[10]

Love and anger (title of a Kate Bush song, by the way) are intertwined in dramas going back to the Greeks, but what most of the channelers of these sentiments might not have known is that they are also very closely related in the brain. The part of the brain that processes rage is linked to the area that processes reward assessment and expectation. "And when people and other animals begin to realize that an expected reward is in jeopardy, even unattainable, these centers in the prefrontal cortex signal the amygdala and trigger rage," Helen Fisher writes in *Why We Love*.[11] In a 2004 article in *New Scientist*, Fisher writes, "In fact, experiments in animals have shown how intimately these reward and rage circuits are intertwined. Stimulate a cat's reward circuits and it feels intense pleasure. Withdraw the stimulation and it bites."

★ ★ ★

I ask Dr. Fisher what it is that makes one person respond to rejection with violence while another person might lick their wounds for a while but rise from the ashes and realize it's not the end of the world.

"The brain is extremely complicated, and let's not forget your childhood," she says. Burt's mother was abusive, hitting him so hard at one time that she displaced his teeth, he says in *Crazy Love*.

"If you grew up in a sort of environment where people were constantly beating each other up, you may be more accustomed to that kind of response," Helen says. The brain system of intense romantic love is full of cravings. "Then you get rejected and not only do you continue to crave this person but you've lost a lot of things. You've lost social networks, you've lost reproductive time if you're young, you've lost the most powerful thing on earth, which is a channel to reproduce your DNA—so people can get extremely angry when they've been rejected, even if the person rejecting them has been pleasant about it."

The person who resorts to violence, she says, "probably has more activity in the amygdala—in brain regions associated with aggressiveness, impulse control, and physical aggression—so that same intense craving and obsession and fury is expressed differently."[12]

When the brain encounters stress or anger, it signals the adrenal gland to release cortisol, the "fight or flight" hormone. The cortisol signals the body to either gear up for battle or run away. Either way, you have a body that's tense, pumping adrenaline, and ready for *some* kind of action. While other parts of the brain have received the cortisol and signaled production to shut down, the amygdala signals for more to be produced. In people with hormone imbalances, while this balancing act is going on "the body never returns to its normal resting state."[13]

The process that happens when people realize a reward is in jeopardy is called the "frustration–aggression hypothesis"—basically, the first causes the second. One part of the theory posits that the closer you are to a reward, the greater your frustration will be when you're thwarted from achieving it.[14] This makes sense. Say you're running late to the airport and you miss your flight by an hour—you're calmly resigned to taking another flight well before you get to the gate. But if you race to the gate only to see the doors close in front of you, missing your flight by seconds, you'll end up as the new viral video sensation when you go psycho on the boarding staff.

POLITICS IS TOTALLY MENTAL

A study by University College, London, involving brain scans of 90 students and two members of Parliament found that those who held conservative views had larger amygdalas (popularly termed the "fear center" when news of the study sprouted on the web) and smaller anterior cingulates, a region associated with optimism and courage. It's unclear, though, whether these dissimilarities were present from birth or were developed through experience, writes Richard Allyene of the London Daily Telegraph, because the subjects were all adults.[15]

The amygdala also seems to play a part in *loss aversion*, the desire to avoid a loss even when there is something to be gained. A study at the California Institute of Technology involved 12 control subjects, two of whom had lesions on their amygdalas caused by a genetic condition, which prevented them from feeling fear. The subjects with healthy amygdalas were less likely to gamble if the difference between potential gains and losses wasn't great, or the potential for loss was greater than the potential for gain. The subjects with the lesions on their amygdala didn't show this aversion, and they gambled anyway.[16]

These two studies sort of make sense together, since the latter is about conserving what you have and the former is about being conservative (which has the word *conserve* right in it) in the first place. Interestingly, yet another study of the amygdala by a team at Massachusetts General Hospital found that the larger the amygdalas of the study subjects, the larger or more complex their social networks tended to be. (But, again, there is the question of whether the larger amygdala is the cause or the result of having more friends.)

Dr. David Carlat, AOL's mental health expert, states, "We believe the amygdala has to do with how we relate to fear. If you have a large network of people around you, there are a lot more opportunities to process the fear response." He adds, "If you think of the amygdala as the fear muscle, there are a lot more chances to flex that muscle."[17]

Maybe. Armchair theory: If, as the first two studies suggest, the amygdala is also about conserving the status quo (which might be thought of as fear of change) maybe the person who ends up with more friends has them because he conserves the old ones even as he acquires the new.

★ ★ ★

Burt was doing well both romantically and professionally and all of a sudden it all seemed to go wrong. He was so close to having it all, and then everything fell apart.

So maybe his amygdala—fear of ruin, fear of loss—was working overtime when he made the decision to have Linda attacked.

Charles Whitman, the infamous University of Texas shooter who climbed the school's clock tower in 1966 and randomly shot people, killing 14 and wounding 31, was found to have a walnut-sized tumor on his amygdala. He also had a brutally abusive background, kept diaries of his violent thoughts, and wrote a note requesting that his brain be autopsied after his death to see if there was a physical cause for these impulses he couldn't seem to control.[18] In an essay titled "The Amygdala and Mass Murder," Dr. Rhwan Joseph writes, "Tumors invading the amygdala have been reported to trigger rage attacks."[19]

It's impossible to say whether the amygdala was going off like a car alarm in Rajini Narayan of Adelaide, but hers is another story of love that erupted in violence. Rajini attempted to set her husband's penis on fire after discovering he was having an affair with another woman. According to Australia's *Courier Mail*, her husband gave her his computer password, which allowed her to find emails to his mistress. When she confronted him and threatened to burn his penis, he said, "No you won't, you fat, dumb bitch." He was wrong. With burns on 75 percent of his body, he died in the hospital. The court heard that Rajini had suffered years of abuse at her husband's hands and that he didn't want her to work less than she did because her salary "was paying for the other woman."[20] Rajini was acquitted of murder but found guilty of manslaughter.

In Rajini's case you could chose from any of a charming bouquet of things that might have ignited accumulated anger and you also can see that she was cheated out of her prize (if you'd call the husband a prize), an expectation gone kablooey, despite the fact that he'd been abusive to her and their children for years.[21]

Not everyone commits horrible violence when they're pissed off, so it's not an excuse, but maybe one day a person's brain structure or chemistry may be at least a partial answer to unanswerable questions like "How could you do such a thing?" And with those answers we might have a better means than we have today (like the antidepressants and antianxiety drugs that were unheard of decades ago) to help prevent tragedy before it happens.

Linda says she dated while Burt was in prison, but no one serious. She was handicapped and didn't think anyone would be serious with her, and besides, she never thought in terms of seriousness. She was just taking it day to day.

"I needed action—life was boring," she says. "You know, you get up, you go to work, you come back from work, you watch television, you have a date here and there—it's boring after a while, so you want a little bit of excitement." She never thought her relationship with Burt would take off as it did, or make headlines. "It just never even occurred to me. I think if I thought that far I would have backed off and not done anything." She admits that she got a little more than she bargained for.

I ask if Burt also provided a comforting familiarity in addition to excitement. They had, after all, been together for some time as a couple—he wasn't a complete stranger. Did she know he'd take good care of her?

"No, I never thought that far in advance."

"Was there affection?"

"Yes, I'd say so, we always cared for each other. The fact that he was a married man in the beginning and wasn't free, well, you know, and that's an old story. I'm not the first case where this has happened—unfortunately it ended so terribly."

I ask her whether the dynamic between them changed when Burt got out of jail. In *Crazy Love* Linda was reported to have worn clear glasses for her first meeting with Burt after his release. He was the only one with whom she could do that instead of wearing her usual glamorous movie-star shades.

"When I decided to go back with Burt I made up my mind: this was gonna be in the past and forget about it, you gotta move on from this point on. So that was pretty much where I was coming from."

She is admirably pragmatic about how people really are, about romantic affairs, the way life goes on, and our imperfections. It comes out when we talk about Burt's affair with Evangeline Borja.

"Might as well be realistic," she says. "This is the fact and this is life, and if he cheated it's not the end of the world. They made a mountain out of a molehill, like he's the only one who'd ever done this. Which was so bizarre, I thought. So, that got me angry."

Does it irritate her when she sees sex scandals in the media—new mountains made out of molehills every day? She considers for a moment.

"I don't judge. I really don't. Because I know from my

own experience. I just listen to what they're saying and, okay, I may think one way, I may not think the right way, but I don't make these judgments."

Some of the excitement that Burt provided was obvious—he a charismatic felon with a sense of drama and a taste for the good life, pursued by the press at every turn. But when I ask Linda what they did together that was exciting, she doesn't bring up jet-setting. She brings up family.

"I didn't have a big family. I had my mother and my aunt. So there never were big parties or events that happened. I was never involved with something like that. His family invited us for Thanksgiving, etcetera, so this was something I was not used to and it was nice. You don't realize you're missing it until it hits you in the face and wow, it's different."

"What was your wedding like?

"My wedding?

"Yeah" I say. And then, in case she forgot, "To Burt."

She screams down the hallway. "BURT! What was our wedding like?"

Then she remembers. "We went to a restaurant."

They were married in a judge's chambers with three friends as witnesses; as ceremonies go, it was the smallest of the small. Their reception was at a restaurant across the street.

"I don't think the restaurant's there anymore. We outlived the restaurant," Linda says.

I ask her what the secret is.

"Fortitude and perseverance." Linda laughs.

"Are you romantic at all? Or just practical?"

"Let me think," Linda says, taking a long pause. "Can I have a little of both?"

★ ★ ★

When I try to talk a little bit more about public perception of her staying with Burt Linda says, very softly, "You don't understand. I don't care what people think. I'm not here to influence people, to change their minds—this is my *personal* life and I do what I want to do."

What does she want to do next?

"Well, Burt wants to make a movie. I want this whole issue to die. I don't want to have any more publicity or anything of that nature. I never wanted that to begin with. But there you are. And here I am. And you're getting an interview. And it's the last thing in the world I want to do."

What can I do with that but wrap it up?

But during the wrapping-it-up chitchat a shift occurs. Now out of the hot seat, Linda starts asking me questions— about my background, the book I'm writing, my love life. It's not an aggressive interrogation. Now we're just talking. She asks if I'm single. I tell her I've been engaged but I backed off of getting married.

"I've been there," she says. "I know what you're saying."

Maybe, I suggest, that's why I was so drawn to her when I saw *Crazy Love*. There was something recognizable about her.

"Something a little familiar," she says.

We talk about our backgrounds and our mothers, about how she loved vacationing in the Costa Brava with a girlfriend.

"I was so much younger and so much prettier, and everywhere we went men would pick us up and would wine us and dine us, it was a whole different life we're talking about, a million years ago."

Linda takes classes. When I ask for what, she says,

"Time and space." Actually it's exercise and communication. She takes a fitness class, and also one about a device called Braille and Speak, which looks a little like a court reporter's keyboard.

"I have to learn how to work this stupid machine," she says. "Once I learn I'm going to be a genius."

After some more chatting I really do have to go because Linda has an errand to run. She is such an accidental celebrity; I don't now how much I'd put up with strangers from around the globe goggling at what I decided to do with my love life. It feels like a rarefied moment I got, talking to her just as Linda, not as part of the notorious *Crazy Love* couple from Queens.

Burt gives me a lift back to the train station. The difference between them is striking, like switching channels between PBS and Spike TV. Linda is sedate. Burt is all energy. He talks about his case, the trips he wants to take, the book he wants to write about judicial corruption, a subject about which he is endlessly passionate.

"I'm not claiming sainthood," he tells me in the car. "All the screwing around I did? I did it."

"When you asked them to do that," I say, meaning to beat up Linda, "tell me what you were feeling. What was going on in your head when you made that call?"

"At the time, I was being unfairly charged with professional misconduct. And at the time, I was young; I wasn't like I am now. I wasn't strong and I wasn't able to handle it."

"How old were you?"

"Thirty. Thirty going on twenty. I never even dreamed it was gonna happen."

He tells me more about being framed for extortion,

about illegal wiretapping in his office, and the raw deal he got, though he never denies the initial offense of paying to have Linda attacked.

"When you say you were thirty going on twenty, what do you mean?" I ask.

"Immature. Very frightened. Try and frighten me now."

"Do you feel it was temporary insanity on your part?"

"No," he says, very quickly. Burt doesn't believe in the insanity defense.

"You knew exactly what you were doing?"

"Yeah, but I was doing stupidity."

"Temporary stupidity?"

"Yeah."

If *that* was a legitimate defense, it would be an instant hit.

"I certainly wasn't looking to have lye thrown in there," Burt says. "I didn't know what it was! I'd never heard of it." His voice is so plaintive he sounds almost on the verge of tears.

"What did you think would happen to her?"

"I thought she was going to be beaten up at the most."

"Like a black eye or something?"

"Yeah."

It was magical thinking, he says.

"Did you think that she would get scared and then want to be with you for protection?"

"Yeah."

"What would you tell a young man now in the same situation?"

"Fuggeddaboudit."

I've never actually heard a New Yorker say this until now.

"Forget and move on to another girl?"

"Move on to another girl. Forget about it. Really, when I see this happen every day I say, What kind of idiots are these? To give away your life by taking away somebody's life. Usually you're taking away the life of a girl with children, too. I mean, what is your point? Come on, wise up, go get somebody else, find somebody else."

"It's a big world?"

"Yeah, and it's got three million females in it. So, this is it, let it go."

Burt's likes to talk, and I think what a great speaker he could be to dissuade people from committing violent crimes for love. But then what would be the lesson if they knew that the woman he targeted ended up marrying him?

It's hard to reconcile thoughts like this with my peculiar fondness for the *Crazy Love* couple, but the bottom line is that Burt did his time, and moreover, Linda is satisfied. This, as she said, is her *personal* life. And she's the only one whose feelings about that really matter.

THE SHAKY BRIDGE

How did Linda Pugach come by her feelings? She is certainly not the only person in the world to have baffled friends and family with a mind-boggling decision about her love life. To get some greater insight into why people choose to pair up with mates the outside world might regard as dangerous, I consult Ian Kerner, a relationship counselor and *New York Times* best-selling author of books such as *Be Honest—You're Not That Into Him Either* and *She Comes First: The Thinking Man's Guide to Pleasuring a Woman*. I send him some information about Burt and Linda and ask him for his thoughts on how the mind works in situations such as these.

★ ★ ★

Some people, Dr. Kerner says, thrive on the drama that their relationship started in.[22] A theory known as Excitation Transfer Theory states that if you have a thrilling experience with someone early on, you'll associate them with that enthralled feeling when you see them later. A study titled "Love at First Fright: Partner Salience Moderates Roller-Coaster-Induced Excitation Transfer" found that single people getting off a roller coaster were likely to find photographs of opposite-sex persons more attractive than those entering the roller coaster; those who were partnered found their mates equally attractive either way.[23]

"They say adrenaline makes the heart grow fonder," Dr. Kerner says, "meaning adrenaline as well as the whole suite of hormones and neurotransmitters that play a role in excitement." So making time for novel experiences in your relationship—to keep it interesting and keep that excitement level up—is a key to continued romance.

A good indication of our tacit appreciation for getting into hot water with someone and getting hot for them as a result is that so many films find two characters facing down murderers, monsters, and nature together just before they fall in love, or back in love: Gail Weathers and Detective Dewey in *Scream*. Drs. Allan Grant and Ellie Sattler in *Jurassic Park*. Charlie Allnut and Rose Sayer in *The African Queen*. Mitch and Melanie in *The Birds*. To say nothing of Mickey and Mallory in *Natural Born Killers*. Danger is thrilling, thrills are sexy, and we can relive them through the person we were with when we got them.

People are brought together by tragedy, Ian says, by violence, car crashes, accidents. "Over the years it is possible—I'm not an expert in this kind of psychodynamic, but it is possible that Burt and Linda were brought together through the tragedy that happened to each other. It's a tragedy and a bond, and there's a muting of the context and their roles in it, so in the end they're brought together by this tragedy. He spent however many years in jail and she lost her eyesight. Forget the fact that he was the one responsible—they shared a tragic thing in their lives and that's what brings them together."

Another study that aids and abets the idea that a little danger is romantic catnip is the Shaky Bridge Study. In 1974 researchers Donald Dutton and Arthur Aron (who has worked on many studies with Helen Fisher, including those in *Why We Love*) did a very sneaky research study on a very shaky bridge over the Capilano River in British Columbia. Actually there were two bridges: one very solid, just 10 feet above the river, and a rickety suspension bridge, five feet wide, made of planks, 230 feet above the river—more a dare than a bridge, really. On one day, single men crossing the shaky bridge were stopped by a pretty female researcher and asked if they'd take part in a questionnaire. At the end the researcher gave them her phone number and said they could call her at home later for the results. The next day, the experiment was conducted on the stable bridge. Far more men who met the young lady on the shaky bridge than on the stable one called her, indicating that the element of danger sparked an element of romance.[24]

Why do girls like bad boys? The shaky bridge might be the answer.

It's just a theory, Dr. Kerner says, but—and qualifying it with the fact that Burt and Linda's story was reported to him and he hasn't met them—it could go a long way to explaining a relationship like Burt and Linda's, where the excitement, the drama, and even the taboo gets placed onto the other person.

Dr. Kerner says you can look at couples in abusive relationships, "where there's lots of fighting and then forgiveness. One theory is that they're just codependent: this is a dysfunctional relationship, she's seeking out the abuse, her self-esteem is so worn down, she's captured in the relationship. The other side of it is that maybe they're both fed by the fighting, fed by the conflict: it excites them, both the conflict itself and the forgiveness and reconciliation that comes from the conflict. People get addicted to drama."

Squabbling couples in drama and fiction are as easy to come by as cliché plot twists, from Beatrice and Benedick in *Much Ado About Nothing* to Al and Peg Bundy in *Married with Children*. Think how many films start with two people who can't stand each other, or at least aren't fond of each other, and end with them falling madly in love? (Partial list: *Two Weeks Notice, The African Queen, Gone with the Wind, When Harry Met Sally, Hannah and Her Sisters, You've Got Mail, Moonstruck.*)

George and Martha from *Who's Afraid of Virginia Woolf?* say it all right here:

George: You can sit around with the gin running out of your mouth; you can humiliate me; you can tear me to pieces all night, that's perfectly okay, that's all right.

Martha: You can stand it!

George: I cannot stand it!

Martha: You can stand it, you married me for it![25]

Burt and Linda were one of my huge inspirations for wanting to study love. I was so taken aback by their story, but now I get it, to a much greater degree than I did when I first read about it. I have clung to more than one man longer than I should have out of romantic desire, and I've looked, to my friends, just like Titania in *A Midsummer Night's Dream*, who took a human-jackass hybrid for a lover. Whether it is because of the Shaky Bridge syndrome, the yin and yang theory, or the flood of dopamine making everything seem more beautiful, love airbrushes away the behavioral flaws that ordinary vision would never overlook, just as it does the obstacles. We're all capable of behavior that seems crazy to others. The Pugaches are not politically correct. But that's what makes them epic. That might bewhat made Cheap Trick write "The Ballad of Burt and Linda":

> Every day is a darker day
> It's always gonna be that way
> One step closer to mine
> I know it's not respectable
> But it is the best of all
> One step closer[26]

For all we can understand via fMRIs, the love of two people is still, and may always be, a unique and private matter.

Chapter 5

Bigfoot the Yenta

LOVING THE ALIEN

In 2009 a paragraph appeared in Chuck Shepherd's *News of the Weird* column about Arthur David Horn, a tenured professor at Colorado State University who was teaching human evolution before meeting his future bride Lynette (a "metaphysical healer") in 1988. With Lynette's guidance, Arthur resigned his teaching post and went on to speak publicly about his realization that "humans come from an alien race of shape-shifting reptilians that continue to control civilization through the secretive leaders known as the Illuminati."[1]

What intrigued me about this story wasn't the Reptile Kings from Outer Space. People believe in much crazier things. People believe that Ed Hardy T-shirts look good, that *The Bachelor* is real and the moon landing is fake, and that not helping the poor helps the poor. Aliens are hardly a stretch. A 2008 Scripps Howard News Service–Ohio University poll says that 56 percent of Americans believe we are not alone in the universe.[2] I know a girl who believes she's been abducted. There are tons of people I wish would be abducted, never to return.

Nope, what interested me about that little *News of the Weird* nugget wasn't the reptiles, it was Dr. Horn's wife, Lynette. Had she turned a man of conventional science into a believer in reptilian space kings? How did she do it?

What kind of sexual sorcery did she practice? And did she give online classes?

Before I tell you about the Horns I want to share an exchange I had with Lynette during the latter part of a long conversation:

Lynette: When Arthur and I were in Montana, I actually left behind my staff that one of my medicine men made for me. He made this staff out of African wood and fastened a little crystal ball to put on the top and gave me lion's balls that I put on there.

Liz: Wait. Did I hear that right? Lion's balls?

Lynette. Yes. (She giggles.)

Liz: Oh. That's *got* to help, right?

Lynette: I guess he thought I needed them. I don't know.

Now, I Googled "lion's balls shamanism" and found no use for lion's balls other than to make little lions, but if Lynette says she owns sacred lion's balls and is casual enough about them to leave them unattended somewhere, I believe her. I'm sure they're dripping with magic. (I hope the lion was already dead and had filled out an organ donor card.) Lynette is a sweet, funny woman and a bit mad, but as Alice's father told Alice in Tim Burton's film version of *Alice in Wonderland*, "All the best people are." If you're not a little crazy in this mean world, you're either too cool or too cold for me.

The Horns would probably both be considered a bit mad in our culture—which is sad for our culture, because the only unusual thing about them is that they are seekers of ideas instead of material things, and in America that puts your marble count in question. When I contacted them in

June 2010, they had between them 130 years of remarkably adventurous living and had been wed 28 years. They were on the road at the time, and Lynette said she would call me on her return. She called early on a Saturday and told me with great deliberation that she had just returned home from her trip. They'd been enjoying their time together, she said. One day Arthur got into the hot tub and was so happy there that he didn't want to leave. She said fine, she'd come back and get him in a bit. She found him later facedown in the pool. He had passed away. The EMTs couldn't revive him.

"And you know that I know if I had stayed with him it wouldn't have happened, and I live with that," she said. "Because there's a part of me that's just, Where is your consciousness sometimes, Lynette? You act like such an idiot! I should have felt him and felt the stress." She said that a group with UFO beliefs similar to hers and Arthur's told her that "there had been a fight to the death with reptilians."[3]

It took two phone calls for us to get to that part; she didn't last very long in the first call that day. I was stunned that she would even keep an interview appointment, but I realized she must be one tough woman. You can't go around inviting the kind of ridicule that might come with talking about alien intervention in human evolution and be a pansy.

"Now, you know," I told her, "I'm going to be asking a lot of questions about Arthur. Are you sure you want to do this now?"

"The best thing in the world for me to do right now would be to talk about Arthur."

So for the next several hours, we did.

★ ★ ★

"I thought they would revive him, because I thought he was having what he would later find out was a near-death experience and that he could come back into his body," Lynette says. She believes there was a fight between good and bad entities over him—but in the end "some very high beings came in and picked up and took him on his merry way, which evidently he wanted to do.

"They took him on, his spirit, into a higher dimension. Liz, I'm sitting here going, What? I can't believe you're telling her this! You really believe this shit? Yes. I do. I was raised with it and I know it's all possible, but it's very, very hard to grasp."

I love spiritual people who curse.

"We sacrificed constantly in our lives to get our work done, to get the books we needed, to do the research, the videos, the whole nine yards. Arthur felt very discouraged." It was so hard to get through to people. Arthur got onto the History Channel once, and it helped, but a little boost on a hard road sometimes wears off quickly. "All he wanted to do was be here and do his research and write his notes," Lynette says, "and though it's hard to imagine going on without him, evidently that is the plan, and it has to be accepted by everybody who's participating. And now he will be able to help me much more from the other side." Lynette believes that Arthur had a "soul contract" that allowed him to do his work and research in this life and have an out when he was ready to leave. She thinks he had a near-death experience in the pool and then could not get back into his body. An autopsy was inconclusive.

When we exchange emails months later, Lynette says the autopsy was finally provided to her in October 2010. The cause was listed as accidental drowning, with complications from serious illnesses that were discovered during the autopsy. Lynette thinks Arthur's blood pressure probably skyrocketed and caused him to faint in the pool.

WA-WA-WEE

Arthur Horn was a tall, dark, handsome man, born in Kansas to a very religious Episcopalian family. He started out as a youthful, Bible-believing Christian, but while pursuing his civil engineering major at Kansas State he had a crisis of faith. By then he had seen and read enough to begin questioning his beliefs, but his real problem was why there had to be so much pain in the world. He was distressed by disease, poverty, and cruelty. He was drafted by the US Army in 1963, by which time he had become an atheist.

While he was stationed in Thailand, Arthur's then girlfriend sent him a book that would change his life: *African Genesis*, by Robert Ardrey, his first exposure to the Darwinian theory of evolution. After being honorably discharged from the army, he studied anthropology, mainly at Colorado State. He moved on to Yale, studying the evolution of nonhuman primates. He was asked to join Dian Fossey studying gorillas but chose to go to Zaire to study bonobo chimps instead; he got his PhD after two years there. He was a tenured professor at Colorado State.

In 1988 Arthur had what Lynette calls "a neurological episode." He woke up one day unable to walk or talk; his doctors told him he might have Epstein-Barr virus. To help his recovery, friends recommended he see Lynnette, who had a home health care business, mostly caring for Alzheimer's and stroke patients. She had also studied alternative methods of healing, including work with Native Americans, and she had studied psychology at UC Santa

Cruz, where Carlos Castaneda was a guest teacher.

Was there a spark when Lynette and Arthur first met?

"Immediately," she says, half laughing. "You know how you don't think you believe in love at first sight? There was just something about him, and I suppose he would say the same thing. He was six feet four and very, very handsome. He was brilliant and he loved the woods and nature. We had a lot of things in common and a lot of things that worked."

But a metaphysical healer attracted to an atheist? You'd think the minute she started talking crystals and he started saying "Prove it," the turn-off would be immediate. But they had at least one thing in common. One big hairy thing.

"I told him about a special place I knew in the Trinity Alps, and he wanted to track Bigfoot there," Lynette says. "I had wanted to do this for years. That was the premise under which we met—we went to that area and camped. And we fell in love." Arthur proposed three weeks later with a ring Lynette tearfully tells me she foresaw in a dream.

"The kids at school would say, 'Dr. Horn, what's happened to you? You look so happy!' " They had a church wedding on the campus of Colorado State, where he had taught for 14 years. They bought a little house and started their marriage but their very different approaches to life stirred a little trouble.

"I had been trained to approach life in a metaphysical way—only serving the divine, that was my whole life," Lynette says. "Arthur didn't believe in God, didn't believe we had a spirit. We were just random beings. We had a very deep love for each other, but he would eat Wheaties all day long and I just wanted to sit on the porch and smoke a cigarette…" "Opposites attract" worked for Arthur and Lynette. Whether it was the Imago, their core yin and yang, a dopamine rush at the novelty each presented the other, or a fifth-of-a-second Roman candle of brain chemicals, it worked.

And Lynette, Arthur writes in his book, *Humanity's Extraterrestrial Origins*, wasn't just any spiritual spouter. "I respected her beliefs primarily because they were neither divisive nor judgmental; her belief system considered all humans divine."[4]

As well as things were going at home, a new crisis of faith was starting to emerge in Arthur, this time in his job. He saw gaps in the theory of evolution and had been impressed by Erich von Däniken's *Chariots of the Gods*, which proposes that human evolution got a shove from extraterrestrials. Then, in 1989, while the couple were visiting a friend's house, Lynette channeled an entity that told Arthur things about himself and his life he had never told another living soul: "It knew things about me that nobody else in the world knew, including Lynette," he writes in his book. The experience was so profound for him that he began to reopen his mind to metaphysical ideas. One day, he came home and told Lynette he was resigning his tenured professorship.

Lynette recounts their conversation that day. "I said, 'Oh, that's wonderful. What are we going to do now?' He said, 'Well, I want to write a book on human origins and have an organic garden.' Other professionals saw that he was willing to take that risk, drop his benefits, his income, and they had huge respect for him. 'Well, that's what I want to do. We'll do it together,' he said. And I said, 'Okay, we'll go to Mount Shasta.' He said, 'Yes, we'll go to Mount Shasta.' Well, of course that's the perfect place; they have all these *wa-wa-wee* things." (*Wa-wa-wee* is Lynette-speak for "metaphysical.") "We found a lovely place that was very, very modest, a little old country two-story house. So our lives began to progress.

"We had to be very strong together and in who we were individually," she says. "We fought a lot early on. It was awful, because Arthur was so set in what he had been trained to know." But Lynette was pretty solid in her own beliefs, which are that our purpose is to evolve spiritually: "To become conscious, to stop being dysfunctional and suffering and hurting each other and killing each other and stand up and be who we are and who we were created to be. And that is only to love. That is the only purpose. There's nothing else."

So, strapped for cash but loaded with ideas and the will to work, the Horns put Arthur's book together. The result was a 363-page opus titled *Humanity's Extraterrestrial Origins*, with a forward written by the formidable Erich von Däniken. I enjoyed the book. It's thoughtful. It's *fun*. And you can tell that Arthur was probably a good teacher by his methodical research and patient approach. It's far too involved to go into deeply, but it boils down to this: There are two types of aliens. One is the reptiles, which Arthur calls—I love this—*lizzies*. The lizzies created humanity to do their grunt work. The good guys are the Pleiadians, who try to help us evolve spiritually and thus save ourselves; the lizzies try to keep us from evolving spiritually, partly by keeping us fighting among ourselves. There's a lot more to it, including black operations, "Vatican moles," and President Eisenhower being in on a big alien cover-up. Seriously—it's complicated. But it's a good read, whether you believe a word of it or not.[5]

Writing their book took everything the Horns had. They self-published it and went all over the place trying to promote it, including UFO conferences—but even there nobody was interested. "Nobody was talking about the spiritual truth about the divine—and how that affects us as a human species," Lynette says. They only wanted to talk about the military and the science, which is too limited an approach, in her opinion.

"If you don't know, 2012 is coming, it's the end of the world."

Finally. I had hoped it would happen at the millennium.

"You have to shift up to the fifth dimension," she says. To be able to hop the train to the next era, you're not going to need things; you're going to need spiritual consciousness.

"The frequency of love is everything right now," Lynette says, "and it's not a BS thing or a wa-wa-wee thing. It's a tangible thing." You can practice it with those who are open to it. If you need it summarized in a single phrase, she says, this will do: "Please don't hurt others now—that's all you need to know."

Now Lynette is on her own. She has friends, family, and colleagues to help and support her, but nothing is the same without Arthur.

"We have no money, no assets, next to no resources, we're in this struggle and all we see is that we have so much more love for each other. It's so wonderful to have come to that place with him. I'm so devastated that he's gone physically. We were coming closer together on every level you can imagine. And he was becoming sweeter, if that's possible. Arthur had the sweetest soul—he was a very gentle man, yet full of fear about loving. He had no clue about what that meant. He thought it was all about sex, as most men do."

Arthur was raised by a generation that went through World War II, a time when people weren't as open about their feelings as they are now. "Arthur's mother told him she loved him, he said, one time. Of course she loved him! His parents were wonderful parents," Lynette tells me. But Arthur grew up not knowing how to be demonstrative. (Interestingly, though I can't find the video, I remember an episode of *Biography* saying that Hugh Hefner was raised in a similar atmosphere of great love but reserved behavior.) "And then I came along—probably a 'woman who loves too much.' When I heard the title of that book I just howled and I thought, Oh no, they named it for me!"

Lynette brought a friend home with her from Nevada, a woman who had also lost her beloved and so seemed a heaven-sent source of support. "I've been telling her, 'I'm thinking about blowing my brains out or jumping off a bridge. I'm not going to do it but I'm thinking about it and I want to tell you.'"

Then suddenly she says she heard in her head: *Wrong! Get up! Eat breakfast! Change toilet paper! Get on with it and stop feeling sorry for yourself.*

Toward the end of our conversation Lynette suddenly starts to laugh.

Lynette: I just lifted my foot up and something in the carpet was scratching me. I hope you appreciate this—it's one of Arthur's toenails.

Liz: Oh, my God.

Lynette: Of course, all the natives and the doctors think that nails continue to carry the energy of the deceased.

They'll keep the master's toenails and their hair—it's really wild. And so Arthur dropped his toenail here for me.

Liz: Maybe he did.

Lynette (who can't stop laughing): It's a little far afield honey, but... Nonetheless, I know he's here and I know he's learning a lot by listening to what's going on with people who are really responding to what happened; it's just fabulous to me.

Did you catch that? Reptilian aliens, lion's balls—and an interdimensionally transmitted toenail is a little far afield. I really do like Lynette.

SENSITIVE SIDEWAYS

Lynette did not blow her brains out or jump off a bridge. She pulled herself together and is going on as well as anyone in her place can, spending time with friends and family and continuing her spiritual practice of life. She's processed those feelings of guilt about not being there when Arthur passed.

"When I found Arthur facedown in that pool, I go back to that and think, You know, if you had just gone back and stayed with him. And then I tell myself, Lynette, that's not what happened. That's not what you did and he chose to do this so you have to let this go and move on, serve where you're able to now." Since our first conversation she's been considering telling me something about the neurological episode that brought her and Arthur together.

"He woke up, he couldn't walk or talk, and that went on for two weeks. All Arthur told me was that maybe he had Epstein-Barr," she says. This was in 1998.

Fast-forward to 2009. The couple were watching basketball on TV and a commercial came on having to do with Asperger's syndrome, a neurological disorder in the autism spectrum that affects how information is processed. People with Asperger's may appear indifferent because they often don't interpret nonverbal social cues, such as body language, very well. They may seem intensely focused on one subject and may seem less interested in emotional interactions. They often have extremely high intelligence and creativity, and they're very sensitive, but because they don't read social cues the way that people without Asperger's do, they don't appear to respond to social interactions in the usual way.[6] Arthur turned to Lynette and said, "Oh, wow, that's what they said I had and that's what I was experiencing."

"I looked at him and I said, 'Arthur, honey, are you telling me after nearly twenty-one years that this was the stronger possibility?' "

He said yes. Lynette was unfamiliar with Asperger's, which was only added to the DSM in 1994. (The *Diagnostic and Statistical Manual of Mental Disorders* lists and describes all known mental health disorders.) Her reading blew her away—it was all so like Arthur. He would sometimes go into rages, which Asperger's people (sometimes called *aspies*, though not everyone likes that term) suffer from out of frustration at not being understood. At the time, Lynette was just trying to "process and shift." She says, "I saw that I needed to find another way with him, and it was very difficult for me. Early in our relationship we had a spat and he said, 'I thought I got a goddess and I got a bitch!' I said, 'Arthur, let me tell you something about women. We all have a royal bitch in us, and if you only go looking for that, that's probably all you're going to get. If you go looking for the goddess and the love in the goddess, that's what you're going to get. So it's really a choice, isn't it?' "

Asperger's explained so much to Lynette. She found

out that people with the syndrome are often brilliant and often consumed with something that is of interest in their life—"like maybe extraterrestrials or aliens! He said to me early on, 'Maybe you could help me with my social skills.' I thought, Social skills? What the hell is he talking about? What does that mean? Everybody has social skills."

But that's not true. Asperger's people don't understand social interaction the way most people do. It's not that they are being willfully unresponsive; they just don't know they're supposed to be responsive.

"The other big one for us was, they have no sense of loving connection or intimacy with their closest beloveds. So all the time I'm living with him, he is struggling, trying to understand. I said, 'Why would you want to be married to me? My whole life is serving God. The divine. You don't even believe in that.' He said, 'Well, you have a superlative nature and I really love you and I need you.' That is probably where he hooked me: that I got through that and came through the other side."

Revealing himself to Lynette this way relieved Arthur of a lot of guilt and hidden feelings, she says.

"Well, I saw that rage in Arthur. It was scary, especially when you didn't understand—you thought it was about you and you were trying to stand up for yourself. So now he was relieved because I knew what he had suspected all along."

Dr. Amy Marsh is a clinical sexologist and hypnotherapist in San Francisco, one of whose areas of expertise is Asperger's syndrome sexuality. She has a web page for it, "The Intimate Aspie." Because Asperger's is a relatively new diagnosis, she says, there are probably more adult aspies than you might think.[7]

"There were probably quite a few people, and still are, who maybe were thought to be odd or quirky but brilliant, and if they were able to socialize enough to get through college and find jobs that were appropriate to their abilities and interests, they probably did okay, at least in their professional lives," Dr. Marsh says. The problems, however, might have been in their relationships. "They don't know why everybody's upset with them or telling them that they're inadequate in some way," and the reason is that they don't read emotional cues the way most people do. Wondering why someone with AS isn't responding to you in a conventional way, from what I understand, is a bit like wondering why your cat didn't bark at the mailman. It's not what they're wired to do.[8]

"The research studies have clearly established that Asperger's syndrome is due to a dysfunction of specific structures and systems in the brain. In short, the brain is 'wired' differently, not necessarily defectively," writes Tony Attwood in *The Complete Guide to Asperger's Syndrome*.[9] (Dr. Marsh highly recommends Attwood and his colleague Carol Gray for a positive approach to AS.) Some famous people with Asperger's include the actor Dan Aykroyd (also a UFO enthusiast), who was diagnosed with a minor case as a child,[10] and singer Gary Numan. (Remember the 1979 hit song "Cars"? And now that you do, can you get its addictive synth-pop New Wave riffs out of your head? No. No, you cannot.) Numan once summed it up with this comment: "For years, I couldn't understand why people thought I was arrogant, but now it all makes a bit more sense."[11]

And then there's Theory of Mind, which Dr. Shrand defined earlier as "the ability to appreciate somebody else's point of view, what are they thinking and what are they feeling." Theory of Mind is critical to development. Aspies are short on this ability and the ability to read emotion in people's faces. An aspie might have trouble laughing at the cartoon characters Wallace and Gromit because so much of Gromit's contribution happens via facial expressions. A 2009 study reported in the journal of the German Medical Association stated that functional imaging showed reduced activity in the left medial prefrontal cortex in aspies while doing Theory of Mind tasks. Further, "the amygdala—an important structure in the limbic system that processes and regulates emotions—and the fusiform face area—an area in the temporal lobe that is specialized for the perception of human faces—also show reduced activity in Asperger's patients or patients with early childhood autism."[12]

This means that people you thought were ignoring you or being rude or who blew off those cow eyes you were giving them may not have been jerks. They simply may not have been able to see you in the way a "neurotypical" person can. Of course they may also have been jerks, but the bottom line is that they may not have been reacting to you because they didn't see you. It's not you. It's not them. It's wiring.

This doesn't mean they're insensitive. Quite the opposite.

"I like to say they're sensitive sideways," Dr. Marsh says, meaning that they're sensitive, but not to the same things neurotypical (NT) people are. They're also not clueless, she says; they're just "not paying attention to the things that the other partner has deemed the appropriate thing to pay attention to. In its own way society—or the social constructions created by neurotypicals—is clueless and narrow and limited as well."

Here-freaking-here. People put themselves in confined emotional spaces all the time when they want to be accepted in certain work or social capacities. The only difference is, the aspies don't have a choice as to what their limits are.

Dr. Marsh compares it to middle school. "Just look at how miserable people are, going through middle school and high school. It's because the social stuff is absolutely so confining and horrible, nobody can stand to be there and everybody's miserable. We can really feel what it's like for a person with Asperger's syndrome if you think back to those days. So that's an example of how the neurotypical world is actually constructed. It's not that much fun for a lot of people; it's super difficult for others."

In an article on Asperger's in the UK *Independent* Dr. Simon Baron-Cohen is quoted as saying, "Passion, falling in love and standing up for justice are all perfectly compatible with Asperger's syndrome. What most people with AS find difficult is casual chatting—they can't do small talk."[13]

If Arthur did indeed have Asperger's, this means that Lynette Horn was actually very intuitive in understanding that he often just needed to be approached differently than a typical person. Dr. Marsh says that very explicit communication, an adjustment of expectations, and thinking strategically are good approaches because a person with AS is "not going to have an easy time with spontaneous emotional requirements."

Interestingly, she says that relationships built on BDSM (the acronym refers to bondage and discipline, dominance and submission, sadism and masochism) can provide good communication models for people in an AS relationship. BDSM relationships require explicit communication for partners to tell each other *exactly* what they want, need, don't want—what their limits are. "I think all kinds of relationships can benefit from that up-front precision," Dr. Marsh says. It could get boring if you had to do it all the time, she says, but a few rules and a lot of talk could be productive in some ways.

Part of the reason communication is so important is that people can be reluctant to engage in it. We'll have sex with people but we don't want to talk to them about having sex with them: talking can feel more intimate than sex. I asked Dr. Marsh if she had any talking points for lovers, whatever their relationship may be.

"If it's an Asperger's person talking to a partner, they're going to be blunt, because that's the way they are," she says. It won't occur to them that someone's feelings might get hurt. NT people can be really matter-of-fact about it too, but if one partner feels he's done all he can and he still can't make his partner happy, that kind of impasse could cause a blowup.

But to communicate things about yourself you first have to know what those things are, and this takes a great deal of self-awareness, especially on the part of the aspie partner. Unless you were lucky enough to have been diagnosed in childhood and worked with therapists to help you integrate certain issues into mainstream life, it can be very difficult, Dr. Marsh says. That's why it's important to consider AS a potential issue in certain relationships. If this is truly appropriate, the AS person can be empowered by a diagnosis and can begin to understand the benefits and the challenges of the condition: "Okay, this is a real thing. I'm not just hopelessly incompatible with everybody."

Dr. Marsh uses the example of sensory dysfunction, which can manifest as an inability to stand certain textures, sounds, tastes, or ways of being touched, a problem that can affect some people with AS. If they can't stand, for example, a slippery texture, oral sex might be a problem for them. For the other partner to understand that it's not *them* the aspie partner has to be able to articulate that *their partner's body* is not the problem; it's that they can't process slippery textures of any kind. That way, Dr. Marsh says, the NT partner will at least be informed about what they're dealing with.

No matter how diplomatic you are, "I *so* can't go down on you" could be a tough thing for the partner to hear. Dr. Marsh recommends a technique called the "sandwich"—you say one nice thing, then suggest a change in the middle, then say something else nice in order to soften your request or criticism. Who in the world couldn't use that one, and not just in bed?

Sexual communication is one thing, but emotional communication is a different kind of intimacy. Some aspie lovers can be totally focused on their partner for a certain amount of time—but when they're back into their interests they're *really* back into their interests.

Dr. Marsh says, "Probably the most enlightening thing that a former partner said to me—a man who was probably very capable of getting an AS diagnosis—was 'I have a limited capacity for emotional engagement.' And though it took me a while to learn this, I found that if I gave him time to transition incrementally from being on the computer to interacting with me, eventually he would be very present, intimate, and emotional with me. But soon enough he would need the interaction to be over, and I couldn't expect anything warm and fuzzy past that point. It was almost like saying, 'Till next time.'"

Considering their social awkwardness and limited

emotional engagement (depending on where they are in the AS spectrum), how do they meet people and get into relationships in the first place?

Dr. Marsh refers to Temple Grandin, who has AS and also has a PhD in animal science and teaches at Colorado State. Her story was made into a feature film, *Temple Grandin*, starring Claire Danes.

"One of the things I really love is where Temple Grandin describes in one of her books how as a kid growing up in the '50s she and her friends would make things together. They'd make kites and forts, and this is how they'd bond and play. When adolescence came along, there was this divergence between what she calls the project people like herself and people who were suddenly going for social interactions. So you might have a couple who meet around a project or a shared interest and maybe one is an aspie and one isn't, but they can create these bonds by sharing their special interests. I think those are the people who are likely to end up with aspie partners: the people who were creative and quirky anyway. They meet someone else who shares their interest and that becomes an overriding joy."

An NT person and an aspie person can grow together in an interest, but, as Dr. Marsh says about her own former partner, the NT person should probably be prepared for the aspie's romantic and sexual attentions to be confined to a certain time and space.

"It hurts that affection should be compartmentalized like that, but on the other hand the outcome is really positive. My sense is that people with Asperger's syndrome are looking for some kind of semiformal structure, as in BDSM relationships or Tantra or a very traditional Christian marriage, where the parameters and the rules are well spelled out and there's less need for spontaneous action, which can be excruciating for the AS person.

"Here in the US and in Western culture we place a heavy value on our lover being able to read our mind and know intuitively when we're sad. We want someone who can come up with special surprises; we think a really good lover is one who is good at these spontaneous shows of affection. There must be cultures where this is not valued as much." Perhaps where there is more value placed on being steadfast, being a good provider.

And indeed, the expectation to be Prince Charming or Cinderella as well as being ambitious, attractive, available, and a good mind reader—it's confining. Who is all that? Who could be?

How the BDSM Model Can Work for Other Relationships

To find out more about whether a BDSM relationship agreement could work for any relationship, with or without the restraints and paddles, I asked a woman I know who is in a BDSM marriage. She told me that the clarity and specificity of the agreement is the helpful part. It makes you really think about who you are as a couple, what you need, and what you are willing to do in order to stay together—things that many couples take for granted. Marriage, after all, implies—what? Sexual fidelity, financial sharing, and kids. The rest of it can be pretty vague.

"We have agreements regarding chores, money and sex, because in my last marriage (not a BDSM relationship) that's where we fought: chores, money, and sex. Every time these came up it became a power play and it killed our relationship," she says. Now their agreements on these issues—in the form of an actual contract—prevent those fights from happening.

"I'm so hard-core when I get angry or feel pushed—there's no lightness in my being and it's toxic for a relationship. So the BDSM model saves me from myself and saves us from me. I have a hard time emotionally disciplining myself. His side is financial; he supports me." He might ask, for example, to see an hour's worth of work on one of her personal creative pursuits, "because when I'm creative I'm a better lover and I'm happier."

The explicitness of their agreements "makes the boundaries of the world clear. There are so many choices—the world is pretty confusing for me. The reality is that it works for me, it feels safer, and I know what I'm supposed to do, and at the end of the day I've gotten more done and my partner and I are happy together and it creates an ideal, fairy-tale world and helps me keep it.

"Marriage doesn't come with a contract; it's just this vague notion that you're going to get married and you're going to live happily ever after. Unless you're religious, where there are built-in guidelines, you're out there on your own," she says. Plus, our competitive, acquisitive, bigger-better-faster-more society says you're forever supposed to be upgrading. "You outlive your marriage quickly because you think, I've done this, so you move on, except you haven't done the 'happily ever after' thing. Just trying to make commitments based on romantic ideals didn't work for me. The modern American marriage myth didn't work for me. Our culture is showing it doesn't work for most people."

And since she mentioned that religious marriages are

often more exacting in their contracts, it may interest
you to know that there are several websites for the
Christian BDSM marriage—and they are not entirely
of the "wives, submit to your husbands" mind-set that
one might think. In fact, ChristiansandBDSM.com
reprinted a thoughtful essay by a woman named Lady
Hellion, which is a little survey course on how to be a
Christian "FemDomme" wife.[14]

"THEY'RE EMBRACING IT IN YOU WHEN YOU CAN'T SEE IT."

So, being specific about what's going on in the relationship
is a big help with an aspie partner, and Lynette Horn was
pretty prescient in realizing that Arthur required an alternative approach before she had even heard of Asperger's,
or learned that he might have Asperger's, in 2009. Their
relationship grew increasingly better in the year before his
passing.

"So here we are, and our love is growing, especially our
lovemaking, which went to a whole other level. He's sixty-
seven years old—this is not supposed to be happening!
But it's getting richer and better and of course it's making
him feel like the great stud that he is, having this amazing
magical time on all these levels," Lynette says.[15]

Having her husband taken from her so suddenly devastated Lynette, and the fact that her circumstances are
reduced in every way makes her resilience that much more
impressive. The Horns didn't have much money, and three
other family members of Lynette's had also died in the
months before we spoke. She isn't sticking by her spiritual
truth from a palatial home or TV studio; she's doing it from

between a rock and a hard place.

Rumi, the Persian poet whose ecstatic twirling inspired the whirling dervishes, wrote this verse about ecstatic love:

> You miracle seekers are always wanting signs.
> So where are they?
>
> Go to bed crying and wake up the same.
> Plead for what doesn't come
> Until it darkens your days.
> Giving away everything, even your mind,
> Sit down in the fire, wanting to become ashes,
> And when you meet with a sword, throw your-
>   self on it.
>
> Fall into the habit of such helpless, mad
>   things—
> You will have your sign.[16]

When you find yourself in what Lynette calls "the meat grinder," when you're at your lowest, she says, "You find the place inside yourself where you feel the love, that only the divine I think, can provide."

What is the divine?

She says it is spiritual connection with higher teachings and truth. "Your teachers, your friends, the men in your life, the women in your life— they all validate it, because they're embracing it in you when you can't see it. They embrace that profound place of love they have for you, and you can only live it when things keep hitting you and hitting you. And by that happening, it's a place of ecstasy, I swear to God."

Embracing the beauty in someone when they can't see it themselves is as satisfying an answer to "What is love?" as I can imagine.

Lynette says she will always grieve for Arthur, but she still has things to live for and be present for. She has no patience with what she calls "the dark drama we can all get into, especially as women. It's sabotage to stay in too much darkness. You have a choice to get out there into the light again and be who you are and be happy—otherwise it's too maudlin and it's not fun. It's not any fun there, girl!"

"I'm going to be seventy-two in a couple of weeks," she says, "and I feel wonderful—physically, emotionally, spiritually. I'm riding on some fast ship with Nikola Tesla and Arthur. That's where Arthur would be and what he deserved and where he'd go in his mind—his brilliant mind."

I really wish I had been able to talk to Arthur Horn himself, especially now that I know them as a couple through Lynette. (Reading his book does make him feel very present.) They certainly aren't the one-dimensional characters I pictured when I read that *News of the Weird* clip. Theirs was truly a tale of a methodical seeker and a wild woman with the balls of a lion, neither of whom let little things like science and religion get in the way of chemistry and spirit.

That Bigfoot—he's quite the yenta.

Chapter 6

Genetic Sexual Attraction

IT SUCKS TO BE EDGAR ALLAN POE

John Lennon was only 26 when he met Yoko Ono, then 33, at an art show at the Indica Gallery in London. John described his first meeting with Yoko in *All We Are Saying: The Last Major Interview with John Lennon and Yoko Ono*, an interview by David Scheff for *Playboy* conducted in their apartment in the Dakota: "It was in 1966 in England. I'd been told about this 'event'—" (There is a shrill scream from outside.) "Oh, another murder at rue Dakota." (Laughter) "—this 'event,' a Japanese avant-garde artist coming from America. She was red-hot. There was going to be something about black bags, and I thought it was all gonna be sex: artsy-fartsy orgies. Great! Well, it was far out but not in the way I thought it was going to be."[1]

The show was titled Unfinished Paintings and Objects. At the time, the avant-garde movement was all about negativity, but this was different. One of the works required the observer to climb a tall ladder to see a tiny placard on the ceiling, which Lennon did. All the card said was "Yes."[2]

The Dakota is foreboding, with its gas lamps, gold sentry box, and wrought-iron demon dragon ornaments: the perfect setting for a less romantic story than John and Yoko's such as *Rosemary's Baby*, which was filmed there. Not far away on West 84th Street is a far cheerier place that pays homage to a far gloomier person, Edgar's Café, named in honor of Edgar Allan Poe, who wrote "The Raven" in the Brennan, the building that houses this charming little restaurant. It's wonderfully snug on a cold, rainy morning, with its French farmhouse feeling, gorgeous pastries in the case, and a large, watery portrait of Edgar watching over us.

I have never thought of Poe as a romantic until recently, but with love's brain chemistry in my brain chemistry I realize that's exactly what he was. He's so often linked with the dark, the dank, and the horrible, with blinded cats, hearts beating under floorboards and premature burials, that it's easy to miss how often he wrote about love. "The Raven," "Ulalume," and "Annabel Lee" are all about death, yes, but the deaths of women so beloved that the lover has been driven to obsession, despair, and madness by their loss, locked in the sort of chemical tail-chasing that lost love would trigger in the brain scans of some of Helen Fisher's subjects 160 years later. Poe's characters seem to experience heinous withdrawal symptoms from the addictive chemicals of love.

In life, Poe was married to his cousin, Virginia Eliza Clemm, who was just 14 years old when they wed. Portraits of her show a delicately pale girl, with long chestnut hair and a face as sweet as Betty Boop's. No one doubted that they loved each other, and despite Poe's constant penury he did his best to provide for her.[3] If only he could have had in life what he would in death: in 2009 an original volume of Poe's first book of poetry sold for a $662,500, a record-breaking price for American literature.[4]

Virginia died of tuberculosis when she was just 25, and

indeed, Poe's works are populated largely with sweet young women who die too young, often of wasting diseases.

From *Eleonora*:
The loveliness of Eleonora was that of the Seraphim; but she was a maiden artless and innocent as the brief life she had led among the flowers.[5]

(Eleonora was the narrator's cousin; only new love could save him from being forever haunted by her death.)

From *Berenice:*
Oh, gorgeous yet fantastic beauty! Oh, sylph amid the shrubberies of Arnheim! Oh, Naiad among its fountains! And then—then all is mystery and terror, and a tale which should not be told. Disease—a fatal disease, fell like the simoon upon her frame; and, even while I gazed upon her, the spirit of change swept over her, pervading her mind, her habits, and her character, and, in a manner the most subtle and terrible, disturbing even the identity of her person! Alas! the destroyer came and went!— and the victim—where is she? I knew her not— or knew her no longer as Berenice![6]

From *Annabel Lee*:
The angels, not half so happy in heaven,
Went envying her and me—
Yes!—that was the reason (as all men know,
In this kingdom by the sea)
That the wind came out of the cloud by night,
    Chilling and killing my Annabel Lee.[7]

★ ★ ★

Jeffrey Savoye, secretary and treasurer of the Edgar Allan Poe Society in Baltimore, directs my attention via email to several passages in Poe's letters where the author's feelings for his young wife are evident. (Poe's letters are available on the Society's website.)[8] The most dramatic is his 1835 missive to Maria Clemm, Virginia's mother and Edgar's aunt, who cared for him in his youth; his own mother died when he was a toddler. Edgar believes Maria is going to accept the offer of a wealthy cousin, Neilson Poe, to take them in and offer Virginia an education. Edgar wants to marry the girl and seems to endure abject terror under the apprehension that he will lose her:

Aug: 29th

My dearest Aunty,

I am blinded with tears while writing this letter—I have no wish to live another hour. Amid sorrow and the deepest anxiety your letter reached—and you well know how little I am able to bear up under the pressure of grief. My bitterest enemy would pity me could he now read my heart. My last my last my only hold on life is cruelly torn away—I have no desire to live and *will not*. But let my duty be done. I love, *you know* I love Virginia passionately devotedly. I cannot express in words the fervent devotion I feel towards my dear little cousin—my own darling. But what can [I] say? Oh think for me for I am incapable of thinking. Al[l of my] thoughts are occupied with the supposition that both you & she will prefer to go with N.

[Neilson] Poe. I do sincerely believe that your *comforts* will for the present be secured—I cannot speak as regards your peace—your happiness. You have both tender hearts—and you will always have the reflection that my agony is more than I can bear—that you have driven me to the grave—for love like mine can never be gotten over. It is useless to disguise the truth that when Virginia goes with N. P. that I shall never behold her again—that is absolutely sure. Pity me, my dear Aunty, pity me. I have no one now to fly to. I am among strangers, and my wretchedness is more than I can bear.... What have I *to live for?* Among strangers with *not one soul to love me* ..."[9]

Poor Edgar! But one has to admire the jab about being assured of their *comforts* but not their *peace.* The ability to instill guilt is a gift beyond price. Virginia did end up with Edgar.

It wasn't perfect, as Poe scholar Richard P. Benton writes on the Poe Society website, though Poe definitely got his romantic heart's desire: "Poe told his best friend in Richmond, John Mackenzie, that the marriage had not been congenial. And he told at least two people that he and his young wife lived together as brother and sister for two years after their wedding."[10] Poe wrote to his cousin Elizabeth R. Tutt, "What it is to be pestered with a wife!"[11]

There's something endearing about that last one, a welcome smack of reality amid Poe's romanticism, as if a character in a Barbara Cartland novel said, "The bonfire of Claudia's passion for Roberto created a corona of light around them, but by morning she was glad he went home so she could get some goddamn sleep."

Benton writes that after Virginia's death, in 1847, of tuberculosis (commonly called *consumption* in the 19th century), Poe told a friend that marriage "has its joys, but its sorrows overbalance them" and that he never fully recovered.[12] Tuberculosis had also killed Poe's mother, Elizabeth, when she was 24 and he was three.

Poe apparently told more than one woman that she was Annabel Lee, which reminds me of Rock Hudson in *Pillow Talk,* writing one song and attaching the name of his various girlfriends to it so that each thinks it's just for her. Two years after Virginia's death, when Poe was arrested for drunkenness and thought himself sick with cholera, he still wrote in a letter to Maria, "It was about Virginia."[13]

So, in modern parlance, it's complicated.

THE LAST TABOO: "IT WASN'T A MOTHER–SON RELATIONSHIP, IT WAS A BOYFRIEND–GIRLFRIEND RELATIONSHIP."

It's impossible to imagine, in our culture, a celebrated public figure married to a first cousin. It wasn't long ago, however, that cousin marriage was no big whoop. Albert Einstein did it. Charles Darwin did it, for goodness sake, and if anyone knew about speciation and what might botch it, it was Darwin. (But he doesn't seem to have been a great romantic. In *Sex at Dawn* Christopher Ryan and Cacilda Jethá write that Darwin made a list of pros and cons for marrying. "Though Darwin proved to be a very loving husband and father these pros and cons of marriage suggest he very seriously considered opting for the companionship of a dog instead."[14])

It's fascinating to think that an urge as primal as sex is vulnerable to the caprices of trendiness, but there it is: cousin marriage was once fine, now it's a Fashion Don't of coupling. In fact, the risk of birth defects or infant mortality as a result of first-cousin breeding is not much higher than average and not much higher than the risk for women who give birth in their forties, according to professors Hamish Spencer and Diane Paul, who argued in a 2008 opinion paper that legislation against such marriages is unfair.[15] What if Edgar and Virginia were "destined" for each other but lived in America today and never considered it an option because of the social taboo? Can destiny be destiny if you can deny it because it's not in style?

There are always some people whose feelings are too strong to get pushed around by culture, the people who openly live a taboo and end up being groundbreakers for the acceptance of previously vilified ways of love such as gay relationships, multi-partner relationships. Just look at what Demi Moore and Ashton Kutcher did to level the field for older women and younger men. They certainly garnered an acceptance, even a hipness, for this type of May–December love that *Harold and Maude* failed to capture.

It isn't always glamorous, though. Sometimes it's painful. Some people experience a phenomenon called genetic sexual attraction or genetic attraction: an attraction between biological relatives as adults, usually after years of separation by adoption or other circumstances. GSA, or GA, got a boost in media attention following the revelation by singer Mackenzie Phillips that she had had an incestuous relationship with her father, rock star Papa John Phillips.[16]

I learned about GA, as Joe Soll, a psychotherapist and lecturer specializing in adoption issues, prefers to call it— in May 2010 after reading about a couple in Ireland who met in a bar, moved in together, and had a child, only to find out later that they were half siblings. The couple, who asked to be called James and Maura, blamed the courts and closed adoption records for enabling this bizarre coincidence.

The couple told how James discovered who his real father was. The story was worthy of *All My Children*. According to the *Daily Mail*, the short version is that his mother got pregnant after a brief romance in the '80s; his father fought in court to have access to his son but was denied. James was raised with another man, who was cold and abusive, as his father. When he and Maura met and became parents, his mother eventually broke down and told him that Maura's father was also his father. James told the *Daily Mail*: "People reading this will think our situation is a one-off and that the chances of this happening are the same as the chances of winning the lottery—but every week someone wins the lottery."[17]

Indeed, it also happened to Patrick and Susan Stübing of Germany, siblings who were separated at birth, fell in love when they met as adults, and had four children. Aida Edemariam and Kate Connolly reported in the *Guardian* in 2007 that the couple's children (two of whom had developmental problems) had been taken into care and that Patrick was in his second year of a jail sentence for incest.[18]

GSA IN ART

The shadow of genetic attraction was present in art as early as the 5th century BC, in Sophocles's *Oedipus Rex*, which tells the tale of Oedipus, King of Thebes. Oedipus is given away at birth by his parents, King Laius and Queen Jocasta, to avoid the fulfillment of a prophecy that Laius would be killed by his own son. They give the infant to a servant to leave on a hillside to die, but the servant can't bear the task he's charged with and gives the baby away. Oedipus grows up with no knowledge of his past, and Jocasta is unaware that her son is still alive. When Oedipus realizes that he *has* killed Laius, his father, and married his mother, he gouges out his eyes with a brooch from Jocasta's dress. (She, meanwhile, has hanged herself.)

Maybe because it's hard to top *Oedipus*, there aren't a lot of examples of GA in later dramas or stories. There's brief sexual tension between Luke and Leia in *Star Wars* before Obi-Wan informs them that they are brother and sister. It also pops up in the film *Soapdish* with some comically nerve-racking sexual tension between Jeffrey Anderson (Kevin Kline) and Lori Craven (Elizabeth Shue) who don't know they are father and daughter.

Psychotherapist Joe Soll was sold on the black market as an infant by a woman who "sold babies for 40 years." She falsified his birth records.

"I don't even know where or when I was born. I don't even know how old I am. It's totally fucked up. I've been searching for almost thirty years and there's nothing, because I have no information."[19]

When he first started looking there was no help for people like him, so he thought he might as well try to help others. In the process he became a specialist in issues regarding adoption, including GSA, which he prefers to call GA because he says it does not always have a sexual component. It's about the attraction people have for each other, he says, when they've never seen anyone who looks like themselves and they don't have the taboo against it because they were not raised with close relatives.

"It goes back to the story of Narcissus looking at his image in the water. If we grow up with people we look like, we get over that. But if we have never seen anyone we look like and we see such a person, what do we want to do?

We want to hold them and touch them and get close—and it turns into sex. I've never met anybody for whom GA really started with sex."

The term *GSA* is credited to Barbara Gonyo, who wrote *I'm His Mother But He's Not My Son*, bravely opening up the conversation about GSA in the 1980s. Barbara says she didn't coin the term *genetic sexual attraction*; she heard someone at a conference use it, a woman who had just met her own brother and found him powerfully alluring.

Barbara Gonyo and Joe Soll are friends, but they don't agree on whether sex should be part of the discussion. Joe feels, as a therapist, that including the word *sex* in the term for this type of attraction weights it too heavily against the people involved. This pull is not their fault, but it is something they are responsible for controlling, and that's where Joe comes in. Barbara, who experienced the phenomenon firsthand when she met her own son when he was 26, feels that if the attraction is not sexual, it's not an issue. "When I found my son the feelings I was feeling for him were sexual," she says. "If they were not sexual, there wouldn't be a problem."[20]

Keeping in mind Dr. Fisher's observation that we are more susceptible to attraction when we're in an agitated or vulnerable state, I ask Joe if the very nature of a first meeting between parent and child or between siblings wouldn't help facilitate deeper feelings.

"Absolutely," he says, and gives an example of an adopted mother meeting her son for the first time since birth. "When a child is born the mother and the child have a romance. It's the most intimate relationship anyone can ever have. The mother holds the child against her breast, skin to skin, body to body, and they have such intimate closeness for the first nine months that the infant doesn't know it's a separate entity."

When they are separated and then reunited, the mind and body want to continue the process. Both parties, Joe says, regress to the ages they were at parting. "The mom regresses to the age she was when she lost her child, so she's a young kid now, and the adoptee's regression is dynamic—which means the kid can be any age, but the one thing they want is to have that closeness they never had. This is nature. This is not about sex; it's about nature's process. What do they want to do? They want to hug each other, and unfortunately when you have two adults hugging each other—nature's process is erotic."

Shortly after my initial conversation with Joe, I read about the case of Aimee Sword, a Michigan woman who, in July 2010, was sentenced to nine to 30 years in prison for having sex with the son she gave up for adoption. An MSNBC story about the case stated that Sword was searching for a reason why this attraction had occurred. Everything about the case of Aimee Sword fits with what Joe says about this condition. I can imagine that it was a product of the frantic chemistry that comes from separation, and worse, being kept in the dark: Sword had been getting updates on her son from his adoptive parents, and when those updates suddenly stopped in 2008, Sword tracked him down on Facebook.[21] It's easy to theorize that this sudden lack of information would fuel an already raw emotional situation—the expected reward didn't arrive. Perhaps it was the panic of abandonment rage, as Dr. Fisher wrote about in *Why We Love*.[22] Or maybe it was "the horror more horrible from being vague, and terror more terrible from ambiguity," as Poe wrote in *Berenice*.

Finally, you have all those unresolved feelings that Joe

says come with GA, and it takes on that "Titanic" quality: so many things could have been done to prevent it but weren't—counseling from a professional, for example. Sword's lawyer, Mitchell Ribitwer, was quoted as saying, "When she saw this boy, something just touched off in her—and it wasn't a mother–son relationship, it was a boyfriend–girlfriend relationship."

Joe says he doesn't see many cases, only about a dozen last year, from people who contact him to help defend them in court. That number is up from two or three in previous years, probably because the media attention has become so widespread. He says he thinks it's a drop in the bucket because most people won't talk about it. He gives an example of a case he might see: "A wife is having an affair with her father and the husband wants to take away custody of the kids because she's a bad parent—she's seen as a sexual predator now."

He continues, "The sexual part is unconscious. The desire to be together I think is very conscious. *Oh, my god! This is my sister; I want to spend every moment with her! Oh, my god, it's like a honeymoon!* Or, *Oh, my god, I've never been so in love with somebody!* All of a sudden it turns into sex. It's fairy tale, puppy love, stuff. Best love they've ever had. The intensity of it is incredible."

Problems come up for people who experience a relationship that crosses the line. Joe says there is "the societal taboo, there's gonna be guilt, you're gonna get tremendous pressure from outside your relationship, people looking at you askance. And if you go back to the story of Oedipus, what did he do when he found out he was sleeping with his mother? He put his eyes out. We have this horrible taboo—people have killed for less. Somebody whose spouse is sleeping with their sibling? People have murdered for less than that, so it's more than just psychological danger."

It's hard not to notice that some of the reasons GA sounds like a bad idea are the same reasons people may have disapproved of interracial or gay relationships a while back. But some cultural attitudes are mutable. Even in a culture such as America 30 years ago, homosexuality was tacitly if not openly accepted. You could never say that about incest.

You might be able to soon, though. As of this writing, Switzerland is considering repealing incest laws that affect relationships between consenting adults.[23]

To Barbara Gonyo, the term *incest* denotes a victim. "There's no victim in GSA because they're both consenting adults. A father raping his child or an older brother raping his sister—that's incest to me and that is a crime." She strongly advises people in the grip of GSA to avoid sexualizing their relationships with a newly discovered relative. "It's a bonding process. If they leave the sex out of it, it will be painful, but it will be more painful if they have sex and continue having it and they end up losing their family or going to jail." The attraction—like most sexual attraction—will pass eventually, she says, and then you will have the brother or sister or other relative you were meant to have.

If GA is so tricky that even people who come to an adoption issues specialist like Joe are ambushed by it, how can it be circumvented?

"Several ways. One way, the first one, is just hold on," Joe says. "Stop the adoption. No, I have to change that. I'm not antiadoption. I'm anti the way we do it," he continues. "If the records were always open, we could have what's called a legalized guardianship with no cessation of contact, meaning people could always be in contact with their siblings and their parents even if they lived somewhere else. We treat it like a divorce. I did part of my training with kids in foster care who had weekly visits with their crack-addicted mothers, but it was the best day of the week for those kids when they got to see Mommy." If we have contact with our family members, the taboo gets set in place; if we don't, it might not.

"Number two is to leave the records open, no matter what. Number three is to educate people about the dangers of GA. Nobody talks about it. They don't want to hear it. When I try to tell people who come to me for help that they need to be aware of this, they change the subject. They go, 'Oh, that would never happen.' They won't listen."

I ask Joe if those people come back to him when it does happen.

"Oh, yeah," he says. "Look, I won't help anybody reunite if they won't prepare in a dozen different ways for four or five months beforehand, meaning reading about what it's like for a mother to lose a child, or the mother reading about what it's like for the adoptee to get in touch with all their emotions about their loss. If they won't do the groundwork, I won't do it. It'll be a disaster. Forget the sex—it'll be a disaster.

"An adoption agency has an obligation to tell people about this if they go for what's called nonidentifying information. The adoption agency has an obligation to tell them, but they won't."

The adoption industry, Soll feels, makes a lot of money, and they want to protect this. "Issues of adoption are so underplayed in this country because adoption is so mainstream and everybody looks at it as this wonderful thing where everybody wins. In fact, the adoptee and the parents always lose, because they've lost each other."

Joe tells me that several countries have shown significant decreases in adoption, including Australia. The *Brisbane Times* reported in 2008, "Thirty-five years ago there were almost 10,000 adoptions in Australia. Last year there were just 568." The story cites better birth control, family planning agencies, better sex education, increased in-vitro fertilization possibilities, and changing social trends as some of the factors that have contributed to the decrease.[24]

What usually happens if the person who has GA is already in a relationship?

"There's another piece to that, too," Joe says. "I don't know what kind of marital relationships they had in the first place. Who knows what was going on in their homes and whether they were really happy or not. And to top it off, adopted people do not pick well. Do you know what repetition compulsion is?"

Nope.

"Okay, here's a Psych 101 quickie. A woman grows up in a home where her father hits her over the head with a wooden spoon whenever he gets angry at her. If she doesn't get help for this, the odds are that she's going to pick abusive men later in life. She could go into a bar with a thousand men, and if there was one guy who would be willing to hit her over the head with a wooden spoon, she'd pick him. Not consciously. The reason is, there's a little girl inside her who wants to correct her childhood experience and find the father who will love her unconditionally. To do that she has to find someone who will abuse her first and then change his mind. So she's going to pick abusive men. And you know that the abusers don't stop—they don't stop unless they go get megahelp. So this is what the adopted person very commonly finds: someone who is unavailable, like Mommy or Daddy. It could be an alcoholic, someone who's abusive, or someone who's just emotionally not present—or halfway around the world." There are a lot of ways of being unavailable, he says.

"And then their relationships don't work well, so when they find someone they love it's easier to stray."

No Kids Allowed on the Moon

My discussion with Joe Soll was my first exposure to most of these issues regarding adoption, and it was part Pandora's box and part Snakes in a Can. I had no idea of the complexities, and I can't know what it's like person-ally. I have friends who were adopted; none that I know of have ever sought out their birth parents. One of my closest friends was adopted and has always been in stable, long-term relationships, so the idea that adoptees don't pick well really surprised me. Of course, Joe sees adoptees and people with adoption issues all the time. But then, I have to wonder if, as a therapist, he's seeing mainly people who *have* issues. Wanting to hear from someone I know is an adoptee and doing well in relationships, and to see how he got that way, I spoke to my friend Charles Martin.

I met Charles when I was about 18 or 19 and he was 22, which I thought was ancient. He wore frock coats and a dangly earring and dyed his hair black and spiked it up like Rick Ocasek. Few people in Orlando in 1983 had that kind of panache, and Charles turned out to be as inter-esting as he looked and twice as big-hearted as anyone can be. He also sustains relationships longer than most people I know do; I've known him for nearly three decades.

Charles's parents couldn't have kids, so all three children in his family were adopted, and the parents informed them of this in a savvy way. The children were told that adopted kids were picked out, so they were wanted even more than regular kids, and they had this discussion when they were very little, about six years old, so they were easily distractible. The conversation went something like this:

"You were adopted, which means we chose you and we think you're really special."

"Okay. What time is lunch?"

Charles's family comes from Georgia, but Charles and his wife of 14 years, Heather, now live in Victoria, British Columbia. I call him to discuss my conversation with Joe regarding adoptees' inability to sustain relationships.

"I don't disagree with him, because he's seen people in therapy," Charles says, "but in my small focus group of three—my brother and my sister and myself—we have exactly the opposite issue. We can't let go of people. It goes right back to what he's talking about, though. It's that rootlessness. Let me put it this way: an adopted person is never going to be the person who sails around the world alone. They want people around."

Both his siblings have also been in happy, long-term relationships.

"In my experience adopted people tend to want to create their own families to give them the roots they don't otherwise come with. I'm still friends with people I went to elementary school with. I have one friend I went to *preschool* with. If someone feels they have no family and no background, they feel like a free agent in the world—they may feel that nobody wants them. But that's a self-esteem issue, not an adoption issue, in my opinion."

Charles has never tried to track down his birth parents. His mother told him his parents were English; they were in America and gave him up for unknown reasons. He feels he's already had enough good fortune with family, between his own and his wife's, and looking for more would be "double-dipping."

"Besides, when you're an adopted kid you build this picture in your mind of why you ended up in the adoption agency, and usually it's because your mom went on to become Princess Grace of Monaco. 'Well, she was Mother Teresa and she had lots of other people who depend on her and she had to give me up.' As for Dad, he had to give me up because NASA said, 'No kids allowed on the moon!'"

"More likely, some English guy came over here and knocked up some trailer trash, and because trailer trash are like the roaches of humanity and survive forever, I'd find them," he says. So the flip side of that dream is the nightmare—reality rarely matches fantasy.

He might get the genetic testing done one day for medical information, he says, but mostly he's afraid he'd be let down to find out who his parents are. "I would hate to find out that my mom had lied to me and I'm descended from hillbillies."

Charles is aware of the story of the Irish brother and sister who have a baby together and want to have another. Charles refers to this attitude as "We're already in the pool. Let's just keep peeing."

He tells me that when he was a kid he was briefly under the impression that he might have a twin. "I always wondered what would I do if I ever met this other person—and being bisexual, would I? If I met him and was attracted to him, would I do it? Hell, yes."[25]

Well, they do say one has to love oneself before one can love another. If they're both the same thing, right down to identical freckles, it would have to be awfully tempting.

Chapter 7

The Greatest Breakup Story Ever Told

"I am enchanted. I am swept away."
—ROGER EBERT, ON *SITA SINGS THE BLUES*

If you've ever been to a film festival and thought, Wow, who picks these wonderful movies? or Jesus, who picks this crap and will they give me my money back? the answers are Someone like me and No. As a member of the various selection committees for the Florida Film Festival over the years, I spent time locked in a screening room watching films with my fellow committee members, which we then deemed as festivalworthy or not. Early on in the season the level of film quality we got was often disappointing. To give you an idea, once during the typically quiet moment we spend writing down comments, my friend and fellow committee member Brian Quain broke the silence with the question, "How do you spell diarrhea?"

One night early in the 2008 season, Brian put a DVD into the player that would alter my life for the better in ways it would take me two years to fully appreciate.

After some clever credits, the screen popped, burst, and sang with vivid, animated images of a peacock, snakes, ocean waves, a sloe-eyed woman in the jeweled Middle Eastern costume of the belly dancer, sensuous Indian music, scratchy 1920s torch song jazz, all in animated, rapid-fire imagery that showed the Indian pantheon and numerous images of the human heart in quick succession. It took me one-fifth of a second to fall in love. And at that point I didn't even know the move included a monkey army.

The film was *Sita Sings the Blues*, by animator and cartoonist Nina Paley, and the tagline was "The greatest breakup story ever told." Based on the sacred Hindu text the Ramayana, the film tells the story of the goddess Sita, wife of Rama, the trials she endures for his love, her kidnapping by a many-headed demon and a variety of other heartaches I won't enumerate because you simply must see it and seeing it is free on YouTube or SitaSings-TheBlues.com.[1]

In the film Sita's story runs concurrently with the tale of a modern American couple, in which the woman's problems with her husband eerily resemble those of the goddess.

Roger Ebert received a copy of *Sita* in 2008 with a note that said it was by "a girl from Urbana," his hometown in Illinois. In his *Chicago Sun-Times* blog he wrote that he promptly filed the film under "movies I will watch when they introduce the 8-day week." When a colleague told him the filmmaker was the daughter of a former mayor of Urbana he was intrigued and reassured that it wasn't some school project. So he had a look. This is what he wrote:

"I put on the DVD and start watching. I am enchanted. I am swept away. I am smiling from one end of the film to the other. It is astonishingly original. It brings together four entirely separate elements and combines them into a great whimsical chord." Ebert immediately invited Nina to come to his film festival in Illinois.[2]

★ ★ ★

Everyone on our committee agreed (which is rare): *Sita* was a shoo-in. I was thrilled. For all the films you sit through on this detail that make you wonder just how chummy you were with Hitler in your last life that you should merit such suffering in this one, every once in a while you get something like this film, and the joy is doubled by sharing it. In writing the program blurbs for the film I found out that the modern breakup story it tells is the story of filmmaker Nina Paley herself.

This, I thought, was as graceful an act of defiance as I could imagine. It was Nina who had gone through the breakup shown on film and when you break up you are *supposed* to be a wreck. You are *supposed* to lose your marbles. You aren't supposed to be a conjurer of beauty, much less of giggling.

Just who was this Nina Paley, I wondered, and what did she know that I didn't?

"Oh, I lost my marbles," Nina tells me on the phone two years after her movie makes my head asplode for the first time and we arrange to meet a couple of weeks later.

"MY BRAIN WAS DIPPED IN HELL"

Nina has wet, curly brown hair, an easy laugh, and a serious need to go get some Chinese food; good stories should never be shared on an empty stomach. We agree on this and, it turns out, have quite a lot in common. Like me, she has a history in the alternative newspaper world: her comic strip "Nina's Adventures" ran in several newsweeklies between 1988 and 1995. She had two other comic strips, "The Hots," syndicated by King Features, and "Fluff," syndicated by Universal Press Syndicate. Her apartment is spare and dominated by work: her drawing table and boxes and boxes and boxes of comic strips, plus images from *Sita* on the walls and *Sita* merch on the shelves. Her cat, Bruno, tries to look indifferent as she goes to leave but fails by staring at her. (It's so hard to look like you couldn't care less unless you really couldn't.)

Nina has been interviewed quite a bit, having circumnavigated the globe doing film festivals in the glow of *Sita*'s success, a journey that has left her happy to be back in her very own neighborhood. She's one of only two people who ever answered "no" when I asked if they had a dream destination.

"I'm a homey gal," she says. "I think it's different knowing that I could leave and deciding not to rather than not having the option and feeling trapped."

That's a relationship analogy if I've ever heard one. While we walk we talk about why some people handle love sanely—or seem to—and whether it's chemical.

"Well, I certainly had the I-want-to-kill-myself chemical," Nina says. "It's like my brain was dipped in hell."[3]

This breakup began, as many breakups do, with a marriage.

"I've actually been against marriage," she says, "because the state has no business interfering with my romantic life or my personal life, but then I realized that the state actually interferes with it whether you get married or not." She cites the case of a lesbian couple she read about where one of the women got seriously ill and her parents blocked her partner from being in on her care.

What pushed Nina and "Dave" (not his real name) toward the altar was his getting a job in India. Nina felt that after five years of dating, including four of living together, they were "functionally married," anyway, "but I was really concerned that if something happened to one of us when we were on opposite sides of the planet, what was the other person going to be able to do?"

Glad you asked.

The Alternatives to Marriage Project is a Brooklyn-based advocacy group that works to protect the rights of unmarried people in matters of housing, health care, and other areas.[4] The organization's webpage dedicated to hospital rights identifies the US states that block unmarried partners and friends from medical decision making, and tells what legal steps to take to protect yourself from having unwanted persons making decisions for you when you're incapacitated. You can download forms for these purposes for free.

Concerned about not having the authority they wanted in case of emergencies, Nina and Dave went ahead and tied the legal knot. But what seemed like just a ceremony for the long-term couple really did have an impact, and not a good one.

"I'm sure getting married contributed to his whole midlife crisis, or whatever it was that led him to push me away," Nina says. "I have no idea what would have happened if we hadn't gotten legally married. He left, and sort of severed every tie that he had. He wasn't calling or emailing anyone; he was not in touch with his family. He just took an axe and chopped it all off when he went to India."

Picture it. One minute you're a solid couple, then—nothing.

Not anything.

Crickets.

"I became increasingly panicked and terrified," Nina says. Friends offered support and theories. "One theory was that he was unemployed for a year before he left. He had talked about it affecting him, but I think for some men not having a job is like an experience of pure failure. I was a witness to that. Maybe he just wanted to forget everything."

The kind of silence Nina is talking about is my kryptonite. Unrequited phone calls make me feel as insecure as the seats on an 80-year-old Tilt-a-Whirl. I call these periods of waiting "the Ghastly Blank," which is how Australians refer to the miles and miles of empty space in the outback.

"Who the hell knows?" Nina says, of Dave's silence. "But then again, that's why I like the Ramayana. It never really explains why Rama does what he does." And in a way I can see that this is more like real life, where we might never get a satisfactory reason for our misery.

When Nina finally got a call from Dave—a month into his trip—she decided to move to India herself. "Bam!" she says. Just like that, she sublet the apartment and hightailed it literally halfway around the world, despite the chilly reception he was giving her. When Nina took a trip back to America for business, he dumped her via email.

Had all this happened in San Francisco, they would have dealt with it, gone to a couples therapist and worked on it. But "he was done with any of that stuff," she says.

"I really don't think he has an evil heart or anything like that, but he just did something that hurt me. He could have let me know before I went out there, but that would have taken, like, balls." Here she can't help laughing. "It would have hurt me no matter what. Anything he did would have hurt me, so he chose the path that would be easiest for him."

While pragmatically searching for clues in Dave's behavior, she didn't shirk any responsibility of her own, and in taking some of the blame on herself she evoked the story of Sita once again.

Nina acknowledges that Sita isn't perfect. She makes mistakes. In the film and in the story, sometimes she is capricious and makes silly demands. She clings to a husband who mistreats her. It doesn't justify Rama's actions, but it does illustrate that while our natural inclination is to rage at the obvious villain, there are always many layers to a breakup. Bitching and blaming certainly feels good, but in the end that compensation fails us spiritually and intellectually. Dave made mistakes, but Nina's acknowledgment of things she would have done differently feels more empowering and more adult than simply pointing a finger and screaming (though that would be really funny).

"I was young and dumb. Seriously," she says. "What do they say? There are no victims, only volunteers. When he didn't tell me his phone number for a month and didn't communicate, and I was, like, I'm going to move in with you in India and get rid of all my stuff, that was something I did. He wasn't saying, 'Oh, Nina, Nina, please come here,' he was giving me lots of subtle messages and I was saying 'Well, why didn't you state it clearly?' "

NEVER GIVE UP, NEVER SURRENDER

"Love is blind," Shakespeare wrote in *The Merchant of Venice*, and it's a truth we all recognize because we've all been there, choosing only what we want to see about the person we adore. Art is littered with examples of this kind of romantic holdout. Scarlett O'Hara refused to believe Ashley Wilkes was not the one for her in *Gone with the*

Wind. On *The Simpsons* Milhouse puppy-dogs around after an uncaring Lisa Simpson. In *Pretty in Pink* poor Ducky has to watch Andie fall for Blaine. Popeye was beloved by Alice the Goon, a bizarre, hulking, trannie-ish female who wore a flowerpot hat and chased after the sailor man. Buddy Holly sang "After all, another fella took ya, but I still can't overlook ya, I'm gonna do my best to hook ya after all is said and done," and then Blondie covered him on it. In *The Witches of Eastwick*, after Alexandra Medford (played by Cher) makes one of the best fuck-off speeches in film, the Devil (played by Jack Nicholson) considers her acidic insults to him and then asks, "Would you like to be on the top or the bottom?"

"The passionate swain," Molière wrote in *The Misanthrope*, "loves even the very faults of those of whom he is enamoured."

 ———————————————

The sharpest of minds can often fail to see the obvious, and having looked at what we go through in love—the addiction, the pain—it makes sense that we might automatically go into denial. If, as we talked about earlier, the dopamine flood gets worse, not better, when we sense the prize slipping away, it makes sense that Nina put more into her relationship not in spite of these subtle rejections but because of them.

"You can't go far in a rowboat without oars," Nina says. I wait for an explanation, thinking this is some ancient Hindu wisdom. "That's what my fortune cookie says," she tells me, and hands over the little slip of paper. She's both amused and annoyed: this is not what she'd call a fortune.

"A fortune is, like, *You will be attacked by a large marine animal.*" Even her cookie is vague.

Nina suspects, and current research supports her, that what she was going through after the breakup was withdrawal.

"I was losing it," she says, "falling apart and crying constantly." She had one affair in San Francisco and then decided to move to Brooklyn, where she began online dating.

"I basically wanted to have sex with every man in New York," she says. She became sexually compulsive. "I suffered greatly from that. It only lasted a few months and then I got help—fortunately I did not get any diseases. I was having unprotected sex with strangers knowing full well how dangerous that was, and when I looked at it with a little clarity I realized that I was just so torn apart by grief that I thought, If this kills me, fine—good. A friend of mine calls it suicide by the installment plan."

Sex was a way of not feeling anything. Once she got past that phase, she says, she got to feel the real grief. She compares it to a tsunami, "a complete breakdown, a really ferocious depressive episode." Depression had been a lifelong issue for Nina, but this time it was more than her system could take. She could barely get out of bed. She couldn't fulfill her work commitments. "It was like I had no skin," she says.

Depression is a serious condition, and 40 percent of people rejected in love go through it, according to Stephanie Ortigue of Syracuse University in an interview in the student newspaper, *The Daily Orange.*[5]

It's easy for the people around you to mistake serious depression for the garden-variety blues, especially after a breakup. It's almost intolerable when you're going through it, though, to have people saying you *just* need to get out, or you *just* need to find someone else, or you *just* need to get over it. Sometimes those things help, but sometimes it's much worse. Then the only good thing about people minimizing your grief is that they shift your focus from hatred of your ex or yourself to hatred of the minimizer.

In a story about depression on PsychCentral News, Rick Nauert writes, "In the general population, depression is still frequently associated with or perceived as a bad lifestyle, impairment of judgment, bad choices, and 'psychological weakness.' However, the results of brain imaging studies demonstrate that depression impacts the brain, and is associated with dysfunction of specific brain regions involved in cognitive control and emotional response."[6]

If you need another reason not to minimize your pain, according to the National Institute of Mental Health "more than 90 percent of people who kill themselves have a diagnosable mental disorder, most commonly a depressive disorder or a substance abuse disorder."[7] One wonders if someone told any of these diagnosable people to "just get over it," thereby compounding their unhappiness by making them feel stupid, but it's not a joke. A little self-medication and friendship goes a long way, but sometimes the old standbys just don't work. If you're suffering, take a cue from the old L'Oreal ad, "Because I'm worth it," and take your misery seriously enough to heal it.

I know I said this wasn't an advice book, but that's not advice. That's experience.

During Nina's depression there was only one thing she enjoyed: working on an animated short version of what would one day become *Sita*. That activity and a change in medication got her out of the hole she was in.

The medication changed everything. "Saved my life," she says, when I tell her my own story of taking Cymbalta in the short term for pain and anxiety. Antidepressants don't work for everyone, Nina says, but when they do it can feel miraculous.

She didn't go from gothic to giddy overnight. But she got functional. She could leave the house. The episode "put into sharp relief the things that made me want to live versus the things that made me want to die."

SEEKING THE LIGHT

What happened next could easily make you wonder if there really are not gods and goddesses who gather to watch human activity the way humans gather to watch *Glee*. Nina went through a compressed recap of her first crippling breakup with her husband. It was much shorter, not shot on location in India, but otherwise it was a mini-sode of the original. She was reliving the Ramayana. So she brokered a deal.

"It was like my offering to the gods: Okay. You guys like the Sita story so much that you are having me act it out over and over again, and I'm tired of acting it out, so what I'll do is make you a movie and you can rewind it and press Play again and again as much as you want. That's my offering to the gods. Let the movie do it for me. I don't want to have to live it anymore."

Most of us bargain with the gods. This is the first time I've ever heard anyone do it the way Nina did. It wasn't "If you give me this, I'll be ever so good," it was "If I give *you* this, you should free me."

"In the Ramayana there are stories about bargains like that all the time," she says. "So-and-so performs these austerities and gets a boon from the gods. And I was like,

Okay, I have performed my austerities. I would like a boon, please." She laughs. "And I did get a boon, it just wasn't the one I thought I was going to get."

For Nina, making the bargain "put it in this great mythological context, so it was comforting, like, 'I am just a pawn of the gods.' It says right in the Ramayana that they love the story! It says it's a great historical story and it pleases all the gods, so here I am acting it out, as are millions of other women."

Now that she had committed to making the film, she decided to think about the nature of commitment. Two committed relationships had eluded her. How to make the one with "Sita" last?

"This is my ring," she grins, extending her hand across the table and showing me the simple golden band she got to remind herself of her commitment to the movie.

"I was inspired by these two monumental breakups, and in both cases it was like, Didn't we have a commitment? When I realized that they felt differently about the relationship, I wanted them to work on it because I figured, well, commitment to someone doesn't mean you're in love with them every day." She decided to commit to the film the way she thought people should commit in relationships, knowing that on some days she would not be in love with it but it didn't mean she would dump it. The ring worked. She kept going, even when she didn't feel she knew what she was doing. There's a sign over her desk that says "If you don't know what you're doing, you're probably doing it right."

"I was trusting my heart. I was seeking the light. That's the one good thing about really severe depression. It's the darkest. It's so dangerous. If I was going to live, I had to go toward the light—and by light I mean anything that gave me a remote shred of pleasure, which was not much. And this film was just the only thing I want to live for. I can't tell you why. I don't feel as if I generated it."

Die to Yourself

Probably the most enduring story arc of all is the one in which the hero or heroine must undergo trial by fire, must die in some sense, to rise from the ashes to greater things. The Bible, John 12:24, says, "...unless a grain of wheat falls into the earth and dies, it remains just a single grain; but if it dies, it bears much fruit." Ebenezer Scrooge is not the same man on Christmas Day he was on Christmas Eve. From *Much Ado About Nothing* to *The Revenge of the Nerds*, we love transformation stories, those that show we must be willing to die to our old selves in order to reach a higher goal.

Nina says, "It's a special state, grief is a really special, amazing state. I hate it, I'm scared of it. I don't want to be in it again, although I'm sure I will, but man, it's amazing." Nina illustrated the state of grief in *Sita* by Rotoscoping the soulful, swirling dancing of Reena Shah with a background of eyes crying fire. "There's all this fire coming up—she's in the fire and there's God there. That is grief."

Back in her cozy apartment, I'm reading Nina's comic strips (my favorite is one about masturbation called "Ménage à Moi") and Bruno is sitting in her office chair chasing his tail as it hangs over the side. The momentum is making the chair spin—it's a million-hit YouTube video just waiting to happen. Nina is not the kind of person to give advice; you can tell that she sees people as too individual for mass-market wisdom. But she tells me the most important thing she thinks the brokenhearted should know. "You feel like you're the most alone person in the world, but that state is the definition of humanity. That's what connects us. So all I'll say is, you're not alone."

We feel alone, possibly, because when other people are going through bad things they often don't let on.

"You can't talk about it at parties," Nina says. "A lot of people are terrified to hear pain; that's just an unfortunate fact about people. You try to open up to them and most people just don't want to hear it. It's like, Snap out of it! Get over it! Well—" She thinks about it for a minute. "No!"

Fortunately, she says, "There are other ways of communicating with people than talking to them at parties. And these include art! And writing! And music! That's why we have amazing art and music about feeling: because there was no other way for people to share it."

In my interview with Helen Fisher I had asked her why some people, like Nina, can turn their misery into creative beauty while others engage in behavior like resorting to violence. She cited both the importance of the person's background and the fact that dopamine is also associated with creativity. People who don't have a physically aggressive past or tendencies can become very creative when they're miserable.

Helen says, "A huge amount of world poetry is about rejection in love. People who have never written a poem before can write a poem when they've been rejected, because the dopamine system becomes so amped up they grow more creative and pour out their passions in poetry."[8]

Nina says she was dealing with depression at an early age, but her family was relatively stable—"normally dysfunctional," she says—so a little calmness and the opportunity for a creative outlet would make all the difference when those rotten gods wrote in the inevitable plot point of rejection.

As for romance, another boon Nina seems to have received from the gods is no desire to be in the game. "Mercifully, my interest in men really waned and I've been celibate for the last year. While I was working on *Sita* I was dating people, but obviously I never got in a lasting relationship."

She adds, "It's just like—grace. I'm just fortunate. About twice a year I go nuts—I have the hormone crazies and just desperately want to get sex. And then it passes. I don't know if it's just age or maturity or a special blessing or what. I just don't have the same need I used to have."

There's not much I wouldn't do for this boon. But there's something sly about this boon business, and somehow I know that the one way I'll never attain such grace is by being too needy for it.

These days, Nina is back in the comic strip business with her new strip, "Mimi and Eunice," and she also works with the nonprofit QuestionCopyright.org.

Has her sense of balance changed since making *Sita*? Does she feel more centered, or better able to know when enough is enough?

"Oh, no," she says. "I've never known that. I believe that I am here to serve the muse. Much of the time I'm between assignments, but sometimes the muse comes and says, 'You are going to do this,' and I say, 'Okay,' and that's what I do. And that's basically how I approach life."

★ ★ ★

Nina's story is an important one, I believe, because if she could thoughtfully and deliberately turn her emotional situation around, that tells us it can be done. By being self-aware both biologically (med-switching time) and emotionally (focusing on what made her want to live versus what made her want to die), she transformed herself. True, she had some advantages not everyone has, but you might have some advantages that she didn't. She used what she had. The devil may be in the dopamine, but the muse is there, too. Maybe in love's misery we should ask not what the gods can do for us, but what we can do for the gods.

Chapter 8

Nikki Reynolds

There is nothing in the world so damaged that it cannot be repaired. I encourage you to know this because without this certainty we should, all of us, be mad.

—HERCULE POIROT IN *APPOINTMENT WITH DEATH*

NEVER A BORROWER

My car is representative of many of the people of the fine state in which we both reside, Florida. It is incontinent, can't go far, overheats quickly, and really only runs to prove a point, a point it can't remember. (I love it anyway.) The bottom line is, my car is unreliable for long trips. When my dad bought a new car and asked if I wanted to drive it for a while, I jumped at the chance because I had a very important road trip to make. I picked the car up in the afternoon. That night, as I was packing for my 6:00 a.m. wakeup call, the phone rang. It was my dad. Someone— not my dad but someone I won't name—had left a gun in the glove compartment of the car. My dad wanted to know if I would take the gun out and leave it in my apartment while I was away.

No. No, I will not. I will not touch the gun that was accidentally left in the car, forgotten. A gun. A firearm. Bang-bang-you're-dead. Left in the car. Accidentally.

I had been driving around with a gun in my possession

without knowing it because someone breezily left this little instrument of death behind like a pair of cheap sunglasses. What if I'd been pulled over and went to look for the registration in the glove box, and opened it in full view of a police officer—and was *surprised* to find a gun there? The negligence of it made me despondent. Of course I won't bring this gun into the house, this gun that gets left lying around like junk mail. Where might it be left next, with my fingerprints on it? This is exactly the kind of stuff that wins people the Darwin Award or gets them in Chuck Shepherd's *News of the Weird* column. I can tell you in my sleep where my cell phone is, and it can't kill another person. My heart hurts.

I call my friend Doug, who is the cool-blue calm to my scarlet rage.

"Am I wrong?" I ask.

"No!" he says. "How do you accidentally leave a gun in the car?"

"And what if I had accidentally taken it to a state prison?"

I was thankful to have the car, but the thought that I came within 10 hours of driving onto the grounds of the Gadsden Correctional Facility in Quincy, Florida, not knowing I had a concealed weapon in the car made me wish that tranquilizers the size of Twinkies came in gumball machines and I had lots and lots of quarters.

My appointment the next day is with Jaquiline Reynolds, a 30-year-old woman currently serving time at Gadsden, near Tallahassee, for second-degree murder. When she was 17, Nikki stabbed her adoptive mother 13 times with a kitchen knife before placing a call to 911 to turn herself in. The transcript of that call is blood-chilling to hear.

Nikki Reynolds came to my attention when her story aired on *Snapped,* a TV show on the Oxygen network that details murders committed by women (and where my information about Nikki's crime came from).[1] Nikki was adopted at the age of three months by Robert and Billie Jean Reynolds of Coral Springs. She went to ball games with her dad and shopping with her mom, did well in school, had friends, and was doted on by her parents, strict Christians who were very involved in their church, as was Nikki. Then along came puberty, adolescence, and Carlos Infante, Nikki's classmate at Marjory Stoneman Douglas High School. Carlos and Nikki were a couple for about two years and he was the first boy with whom she was sexually intimate.[2]

Even for adults, sexual intimacy triggers a tidal wave of those addictive chemicals that come with love. Those of us who have been in battle with these chemicals know all their tricks and still have a tough time fighting them off.

Nikki was a young girl experiencing this flood for the first time, and she was largely experiencing it alone. She didn't want to discuss her sexual activity with her parents, fearing it would disappoint them. She isolated herself from her friends; her world was Carlos. She feared pregnancy but also feigned it strategically, once even making up a story about being raped in order to protect Carlos in case she was pregnant. The story fell apart when the police questioned her rape story and told her parents that she had lied.

Billie Jean didn't want Nikki seeing so much of Carlos, but Nikki was having none of it. To her that was like asking if she could breathe a little less. She slept a lot. Her grades deteriorated. Nothing interested her. She was exhibiting signs a lot of people in our syndrome-savvy culture would take for depression—but depression looks a lot like ordinary American adolescence, so it was probably tough to tell how troubled she really was. All she cared about was Carlos. Sometimes he would say he wanted to break up, but she would tell him she was pregnant and he would stay with her. In the end that was why he left her: she was the girl who cried wolf one too many times. Her idea of trying birth control was to get the pills from a friend, but they made her break out in hives. (Birth control pills require a doctor's prescription to ensure that the woman receives the correct medication and that she's healthy enough to take it.)

In May 1996, when Nikki concocted yet another pregnancy story, her mother and her boyfriend had had enough. Carlos was sick of the lies. He said he wanted nothing more to do with her and it was only Nikki he was mad at, not her mother. After apologizing to Carlos for Nikki's behavior, Billie Jean decided to take Nikki to see the church counselor, unaware that Nikki had just taken an overdose of aspirin in a suicide attempt.

The counseling session went badly and Nikki and her mother went home. Nikki thought the aspirin would kill her. When it didn't, she formulated a new plan: to kill Carlos. If she couldn't have him, no one would. There was an obstacle, though: the family was scheduled to meet with the high school counselor the next morning. Nikki decided the best plan was to kill her parents, which would free her to go to school and slit the throat of the boy who had scorned her.

Nikki had broken from reality enough to see murder as her only option but she was still grounded in reality enough to plan it. When her father went to church that evening, Billie Jean stayed at home. While cleaning the kitchen, Nikki got the idea to kill her mother first, clean up the mess, and then kill her dad when he got home; this was easier than her original idea, killing them both in the night. While her mother sat at the computer Nikki attempted to slit her throat. When that didn't work, Billie Jean had a minute to try to get away. Nikki stabbed her repeatedly, asking her, "Why am I doing this?" and saying she was sorry but she couldn't live without Carlos. She said, "Are you dying? Are you dying?" realizing her mother was suffering and wanting the suffering to stop. She stabbed her 13 times. Before Billie Jean died she told Nikki that she wanted her to get help and that she loved her and forgave her.

Horror struck. Hurled back into reality by the carnage committed by her own hand, Nikki called 911. The call is harrowing to hear. Between sobs and screams Nikki tells the operator she's stabbed her mother and there's blood everywhere, to please come and save her. They were too late.

Nikki was taken into custody. In a taped stream-of-consciousness confession she told them everything—about the plan to kill Carlos, about killing her mother. She suddenly began to vomit—the aspirin overdose had kicked in. She was taken to the hospital, treated, and released the next morning into police custody, charged with first-degree murder.

Two years later, Nikki went on trial. Her defense attorneys pleaded insanity, hoping to keep her from life in prison, a defense Nikki now says she feels was right ("What sane person would stab a person they love, and keep going?") though she accepts and always has accepted the responsibility for her actions.

The defense offered the testimony of two psychiatrists who said that Nikki was not in her right mind. They said she had borderline personality disorder, a mental illness that typically presents itself in adolescence or early adulthood and is characterized by an intense fear of abandonment, a clingy disposition, neediness, low sense of self-worth. People with borderline personality disorder often push others away out of fear of rejection, then go to extreme lengths, including suicide attempts, to get them back.[3] On *Snapped* Dr. Benjamin Barnea stated that an aspirin overdose could cause "metabolic derangement" and caused Nikki to experience "a mini-psychotic episode."

But the prosecution had two psychiatrists who were able to testify that Nikki knew what she was doing. Under Florida law, insanity can be established if the defendant has a mental illness that prevents her from knowing what she is doing or from understanding its consequences, or if the defendant didn't know that what she was doing was wrong.[4] Nikki, they said, knew what she was doing, right down to testing the knife to see if it was sharp enough. The jury deadlocked and a mistrial was declared.

Nikki was retried in the same court in November 1999. In this round, the defense had a new witness. They had tracked down Katrina Ramos, Nikki's biological mother, who testified to a family history of mental illness and to self-inflicted violence—trying to induce a miscarriage while pregnant with Nikki by punching herself in the stomach and falling down on purpose.

In the end the jury would decide that Nikki was not insane. She was found guilty of second-degree murder and sentenced to 34 years in prison.

When I saw Nikki's story on television it scared me to think how easily that could have been me. I'm not homicidal, but I recognized myself in the teenager Nikki was, the baby-faced naïf—I recognized her anger, frustration, and fear as one recognizes a member of one's tribe. I had a great many more outlets than Nikki, but I still felt that operatic frustration when I was young. Many of us have been torn apart by love and feel as if we're going to do something desperate, even if we don't know what. Nikki actually did it. I had to wonder how this girl who went over the brink felt about love today.

LEARNING TO FORGIVE YOURSELF: "I USED TO GET ANGRY WHEN PEOPLE SHOWED THAT THEY CARE ABOUT ME."

Gadsden Correctional is in Quincy, Florida, just outside Tallahassee, in the northern part of the state. I'm 100 percent sure that I'm the only person in the world who has ever been this happy to pull up in front of it. I feel that Nikki has something really important to offer: having been inside insanity, she can help pull other people away from it. Like a character in Dante's *Inferno*, Nikki can speak directly from hell and maybe help someone else avoid it.

My friend Sam comes on this trip with me, too, and he drops me off in the company of Unit Manager Richard Krutcher, a big man with an odd kind of warmth, which is probably just about right for a place where you're not sure how warm you ought to be. I go through the security gate and deal with one of the prison guards, a wall of female who is a perfect ad for never doing anything to end up in jail. (Everyone else at Gadsden was as nice as pie and ice cream.) Mr. Krutcher takes me to a big, open room that looks like a school cafeteria, with lots of vending machines including ones that sell frozen meals. He asks where I would like to speak to Nikki and I spot a little room off to the side painted with animals and full of books and toys, a playroom for children who have come on inmate visits. This room is small and I feel it will be easier to establish a comfort level in it. Mr. Krutcher obligingly brings in a table and three chairs. Why three?

Because, he says, there will be a counselor in on the interview. She will not speak for Nikki or be part of the interview, but she will be there for Nikki's sake and my safety.

"Wow," I say. I can't help laughing, but it never occurred to me that I might be in any danger. "I never even thought about my safety."

"We did," he says. "She wasn't on *Snapped* for nothing."

And suddenly, there she is.

She's not the pale, baby-faced teenager of 13 years ago: she's as tan and slender as a wooden flute and her face has thinned out in adulthood. She's beautiful. She wears her pencil-straight, shiny brown hair waist-length and has on the standard prison uniform of a shapeless blue smock.

Nikki and I sit catty-corner from each other at a long conference table while her counselor sits away from us, skirting the wall, and observes. Since we've been corresponding, it's easy to break the ice by talking about things like the prison softball team, for which she keeps the stats, and about being part of the prison's dog program, one of many across the country where former racing greyhounds are trained for domestic life by prisoners. Nikki adores her dogs and has sent me lots of pictures of them. Soon it feels natural enough to segue into asking about the episode of *Snapped* that alerted me to her story. Does it seem like a lifetime ago? What was it like to watch?

"I had different opinions of myself. I wanted to say I hated the little girl I was looking at," Nikki says. Her voice is soft but clear and she speaks quickly but with a rich Southern drawl. She says she also sympathized with the pain she was in, and though it seemed like a lifetime ago, seeing her family made it vivid, as if it happened yesterday.

She appreciated the accuracy with which she says *Snapped* showed her story but it did bring it all closer to home.

She's doesn't demure from the subject of her mother's murder. The guilt she carries is so severe that her doctor feels she has posttraumatic stress as well as depression, for which she's recently started taking Zoloft. I ask if she has days where she relives the murder and whether she has to distance herself from it.

"Every time I go to thinking about it, I'll block it out, because if I really sat there and cried it out how I really felt, I'm gonna have a disorderly conduct," she says. Sometimes when she can't control it she cries about it silently, but she still has a lot of anger and a lack of forgiveness for herself. She can't change the past, she says, but she can do her best to improve the present.

"She was an innocent person," Nikki says, referring to Billie Jean. "It's not like I brutally stabbed a woman who abused me—she was perfectly innocent, had nothing to do with it, had nothing to do with it even in my thoughts. But at that time I was so focused on the loss of Carlos it never registered what I was doing, what it was costing me. It was just, as long as I get to him, no matter what it takes, that's what was gonna happen. Forgiving myself for that is so much more difficult than forgiving yourself for killing someone who beat the crap out of you all your life, or that you got in a fight with. The woman loved me till her last breath… So it's very hard."

She goes on, "I would like to say that in order to forgive myself it would definitely help if my dad was still in touch with me. It helped me when I was in the county jail and he would write to me, the words that he wrote and the cards that he sent let me realize that I could still be loved."

Nikki's father stopped communicating with her after she

was convicted in December 1999. She got one last letter. "That letter was the first time he ever really described any pain he had felt. He said I'd pretty much have to start looking out for myself, but he'd be here and there for me." But when she tried to write him from prison, she says, "I never heard back from him. Not one time." She recently called her former church pastor and asked after her dad, but he had not heard anything from him.

Nikki has never received a negative piece of mail. We talk about the empathy expressed by people who have seen her story on *Snapped*.

"Sometimes I used to get angry when people showed that they care about me," she says. Her self-hatred makes it hard for her to understand why people would care, but she tries to involve herself in activities that feel positive, like her dogs and the people on the softball team who rely on her. "Those things are like, okay, I'm still important to the world, you know?"

"QUIET LITTLE WHITE GIRLS"

How important Nikki has the potential to be is evidenced by a melodrama in which she was recently involved. I asked her what she would recommend to the parents, teachers, or friends of someone who was experiencing what she did— who was so besotted with another person that they weren't connecting with reality.

"I actually had an opportunity like that when I was in that other facility. A girl's daughter was screaming and ranting and raving on the phone: she wanted to harm her grandmother, which was my friend's mom. And my friend was like, 'Nikki, she's gonna do the same thing! She got a knife!' I got on the phone with the girl and she's like, 'You don't understand!' and I said, 'Yes, I do.' I put myself out there. I went through the emotions that she was going through at the same time instead of just saying 'Don't do that, that's wrong!' Sometimes you've got to really *go wrong with* somebody."

The blunt emotional force of Nikki's hard-core empathy disarmed the girl—it was her own personal *Scared Straight*. Nikki feels that "it was a God thing," that she was meant to be there to help this girl.

"When I first got locked up, because I was so young, they used to bring juvenile tours through the county jail and they would pull me out because I was the same age as them. They might be juvenile delinquents who have done drugs or stolen. I'd say 'I never did drugs, I never was out there stealing, but I done took a life, an innocent life, because of the relationship I was in.' " She tried to tell them how behavior they might think is simple, like stealing, could lead to killing someone. "God, if it can happen over something as simple as a relationship, it could happen more so if I'm high on drugs—or *they* could get killed."

She says, "Everybody has a different way of raising their kids, but sometimes you've really got to *take it* there so they realize the severity of it, instead of sugarcoating it: 'No, baby don't do that,' and just sheltering your kids like that." Her voice goes very soft and she adds, "A little bit more of an emotional level, because that's how some people relate, on emotion."

The difference between Nikki and the 14-year-old girl on the phone was that "she had that anger and rage toward the intended victim, which I did not. It was more, If I can't have Carlos, no one can, and whatever got in my way..." Her anger wasn't toward her mother, but she understood the intensity of it, and that's what she needed to make the younger girl understand.

Nikki uses, without any evident awareness of it, a

striking metaphor when she talks about understanding the girl's feelings: "I can still see the separation anxiety that she was feeling in all of that. It's the anger... See, my anger was at Carlos and myself, but there was still that rage and that overwhelming feeling you just can't control anymore. You're losing your senses. So you have to just pierce them in that sense emotionally, make them realize, instead of just saying, 'I understand,' show them why you understand."

Does she encounter other women in prison like herself, who nobody would think was capable of such an act? "Oh, the majority. When I first got locked up in the county, it seemed like every girl I met who was in for murder—they were the ones you would have least expected that from. Quiet little white girls, you know what I'm saying? It's amazing. And that comes from holding things in—you don't feel like you can talk, and eventually you're going to explode.

"One girl, her boyfriend killed her husband because supposedly her husband was beating on her. Another lady, it was drug-related. She was in the car with a girl who stabbed her with a syringe needle, so she pulled out her gun and shot her. They're people who never had a violent past, never had any priors, just quiet normal women."

See what happens when you have a gun in the car?

"So many of them come back. I'm still here and they come back and back and back. They have to find something else to focus on. Anybody's capable of being in prison. People make bad choices."

Nikki's home environment was stable, but she didn't understand her parents' even-tempered way of seeing things. She saw more of her emotional self in her biological family. "Every time they were in a relationship and a person broke up with them, they wanted to die or it was the end of the world. I definitely believe in the genetics."

She takes her rehabilitation very seriously and worries about keeping a grip on herself. "Like, if you're in a relationship and you walk in and your man is sleeping with another woman, how do you just close the door? I want to know how to just do that!"

Most of us would have a pretty hard time with that, but Nikki is right to be concerned about that raw, out-of-control feeling: she doesn't want to repeat her past. It's easy to hear how intense it was for her when she talks about certain instances, such as when she chose to lie about being raped. "I didn't even wait to see if I was pregnant. I started to think, What if I'm pregnant? What if I'm pregnant? What can I do? And I started looking in the Yellow Pages for these abortion clinics. I remember making a phone call, the lady telling me about a 'twilight special,' they call it. It can be confidential, whatever. But I was just freaking out. Who's going to take me? And how am I gonna pay for it? So then I thought, Well, let me just say I was raped. It doesn't put Carlos out there, and my parents will still think I was their good little girl. When I spoke to the rape counselors they made me feel like I could tell them the truth. They said, 'We're not saying this is the case, but a lot of girls do this to protect their boyfriends, and if that's the case we'll just tell your parents and you can get your clothes.' So I told them the truth. And of course they told my dad."

Nikki was a smart girl, yet that fear response overrode her reason to the point that she evidently didn't even think of getting a pregnancy test. "And then in the end I wanted to get pregnant because I wanted to keep him," she says. But her parents would have been angry with her. In their religious household she didn't have open conversations with her parents about such things. "It was always just about God and how we should live," she says. She still finds strength in her religious beliefs.

I ask if she thinks any of what happened to her was destined to be her fate.

"No, I definitely think it was my decision that did it. God allowed it. He sees the whole picture. I don't." This gives her some ability to let go of things, like whether or not they will get the dogs back. The dogs have already allowed her to become more pragmatic about relationships. "I like to see them go because they're going to homes; other people break down something serious," she says. "It's definitely helped with detachment—because they have an unconditional love and it's the best kind of love I've gotten since I've been locked up. I could look at that in future relationships: if it doesn't work out, then okay, whatever, it's not the end of the world."

Nikki knows what a high price acting on the impulses of mad love can exact, so I ask her what she thinks people can do, for themselves or others, not to end up going over the edge—not to end up as she did. She advises a few things:

> ▶ Think about the last person you thought you couldn't live without, until you did; it will help you realize you'll be OK without this one.

> ▶ Involve the brokenhearted or obsessed in activities they used to love, so they can realize there is more to life than a single human being.

▸ Talk to someone who has been where you are so they can empathize with you.

▸ Graphically go through the steps the troubled person wants to take. If they say they want to kill someone, say, "Okay, how is it going to feel that the next step is prison?"

Nikki sums it up: "What makes this person so great that you cannot live without them? Now, some people might feel this way because we're talking about their financial security. 'I can't live without him because if he leaves me I'm not gonna have a house!' That's different than the emotional 'I can't live without him.' I think they need to focus on themselves, the self-love. When you lose yourself in another person you lose your self-love."

I have unquestionably lost myself in love, was thrilled to give in to the emotional current and get pulled out to the depths, never caring if I came back. All my beautiful work, my brilliant friends, the people who loved me lost their substance when I was high on that chemical. We have all been there. The weighty responsibility of being yourself is lifted in those moments you entwine with another. I think Nikki lost herself in obsessive love and didn't want to get back or didn't know how to get back. I think she is trying as hard as anyone can to be better. How could anyone not want to recover from that?

"IT WAS AN OBSESSION"

And what of the love that caused it all?

Carlos seldom even crosses Nikki's mind these days unless someone asks her about him. Seeing him on *Snapped* didn't jar her in any way. Does she still view the feelings she had for Carlos as love?

"No, no," she says. "It was an obsession."

What she was feeling, she now sees, was not so much love as fear of rejection. "It was a control thing for me, he was my possession. I didn't want him to have any friends, I didn't want him to have anybody. I wanted to eat, sleep, and breathe Carlos, and that wasn't love at all. Also, I think if you really love somebody, it lasts. Once the crime happened it was almost like a switch went off. All this happened over somebody I only think about unless I talk about him."

When I ask if her youth and inexperience played into her spiraling out of control, Nikki brings up the notion of chemistry.

"I actually heard this recently, that when you first have sex with someone your body releases a chemical and it makes you a whole different being. I don't want to turn this into a biblical thing, but I know that when you become one with somebody you change. That's why God cherishes love so much, because it does something to you inside with your emotions."

Two chemicals that might help explain what Nikki is describing would be dopamine, the pleasure-releasing neurotransmitter, and oxytocin, the bonding agent and "cuddle hormone." But Nikki was also carrying some pretty serious preconceptions about what a sexual relationship should encompass.

"I thought, Okay, now that I've been intimate with him, this is a forever thing, because I always believed in no sex before marriage. After we did it, I thought, I've definitely got to marry him now to make it right."

When I ask her if she's nervous about getting into relationships when she gets out of prison I get the fastest "Yes" I've ever heard in my life. "I can't sit here and think I'm gonna take another life," she says, but she still has insecurity and rage and is working on learning to control her emotions. She has four years to get it right—Nikki is eligible for parole in 2015.

Relationships are hard in prison; you can't trust people, because they turn on you. Nikki's last girlfriend was released, and that didn't bother her at all—in fact, she shows the same pragmatism she shows about the dogs. "I can't control what she does out there," she says. The girl did keep in touch, but "her world is different, she's got kids." Like the dogs, the girl has moved on to a home and a better life. Nikki doesn't want to think of herself as bisexual, because it's biblically wrong, and she does want to be married and have children someday. Her relationships in prison have helped show her that she has changed, but because she was locked up so young she worries that she may have no idea how to have a relationship, or anything else, as an adult.

But she's not interested in finding someone to take care of her before she leaves. I ask if men have seen her on TV and written to her.

"Certain men, of course, through the years, they want to devote their luuuuuv to you! And all this crazy stuff. I don't want that when I get out," she says. She just wants to know what it's like in what she calls "the free world." She looks forward to shopping, buying hygiene and beauty products, and new technology, like digital cameras, which she's totally captivated by. When she went in, she reminds me, technology was VHS tapes and—a word I haven't heard in forever—cassingles.

She's nervous but excited about the prospect of being back in "the free world."

"I'm pretty good with challenge. I look forward to that. And I like to feel responsible—like when I do the softball stats, or when I had my dogs. Feeling responsible for a life."

TWO VIEWS ON THE TEEN BRAIN

Nikki had a problem with an addictive love, a borderline personality disorder, anxiety over displeasing her parents, over losing Carlos—at first it doesn't seem necessary to look beyond these issues to understand why, as the show's title so aptly puts it, she snapped. Then I ran across some information about the teen brain that made me wonder if there wasn't just a little more to it. It's easy to see, quite vividly, in fact, that teenagers act differently from adults, so why wouldn't there be differences in their brains that make them act the way they do?

On CNN's AMFix series on teens, *Walk in My Shoes*, Dr. Jay Giedd, a neuroscientist at the National Institute of Mental Health, talks about teens dealing with violence. He says the frontal lobe doesn't mature until very late, about age 25, so teens are prone to act more impulsively. "Whenever there's high emotion, this part of the brain is really taxed. It really has to work extra hard to sort it all out."[5]

In 2002 Dr. Giedd also appeared on a PBS report, *Frontline: Inside the Teenage Brain*, which discussed some of the reasons teens appear more impulsive, moody, or sleepy than their parents might prefer. What teens are doing during those years can also affect their capabilities in the future, because while there is growth there is also "pruning"—the brain has a "use it or lose it" attitude and will get rid of cells that aren't being engaged.[6]

I wondered if this might have some bearing on what happened to Nikki, so I asked two experts, Dr. Robert Epstein and Dr. Joseph Shrand.

Dr. Epstein is the founder and Director Emeritus of the Cambridge Center for Behavioral Studies in Massachusetts, former editor-in-chief of *Psychology Today*, author of *Teen 2.0* and the forthcoming *Ageless Society*.[7] He isn't buying it.

"There is no evidence whatsoever that the problems in our teens are caused by their underdeveloped or faulty brains," he says. "You'll see slight differences between teen brains and younger and older brains because the brain develops throughout our lives, so there will be changes with age, but it's also true because we've been treating them a certain way. When you treat people a certain way, experience shapes the brain, experience changes both the anatomy and physiology of the brain." Dr. Epstein believes that culture shapes the brain and that ours isn't doing very well by teens.[8]

Cultures where teens are integrated earlier into adult society don't see the behavior we associate with American teens, Dr. Epstein says. Our culture infantilizes and separates teens, isolates them in an environment where they only socialize with each other, not with adults, and offers them only the most inane role models. (Lindsey Lohan is mentioned.)

"There is a kind of constant competition going on among teens to drive faster or smoke another joint," he says. "There is pressure to take risks, but it is a side effect of being isolated from adults and trapped with other teens." And teens have twice as many social restrictions as incarcerated felons and ten times as many as adults—all because of their age and despite the fact that they are just as capable and competent as adults.[9]

In many cultures, Dr. Epstein says, there are rituals marking the moment when the teen enters adulthood at puberty; there is also "a continuum, wherein from the time they're very young they're allowed and encouraged to take care of younger siblings responsibly." Responsibilities are bestowed by recognizing competence, not by imposing arbitrary age cutoffs. Even in the Bible, he notes, "You can be very young and be a prophet. You can be very young and be a king."

In *Ageless Society*, Dr. Epstein envisions what life would be like if, from "birth to death, we never judged people by their age, only by their competence. I think that would be a very, very interesting place." Worldwide, we have been moving away from judging people based on other arbitrary conditions like race or sex, he says. "If you throw away all women, which by the way most of the world does still, you literally are throwing away half of your human resources."

The frustration that infantilization causes is palpable: I can remember the resentful sensation of being a teenager, and I've been out of high school for about 30 years. (My hand to God, I have never used algebra and I'm still pissed at the time of my life that was wasted on it.) Dr. Epstein says that teens figure they can reach "instant adulthood" in two ways: by getting pregnant or by committing a crime.

Of course, not all teens respond to their restrictive situations negatively—or to their freedoms positively—but the notion of lifting restrictions where capability is demonstrated is certainly worth looking into. There must be jobs that younger people are capable of besides McDonald's cashier and movie star.

In *Teen 2.0* Dr. Epstein says he reviewed research "which shows pretty clearly that the love that teenagers experience is indistinguishable from the love that older adults experience. It's exactly the same." In his research for *Ageless Society,* he says he interviewed people "who are in their 80s and become obsessed, who become jealous over a lover and who commit murder."

For a second point of view on how the teen brain works, I spoke to Dr. Joseph Shrand, who gave us such a great tour of the brain in chapter 1 and who works with teens as the medical director for CASTLE—Clean and Sober Teens Living Empowered. I wanted to ask him about the things that might drive a teenager over the brink. Obviously adults commit plenty of murders, too, but are there specifics that might make a teenager more vulnerable?

The neocortex (new brain!), he says, continues to myelinate through development, because the teen limbic system (fight, flight, reward, pleasure) is "relatively and differentially myelinated compared to their prefrontal cortex" (problem solving, anticipation of consequences), which is still developing. He says the teens in his substance abuse program are seeking the rush of dopamine, which he describes as "the chemical of internally driven pleasure."

This gets to a really important component of our makeup: "Human beings like to experience pleasure—the adolescent likes to experience pleasure, likes to take risks, but also likes to be social. These are the three main hallmarks of adolescence. We are all like this, but in adolescents especially the social component can be very powerful, and then another chemical comes into play called oxytocin."

We met oxytocin back in chapter 1: it's a bonding chemical, "the cuddle hormone." The one that makes you stick around. Not being very strong or fast, early humans at least had the power of bonding together and working together.

"So there's a huge evolutionary premium on being part of a social group, and this may have something to do with why oxytocin is so powerful: oxytocin binds people together, so you begin to experience the pleasure of this social interaction, not just the internally driven dopamine pleasure of eating a good mango."

One thing CASTLE's substance abuse program tries to do is to shift the dopamine craving for drugs or alcohol in the dependant teens to a craving for oxytocin: the pleasure of social interaction.

"They begin to feel valuable to other people," Dr. Shrand says, like having someone say, "You did a great job," or "That's a beautiful piece of art," or "Wow! You really scored that touchdown!" They begin to feel the value through oxytocin and the prosocial prefrontal cortex part of their brain. And because they have an intact Theory of Mind, they're interested in what other people think or feel, but human beings are particularly interested in what are you thinking and feeling about *me*. And that, I think, is what drives all these interactions: we want someone to see us as valuable, and if we don't feel that way, all sorts of things happen.

"For instance, when was the last time you got angry with someone who was treating you with respect? You don't, right? That is a brain thing—the human brain will not activate anger if it feels respected because respect tells the person, 'You are valuable and I see in you something that has potential.'"

Though they are coming at it from different angles, Dr. Epstein and Dr. Shrand seem to arrive at a very similar point. Whether it's by making teens feel valuable through social situations or by not infantilizing them, it comes down to according teens respect.

As far as love is concerned, Dr. Shrand says that adolescents are able to conceptualize time and understand abstract thought in a way that children, for whom everything is about the here-and-now, cannot.

"But sometimes," he says, "there's still this residual of the childhood concrete operations—of everything here and now—so it's sort of like two tectonic plates of the earth crashing up against each other. These two major forms of thought collide and the adolescent may begin to think about the future, but all they can see in the future is more here and now. That can lead to despair in some of these kids. They feel, *If somebody deprives me of access to this person I will never be loved again*, and that's intolerable."

That kind of obsession obviously happens in adults, too. We can experience what Dr. Shrand calls "an irrational limbic trigger," where we feel that panic of *No one will ever love me again*, and we simply have to work at overriding it with our prefrontal cortex—our problem-solving, consequence-seeing abilities.

To me, the idea of controlling my emotions by thinking, *Just fight it* is a losing proposition. But somehow, *Just fight it with your prefrontal cortex* makes it almost an obligation. Why did we bother developing that big new brain, if not to keep us from going to pieces?

So what can parents do if they see a problematic romance developing? Dr. Shrand says they can recognize that their adolescent may not appreciate the consequences of their decisions.

"And that's not the teen's fault, but it does still hold them responsible and accountable," he says. "It's not a free ride just because of the way our brains are evolving. The more we know about it, however, I think we can actually help adolescents shift and exercise the prefrontal cortex." That's part of the name of his program: Empowered. "And knowledge is power."

If parents can understand that teenagers aren't purposely trying to undermine them, Dr. Shrand says, it's going to be a huge help. He is currently working on a book about anger for Harvard Health Publications. "If the parent thinks the kid is being disrespectful, it's going to activate the parent's limbic system. Now you have *two* angry brains. If the parents can use their prefrontal cortex, which is meant to be a bit more developed in adults, they can sit back and say, Hey, this is my kid's limbic system. They're not necessarily purposely trying to be disrespectful. This is the best they can do right now. It's up to *you* not to activate your limbic system, just keep your prefrontal cortex activated and treat your child with respect. You don't get angry at someone who is treating you with respect."

Sometimes we speak humorously about teens living in a dark place, but Dr. Shrand reminds us that they are truly remarkable. "I really believe people are always doing the best they can, and I think when we start looking at people that way it's going to change everything."[10]

Chapter 9

Down for the Count: Love and Draculacon

SOME PEOPLE JUST CAN'T TAKE DEATH FOR AN ANSWER

The year is 1982. War rages in the Falklands, Jermaine Jackson guest stars on *The Facts of Life*, and I'm about to graduate from high school with a GPA that's about the same as my BAL.

Drinking was my thing. Drugs weren't a problem for me, but they were a problem for the Florida Keys that year, when the US Border Patrol set up a blockade just north of the islands, treating them as if they were a foreign country, stopping and searching every car that exited or entered. The traffic jam became big news and the Keys felt the squeeze in the loss of tourist dollars.

Key West residents decided that if they were going to be treated like a foreign country they might as well be one. They renamed themselves the Conch Republic, seceded from the United States, broke a loaf of stale Cuban bread over the head of someone dressed like a member of the US Navy, and then surrendered, asking for $1 billion in war reparations. That stroke of mad genius set the tone for everything that happens in Key West, and the town's free spirit is one of the reasons some people go there for vacation and never leave.[1]

In 1926 scientist Carl Von Cosel (aka Carl Tanzler, aka Count Carl Von Cosel)[2] decided he liked Key West too much to leave it, too. Von Cosel had sailed for Key West from his home in Germany, leaving his wife and daughters to join him later. Shortly after arriving in the Keys he traveled to his sister's house in Zephyrhills. His stay there didn't last long. When the rest of his family finally joined him, Von Cosel left and returned alone to Key West.

In 1930, during the course of his duties at work as a radiologist in a local hospital, Von Cosel met a tuberculosis patient named Maria Elena de Hoyos, a great local beauty, just 22 years old. Photos of Elena show a thin, sultry woman with sharp features and a unique charisma behind her large, dark eyes that's evident even in an antique still photograph. Von Cosel became smitten and wanted to marry Elena, but she died before he could even ask. Her family consented to inter her in a crypt that Von Cosel had built for her to keep her body aboveground. He visited her in the tomb day after day, eventually leaving his job and installing a phone line in the tomb so that when he returned home they could still chat.[3]

So, OK: Von Cosel is a genuine German cuckoo clock. But calling a dead girl wasn't the half of it. Eventually he took her body home.

In his book about the Von Cosel case, *Undying Love: The True Story of a Passion that Defied Death*, author Ben Harrison quotes Von Cosel's memoirs regarding the night he spirited Elena out of the graveyard: "All of the cemetery was alive with souls which came out from the graves on all sides, moving and thronging all around us...It was like a divine spirit wedding march for me, taking place..."

As the body of the corpse bride began to deteriorate,

Von Cosel preserved it by replacing her rotting eyes with glass ones and making a wig of her hair when it fell out. As her flesh began to go, he replaced it with oiled silk. In 1940, when Elena's sister Nana suspected something was up and found Elena's body dressed in a silk gown on Von Cosel's bed, she called the police.

Harrison writes that at a time when the news was an endless stream of World War II horror, Von Cosel's story was a welcome change. "Newspapers likened von Cosel to Don Quixote, the hopeless romantic tilting at the windmill of death."[4]

That's quite a dashing image for someone who inserted a vaginal tube into a rotting corpse to facilitate sex with the remains. Katherine Ramsland, associate professor of forensic psychology and criminal justice at DeSales University and author of *The Science of Vampires*, *Ghost*, and 38 other books, wrote about Von Cosel for TruTV's True Crime library. She reported that Von Cosel was found to be sane but the statute of limitations on his grave-robbing offense had run out, so he was let go. He moved to central Florida (lucky us) and 21 years later was found dead in his home holding a doll wearing the death mask he had made of the beautiful Elena shortly before she died. Which of course, he must never really believed that she had.

Some people just can't take death for an answer. Understanding what we now do about the desperation of the brain in love allows us to see people who have such a hard time letting go as figures more of pity than of censure—except perhaps for the sex with the rotting carcass part, in Von Cosel's case.

★ ★ ★

Von Cosel is not the only one who felt he never could say goodbye. On July 6, 2010, a story broke about a sweet little old lady who was keeping her dead husband and twin sister in the guest room and garage, respectively. Jean Stevens paid to have an anonymous helper dig them up shortly after their embalming and burials, his in 1999, hers 10 years later. Jean was pi-issed at whoever snitched on her. "I think that is dirty, rotten," she said in a story in the *New York Daily News*. The claustrophobic woman found the idea of her beloveds buried under the ground in a box too difficult to bear; having them above ground made it feel as if they weren't gone. "Death is very hard for me to take," she said.[5]

Mrs. Stevens's case was compassionately handled by Bradford County (Pennsylvania) District Attorney Daniel Barrett, who said she would be allowed to keep the bodies as long as she built a crypt to keep them in.

Then there's Le Van, a 55-year-old father of seven in Viet Nam whose wife, Sang, died in 2003. At first, he slept on top of her grave. Then, worrying about the weather, he tunneled into it, molded clay around her remains, dressed her, and slept beside her. When his kids found out and prevented him from visiting the graveyard, he just took his statue-wife home and slept beside her there because he wanted to be able to hug her. His youngest son, who was 12 at the time, sometimes slept beside her, too.[6]

Every once in a while, in fact or fiction, a story of a trau-matized survivor like Jean Stevens or Le Van comes along, and it's enough to make even the flintiest soul in the world burst into tears. In fiction, the most famous lovers in litera-ture, Romeo and Juliet, willingly follow each other to the grave. (If that sounds impossible, trust me, it's complicated.) Who can forget Leland Palmer in *Twin Peaks* jumping onto his daughter Laura's casket as she was being lowered into the ground, his wife Sarah screaming after him, "Don't ruin this, too!"[7] Then there's *Ponette*. OMG. *Ponette* is a French film about children trying to understand death. In the end (spoiler alert) little Ponette, who is about five years old, visits the grave of her mother, who was killed in a car wreck. The little girl becomes so distraught that she plops down beside the grave and starts digging with her bare hands, crying "Mommy! I'm here!" I didn't watch another French movie for seven years.[8]

Lovers often feel that the fearsomeness of death is better than a life without the one they love. In 2009, Sir Edward and Lady Joan Downes elected to die together in Zurich after 56 years of marriage with the help of Dignitas, a Swiss assisted-suicide organization. Joan Downes, 74, was fighting cancer and her husband, 85, a celebrated conductor, had failing hearing and eyesight, which made conducting difficult. They were, by all accounts, an extremely devoted couple. We usually think the survival instinct is the strongest thing in the world. For this couple love was stronger.[9]

A 20-year Swedish study of the rate of suicide among spouses of the recently deceased found that "standardized mortality ratios were considerably higher for those under the age of 59, being about 90 times the average rate for men and 120 times for women, in the first week after the event," according to Medscape.com.[10] A 1991 study of rates of depression among widows and widowers in the weeks following the death of their spouse found them to be "substantially higher" than the rate for those whose spouses were living—24 percent at two months, 23 percent at seven months, and 16 percent at 13 months.[11]

"The great love of Gertrude's life was denied, and she closed herself off in that house and didn't want to leave it, even in death," Dr. Hans Holzer, author and former parapsychology professor, said in the *New York Times* of one of the most celebrated ghosts in the city, Gertrude Tredwell.[12] The story goes that Gertrude's mean, miserable father, Seabury Tredwell, denied Gertrude's young suitor Lewis Walton her hand in marriage, and Gertrude, who was in her twenties, never left the house again. She died at the age of 93 in the same bed in which she was born, and some say she's still there.

It Had to Be Her

If there is anyone who can tell me about the extremes to which people go, for love or anything else, it's probably Katherine Ramsland, who wrote the entry on Carl Von Cosel for TruTV Crime Library. I interviewed Katherine many years ago, when I was a columnist for the *Orlando Weekly,* about her book *Piercing the Darkness,* which described her work infiltrating the vampire cults of America. I like Katherine. She's as productive and macabre as Stephen King, but the tales of terror told by this petite, tireless author are true.

Katherine is the person to contact, not only about Von Cosel but also about hybristophiliacs: individuals who fall in love with or are turned on by people who have committed violent crimes. When I read that she is speaking at something called "Draculacon II," I think that sounds like an ideal environment in which to chat with her. I love a good convention, and one teeming with people geeked out on vampires sounds like a great time waiting to be had. I picture some Doubletree in Pittsburgh with a huge over-air-conditioned meeting room crammed full of *Twilight* merchandise and one old dude with a card table selling pictures of Bela Lugosi. As of this writing I've never seen a *Twilight* film, but that's not the point. I love fans. Fandom turns adults into 10-year-olds, disables their embarrassment mechanism, and gives them permission to show unabashed love without caring how goofy they look. It makes the world friendlier.

FANBOY LOVE ASSOCIATION

It never occurred to me before that fans might experience a chemical surge similar to lovers when they see their love object, but an article by Andrew Groen on GamePro.com suggests that this might be the case. His analysis of the attachment of gamers to particular brands and consoles can easily be extended to pop cultural icons (vampires or sci-fi shows) or simply to other people.

"They start the dopamine drip," Groen quotes Patrick Hanlon as saying of gamers' emotional involvement with their interactive consoles. Hanlon is the author of *Primal Branding: Create Zealots for Your Company, Your Brand, and Your Future*. The identity of a brand loyalist becomes wrapped up with a particular product. He or she becomes part of a community that is difficult to leave because of all that would be lost, including a sense of belonging, bonding, and being valued by others. Sounds like oxytocin to me.[13]

Katherine tells me this isn't exactly one of those big, shiny conventions. It's not in a posh hotel or even in the city. It's in an old mining town in the Pennsylvania foothills and it isn't expected to be huge, which kind of makes it more intriguing though also more daunting. My expectations are reversed—there will likely be a multitude of Lugosi disciples and maybe one Twihard. David J., formerly of Bauhaus and The Jazz Butcher Conspiracy, is going to be there. Sold.

But a vampire purist convention in an old mining town 836 miles away poses one problem: How am I going to con *anyone* into doing this con with me?

If ever there was a Samantha and Serena pair of friends, it is my friend Elizabeth Levensohn and myself. She's my oldest friend—31 years and counting. Elizabeth has a wild, ethereal kind of beauty. She has a tumble of blonde curls, the biggest, friendliest smile I've ever seen, and lots of colorful elaborate tattoos; my style is controlled and aloof, hair straight as a runway, tailored black jackets, and one discreet tattoo—her gift to me for my 28th birthday.

We also differ in how we find comfort. Her nonchemical escapes have always sought the light—Buddhism, surfing, and women's music festivals. My nonchemical escapes have always sought the dark—crime, the occult, scary movies. Horror films make me feel as though no matter what is happening to me, at least no one's chasing me with an axe. Elizabeth hates all that, so I tend to try to keep her out of it.

But something happened last year that made me think she might be willing to join me at Draculacon. One of the people Elizabeth has known longer than she's known me is Jonathan, whom she met when she was seven. They grew up together—same schools, neighborhoods, and circles of friends. Their paths separated in adulthood—college, marriages, and children, the carving out of one's place in the world—but they saw each other from time to time. Jonathan moved to Pennsylvania, and both eventually divorced their respective spouses. After dating for a few years, Elizabeth told me that she was through with love until she knew she had the real thing. The next *day,* she says—the next *day*—Jonathan came to visit and they both knew this was it: a sudden romance 37 years in the making. Timing, someone said, probably a watchmaker, is everything.

That is a mystery even Agatha Christie and Dr. Fisher working together would be hard pressed to solve, I think. How did these two puzzle pieces come to fit together so well after floating around each other for so long and not finding that just-right fit? There are films about such attractions—*Hannah and Her Sisters, Drop Dead Fred*. It's nice to know they happen in real life once in a while.

And in another nod to timing, Jonathan was living in Pittsburgh, not too far from Windber, where this Draculacon II event was to take place. And Jonathan likes vampires. Now not only did I have traveling companions to Draculacon, I had perfect traveling companions. It was so meant-to-be I'd be surprised if Nostradamus didn't jot it down somewhere. Someone should look that up.

It's as cold as a corpse when we arrive in tiny Windber, Pennsylvania, the kind of gray where it seems like 7:00 a.m. all day long, a persistent dawn or dusk feeling perfect for the event at hand. Draculacon II was being held at the Arcadia Theater, a small, stand-alone brick building where the people of Windber saw their first talkies in the

1920s. It didn't look as if it had changed much since. The people in the lobby, too, looked like they had come from another era.

My favorite Draculaconer was, instantly, a girl dressed as a 19th-century zombie servant. She looked as if she'd walked straight out of Disney's Haunted Mansion and all the way to Windber. She had a gray face, a bleak little hair ribbon, and a long, dour, dark-green maid's outfit. She rather looked like she could use a good cleaning, herself. She had an atmosphere, which is as high a compliment as you can pay anyone. The girl behind the swag counter was pretty good, too: I don't recall her outfit, but she had an axe handle protruding from her chest, dripping with dotingly applied FX gore.

Katherine Ramsland is signing books and talking with fans. When she has a lull, she pulls up a chair for me to sit at the vendors' table with her. We start talking about Von Cosel and all of a sudden she smiles. "Look! He's right there!" she laughs and points across the lobby, where the emcee is walking out the door, wearing a suit and a demonic mask—goatee, bushy brows, and long pointy nose. It has a seeping creepiness that's definitely worthy of the Count; Von Cosel called himself "Count Von Cosel," though there's no record that he was one.

He also wasn't a necrophile, according to Katherine. "Not really," she says, "because he was totally in love with *her*. It was an obsession and in that sense, a paraphilia. It's just that she died."

I think he's getting off on a technicality, because he *did* get off on a corpse. I'd have thought that that was the only requirement for being considered a necrophile, but Katherine thinks otherwise. It was the living Elena that Von

Cosel fell in love with and Elena that he was obsessed with. To him the fact that she was dead didn't change the fact that she was Elena. It wasn't just any old corpse—it had to be her. Von Cosel may just be the ultimate monogamist.

> **"Do not let evil into your heart. It will make a home there."**
> **—HERCULE POIROT IN *DEATH ON THE NILE***

Katherine Ramsland knows from necrophiles. She reminds me of the story of Leilah, whom she interviewed in her book *Cemetery Stories*. Leilah lived in New Orleans in a house named Westgate and was in love with Azrael, the Angel of Death. Her website (www.westgatenecromantic. com) tells her story and shows exquisite death-related artwork, often picturing the skeleton figure of the grim reaper and a ripe young maiden.[14]

"Leilah would go to the cemetery and lie with bodies and kiss them," Katherine says. "Imagine it." I do, and I feel barfy. I'm pretty open-minded, to each his own, nunna my beeswax, etc., but I think *flatline* is a fine place to draw the line. It just seems woefully unsanitary, for one thing—I mean, Jeez, there might be *bugs* in there.

"Her favorite birthday present was brought to her by a friend of hers, a gravedigger. They were moving a potter's graveyard elsewhere to make room for housing units, and he comes knocking on her door on her birthday with a freshly exhumed corpse wrapped in a big red ribbon. 'You can have it till Monday. Do as you like,' he says. She put it in bed, bathed it, made a death mask of it—she showed me, I saw it." This was the most magical present Leilah could imagine.

"I know others who have done that," Katherine says.

"Jeffrey Dahmer did that. John Wayne Gacy did that. Dennis Nilsen did that."

Katherine knows everybody.

Leilah isn't the first woman to do this kind of thing, either, she says. There's Karen Greenlee, a mortuary worker in California who took off with a corpse she was supposed to be delivering to the cemetery and wasn't seen for days. "She thought he was so beautiful. She was driving him to the cemetery and she just took off," Katherine says with a laugh.[15]

In an essay in the book *Apocalypse Culture* titled "The Unrepentant Necrophile," Jim Morton writes that Greenlee left a letter in the coffin with the body confessing to erotic escapades with dozens of dead men. "The letter was filled with remorse over her sexual desires," Morton writes, quoting Greenlee's missive: "Why do I do it? Why? Why? Fear of love, relationships. No romance ever hurt like this. It's the pits. I'm a morgue rat. This is my rathole, perhaps my grave."[16]

Morton writes that Greenlee has now come to terms with her sexuality—and that there's a lot more of it going on than people might imagine.

Katherine's friend, colleague, and fellow speaker, Rosemary Ellen Guiley, author of *The Encyclopedia of Witches, Witchcraft, and Wicca* and 39 other books about the paranormal, kicks in a thought about loving the dead. "They don't talk back," she says. "They don't get up and leave."

"That's part of it," Katherine says, more seriously. "Their whole thing is, *I now possess them, they'll never leave me*. She brings up the Hungarian aristocrat Vera Renczi, who kept the corpses of 35 men in zinc coffins in her basement. She killed them because she (usually wrongly) suspected infidelity and was afraid they would leave her. "Her son would say, 'You know what? I'm going to turn you in,' which was a stupid thing to say to a killer. He didn't get the chance. She killed him.'"[17]

"Erich Fromm has a theory about the necrophile's character," Katherine says. "The type of person who embraces what death means—disintegration, decline, termination—there are people who are attracted to that, so some of them become necrophiles, some of them become killers, some of them become politicians who cause chaos in the economy. They like that stuff, the things that disintegrate wholeness and bring in chaos. So now if you're in love with death as a figure, you're projecting onto this figure your sense of what you're really embracing—the chaos and the decline, dissolution, decomposition of everything, you're really in love with that stuff—projecting it into a figure the way we do gods and goddess. We have Zeus, Hera, all of these who embody our psychological projections. So for Leilah, that's what he would be. She would say, of Azrael, 'He comes to me. He's real.' He has to use a corpse to do it but he does."

Fromm wrote that the necrophilous person is not just attracted to death, but to destruction, stasis; they're afraid of life and its unpredictable, uncontrollable nature. Fromm also distinguished actual sexual necrophilia from necrophilic characteristics such as a love of destruction and an attraction to decay, to anything mechanical.[18]

Fromm's 1964 essay "Creators and Destroyers" is a eerily portentous of an age in which none of us are complete without machinery. The necrophilous character isn't just concerned with death but with all that isn't alive—with machinery and order—over the chaos and unpredictability of living things.[19] The biophile, on the other hand, prefers the process of life and wants to "influence by love, by reason, by his example, not by force." In *Sexual Selections* Marlene Zuk refers to *biophilia* as "a term that has caught on to express our emotional attachment to animals, landscapes, and wilderness." She writes that "tapping into these feelings is essential to efforts to preserve biodiversity."[20] Bureaucratic, industrial societies like ours, Fromm writes, produce "the organization man" and *Homo consumens*, also *Homo mechanicus,* "gadget man." We become preoccupied with mechanization and view people as commodities.

Now, half a century after Fromm's essay was published, there is no question that we have become more gadget oriented. We are inclined to nip, tuck, and Botox our natural bodies until they look like objects. There is even an app that will make a marriage proposal for you.[21]

PAST PERFECT

A certain type of person, I believe, fits Fromm's necrophilous character theory, the kind who tries to influence American culture and politics by pulling us back to where we were in the 1950s, or simply the televised image of the 1950s. They seek to keep culture from growing. They're terrified of the uncontrolled. In Fromm's words in *Creators and Destroyers,* "The necrophilous dwell in the past, never in the future. Their feelings are essentially sentimental; that is, they nurse the memory of feelings which they had yesterday or believe they had."[22]

Call him *Homo dobiegillis.*

★ ★ ★

That was a fun detour into psychological necrophilia, but back to Von Cosel. Katherine observed that he is outstanding in his category because his fixation was on Elena herself, not on death or the dead, and that is what turned him into a ghoul. Had he never met Elena, he might never have whispered sweet nothings into cold blue ears.

Not being able to let someone go even when they're dead certainly points to love as addiction. The trouble is, as Katherine has said about hybristophiliacs, people who fall in love with violent criminals: what love addict is going to think they have a problem?

On the subject of what is and isn't addiction I agree with Yippie cofounder Paul Krassner, who once told me in an interview, "What addiction has meant for me is that you start something for pleasure and then you continue it in order to avoid pain."

So when you find yourself calling AT&T to check the price of running a phone line to a coffin, it might be time to go to a meeting.

"The Carol Bundy–Daniel Clark story is very instructive," Katherine says when we discuss the mental state of a character like Von Cosel, who would never have done anything so bizarre under normal circumstances. In the case of Carol Bundy it was her boyfriend, Daniel Clark, who was the catalyst for her criminal behavior. Bundy and Clark (whom Katherine wrote about for TruTV Crime Library) were convicted of killing two people in 1980 but were suspected of more murders. In the case of 20-year-old Exxie Wilson they kept the severed head in the freezer. Bundy put makeup on it and Clark used it for a sex toy.[23]

Carol Bundy would never have done any of it on her

own, Katherine says. In her book *Inside the Minds of Sexual Predators,* Katherine and her coauthor, Patrick Norman McGrain, enumerate the findings of Robert R. Hazelwood, a former FBI agent with the Behavioral Sciences Unit, in a study of how the wives and girlfriends of sex offenders are manipulated by their romantic partners into joining them in their crimes.

"The researchers identified a five-step process that turned these women into accomplices," Katherine writes, including identifying an easily controlled person, seducing her, reshaping her sexual norms, cutting her off from other people, and finally, "punishment: physical, verbal, and sexual, which further erodes the woman's self-esteem and ability to act on her own. In short, it's a relationship of dominance and submission, which means that one person is assertive and the other submissive as a means of achieving intimacy or greater sexual satisfaction. (This dynamic is different from, but often coincides with, sado-masochism)."[24]

We talked about the Shaky Bridge Theory and how the element of danger can be arousing. Give a girl a choice between Potsie and Fonzie and, well, she'll accept the Fonz's classic offer to sit on it. But how bad do they actually need to be? Fonzie was actually a good guy, albeit a thief of jukebox tunes and a monopolizer of the bathroom. A certain roguish charm is one thing, but how do women end up falling for men who are *really* bad, anywhere from verbally abusive to criminal, to violent criminal, to serial killer? The five-step process outlined above is certainly instructive, but it includes the targeting of a partner who will participate in the criminal's crimes. What about a seemingly average woman who suddenly falls for a murderer?

Dr. Anandhi Narasimhan is a clinical instructor at Cedars-Sinai Medical Center, has a private practice in Los Angeles, and is a child and adolescent psychiatrist for the nonprofit Aviva Family and Children's Services. She used to work in the federal prison system, doing forensic evaluations to determine competency. She spoke to me about why it is that, against all their instincts, some people give their hearts to criminals.

"Some of these men I know because I've treated them and met them. They can be very charming people; a lot of them are con artists, and that's how they victimize people by somehow roping them in to begin with, whether they're going to rob from them or take advantage of them." It's not difficult for these men to learn the skills of manipulation they need to continue having a criminal career, she says.

Dr. Narasimhan cites the novel *The Lovely Bones*, by Alice Sebold, in which she says the author does a great job of describing the criminal.

"In general we have this unidimensional view of criminals, like they're just murderers, nothing else about them can be enticing to anyone—which is not true: a lot of them do have characteristics or social skills that make them appealing and that can be very powerful and influential. I deal with women all the time, more or less law-abiding citizens, who get themselves involved with criminals, knowingly or unknowingly, because they're influenced by them.

"I think our first instinct is, That's just awful! How could you even entertain that? But as Alice Sebold describes in the book, there can be multiple dimensions to the way criminals interact with the world." The killer in Sebold's novel is portrayed as a quiet, law-abiding middle-aged man, an odd fellow who lives alone and spends his spare time crafting exquisitely detailed dollhouses for which the wealthy pay good money, someone who has no trouble going unnoticed when he leaves town or when he arrives in a new one. His mild persona makes it easy for him to get away with murder over and over again.

Even Dr. Narasimhan is surprised by the dichotomy in someone who can kill but seems to have all the normal sensitivities the rest of us do, especially in regard to love.

"A lot of them may have committed murder, but they will also talk about how close they are to their grand-mother who recently passed away, and some of them who have children, how much they love their children. It's kind of bizarre. Okay, you were in the mind-set to cause bodily damage that was or could have been fatal, and now you're talking about the love you've got for other people. It's hard to imagine that they would have feelings of love or compassion toward anybody. I mean, there are sociopaths out there who are vegetarians; they think it's wrong to kill animals, but they're sociopaths."

Is that dichotomy indicative of a brain chemistry issue?

"I think the research is still in the developing phases of studying the morphology or the biochemical nature," Dr. Narasimhan says. "We know that a lot of these people have comorbidities. Somebody who has attention deficit hyper-activity disorder can be very impulsive. That, coupled with sociopathy and a lack of empathy for others, can drive them to commit an act without utilizing proper judgment. The combination may make it worse; comorbidities with other symptoms can drive them into more extreme behavior."[25]

A study reported in Elsevier's journal *Cortex* in May 2010 tested the emotional and cognitive aspects of the Theory of Mind, the ability to understand that other people have separate thoughts and feelings from us, in psychopaths. The psychopaths' test results were similar to those of subjects who had frontal lobe damage.[26]

Why people commit crimes is one thing. Why people *marry* people who commit crimes is another, along the lines of Ben Kenobi's "Who's the more foolish? The fool or the fool who follows him?" Who's harder to comprehend? The psycho or the person who marries the psycho?

Author Sheila Isenberg has written one helluva page-turner, *Women Who Love Men Who Kill*, that makes it easier to understand women who marry men who are in prison for horrendous crimes. It's a compact little volume packed with explanations about how women get into relationships for which most of us have a natural revulsion.

For one thing, these women don't see the bad things in their men—they see everything *but* the bad things: if they are aware, say, that he shot someone, they'll find a million excuses for him or reasons why he did it. He didn't know the gun was loaded. It was an accident. He *had* to do it. As Dr. Narasimhan pointed out, they're not seeing him *just* as a killer, the way most of us would.

Dr. Isenberg writes about Maria, whose abusive, domineering husband became incapacitated after an accident and was thereafter dependent on her. She also had a boyfriend, Phil, who was in prison for murder. Two captive men who couldn't get to her sexually were fine for a woman who'd been pawed at, date-raped, and harassed. The night Maria lost her virginity her father had a heart attack. He allowed her lover—but not her—to come to the hospital. Now Maria had two men whose relationship with her she controlled and from whom she was physically safe.

There was Lori, who had a nightmare childhood of sexual abuse by her father and emotional and physical abuse at the hands of both alcoholic parents. She married at 18, but her husband was cold toward her. Then she met Kevin, who was in jail for murder, after reading an ad he had placed in the classified section of the *Village Voice* in 1987. He was emotionally gentle and doted on her. He stood up for her, even to herself. This sort of kindness was a totally new experience for her, at the age of 38. Plus, since he was in jail, he couldn't hurt her.[27]

"For some women it is thrilling to dance with the master of death," Isenberg writes—to have some power over a killer. But killers aren't really powerful or manly, she says, and women who love them don't really experience mature, adult love, with its complexities and problems. They're usually women with harsh pasts—absent or domineering fathers, domineering mothers, often "raised as Catholics, severely affected by oppressive church teachings, including sexism, subjugation of women, and repressive sexuality." Like the knights and ladies of olde, they won't have sex or true intimacy to enjoy—or worry about.[28]

I ask Katherine Ramsland to talk a bit about love and brain chemistry.

"There's the settling in, and when the infatuation wears off the hormones change, the neurotransmitters change," she says. "Then you decide that love is not just infatuation, the dopamine rush—it's about commitment and actions and recognizing who the other person really is, not who the infatuation/dopamine made that other person into."

Dr. Fisher compared love to cocaine. When I ask Katherine if there's a drug she'd compare love's blood chemistry to, she has a different idea.

"Yeah. Infatuation is like the drug Ecstasy. Ecstasy makes people feel all warm and cozy; they can embrace the whole world and feel larger than themselves, the way love makes them feel." In fact, it's an excess of the love chemical serotonin that causes the Ecstasy high. (But those large releases of serotonin evidently cause a depletion that can show up later as depression.)

So with someone like Von Cosel, who had no idea when something was dead, much less romantically finished, does that chemical flood, that high, just keep coming and coming?

"Well, we're finding with addiction that some people have fewer dopamine receptors, so they're constantly sucking at it to get as much as they can. Dopamine floods the brain and doesn't get cleaned up," she says.[29]

"Obsessive stalkers have an addiction. They live for that high of being near the person they've chosen, and no one can talk them out of that delusion. Nobody. So I think the fixated stage that Von Cosel was probably in would very likely have some relationship to a dysfunction in the neurotransmitters."

Erotomania is an awesome word for what Katherine says is a very dangerous form of stalking. Just a glimpse of a person to whom one is dopamine-addicted might be enough, for a while. "First they approach in a friendly way. If that doesn't work, they become belligerent and angry and intrusive. It depends on what they're after—different stalkers want different things: to be loved back, just to be important to their love objects, or just to have them thinking about the stalker. Erotomanic stalkers believe the object of their fixation loves them, no matter what they say. *We belong together (or we were in another life together), so you will come to see and recognize that we are bonded, body and soul, and you must respond to that.* That's erotomania."

And it is a disorder that's very familiar to movie audiences: *Fatal Attraction. Play Misty for Me. Single White Female. The King of Comedy. All About Eve.* Or Nick Swardson stalking Jon Heder in the comedy *Blades of Glory,* exiting on the line, "Bye, Jimmy! I'm still gonna kill you one day!" We like stalkers—when we're safely watching them on a screen.

Von Cosel wasn't erotomanic, Katherine says; he was fixated. "He's not a stalker, but he's clearly having the same brain dysfunction as a stalker because the erotomanic fixation is very similar. Let's say she didn't get sick. Let's say she decided to leave him. Yeah, I bet he'd be a stalker."

Katherine won't venture to guess what Von Cosel's reaction would have been had Elena lived to a ripe old age. "We don't know what the nature of his fixation was," she says—whether it was Elena herself, her age, her appearance or something else. The one thing that made her the center of the world.[30]

"IT'S NOT OKAY NOT TO BE LOVED."

The center of the world is what most of us want to find in our beloved, right? Someone to share the world with. We say "my other half," or "my better half," as though we are not whole without the other. The most popular romantic line of the last 15 years was Jerry Maguire's "You complete me."

In *The Symposium,* Plato tells the story of how humans started out as a creature of both sexes, androgynous, but to humble them Zeus separated the sexes. In trying to get their lost halves back they became "entwined in mutual embraces, longing to grow into one; they were on the point of dying from hunger and self-neglect because they did not like to do anything apart."[31]

In that story Plato spoke with the utmost eloquence of love's beautiful addiction. "When one of them meets with his other half, the pair are lost in an amazement of love and friendship and intimacy, and one will not be out of the other's sight, as I may say, even for a moment; these are the people who pass their whole lives together; yet they could not explain what they desire of one another."

Our culture follows that Platonic vision: in every fairy tale, in every description of a happy family or a great relationship, in any depiction of normalcy, we want someone who will complete us. It's a tall order; it's not like we're born with a claim ticket in our hands. (Maybe this is why we enter the world crying.) Does the cultural expectation that we should all find one true love and hang onto it with all our might screw us up as much as it seems to?

"It certainly can," Katherine says, "because if culture has given us an idea of what perfect love is, a perfectionist or someone with a controlling nature must attain it because that's part of their self-image. They need to achieve it and control it, and such people are typically unyielding. Not to attain it is a failure, it's not tolerable to them. So there you have the making of a potential criminal."

For the noncriminal, the cultural mandate can just be dispiriting.

"It's not okay not to be loved," Katherine says. "Something's wrong with you if there's no one in your life you can point to who loves you. It has nothing to do with the way circumstances fall in your life. It has to do with the belief *You are not lovable.* That's how it's interpreted."

And this is how prison groupies get involved with the objects of their affection. "Now they at least have somebody who can't get away!—someone who's thinking about them all the time. They have no accountability to that person, but they can say, 'Yeah, I have a boyfriend, I have a husband. You'll see a lot of this in the self-help section. 'How to marry the man who completes you.' So much of therapy is about working on you so you can attract Mr. Right." I remember, with a little shudder, the Dean Martin lyric "You're nobody till somebody loves you, so grab yourself somebody to love."

It's also in the stories we start absorbing almost before our fontanelles toughen up. Katherine says, "Well, you have Cinderella, but there you also have a bunch of ugly step-sisters who don't have beaus." These are the ones who will never get the prince "because they are unlovable, they're horrible, shrewish people who are never going to get the prince no matter how much they try to put their foot in the shoe. You just have to recognize what the story is about."

One of the things Katherine notices when she watches those romantic comedies that end with the couple getting together is this: "What are the chances of them staying together very long? Not very good. Like *Jerry Maguire*—no way is that going to last! So it might be a happy ending, but give it about two months and you'll find out it's not going to work."

I can't help laughing: two months is my relationship probation period. If it's not going to work, I know two months in.

"People don't think long range," Katherine says. "They're so in love with the idea of love. They think, once you get that, you've made it! And you could get it with a serial killer."

"We have a peculiar relationship with permanence and transience," says Katherine. "We love the transience because that's where we feel alive. That's where edginess is. That's where we don't know for sure what's going to happen, that's where it's exciting. Permanence makes us feel safe, but if you feel too safe, you're bored, and then you go out looking for something unique and unusual. Then, when that starts to feel a little scary and unsafe, you go back."

You may remember that we are having this conversation at a table of books on the paranormal in a century-old theater at a vampire convention. Most people have been inside watching a movie, so Katherine and I have had some good quiet time together. Now there is some kerfuffle behind us. Someone in the lobby is shouting about a missing cell phone. A young man named "Jack" (not his real name) recognizes the phone and he's freaked out by it. He swears up, down, and sideways that he left that phone in Los Angeles.

"We've been kicking it around on stage for the last half hour like a hockey puck," one of the Draculacon staffers says. Jack is positive: he did not have the phone with him. His hands are shaking.

"It wants to be with you," Katherine says in an amused and knowing way. She tells him she thinks this is what's called an *apport*, the spontaneous appearance of an object, seemingly out of thin air, by paranormal teleportation. She says she's been getting similar things—pennies and dimes appearing out of nowhere—since she's been working on her latest book, and that it's happened to her here in Windber before, while staying at the highly atmospheric Grand Midway Hotel, whose owner, Blair Murphy, is the Draculacon II organizer. On that occasion, Katherine was missing a pair of gray pearl earrings. She turned the room upside down looking for them, packed and unpacked— they didn't turn up. When she got home and opened her suitcase they were right on top.

This happens to me all the time too, only I attribute it to my disorganization. I want to believe Jack's cell phone appeared spontaneously, but there's that little voice inside me that says he just may not have realized he brought it with him.

Jack is still shaking, and I encourage him to go find the bar and do a shot. But Draculacon is one of the few places where a Roman Catholic Demonologist might just drop in, and that's exactly what happens. Katherine snags demonologist Adam Blai, who has just come into the lobby, to chat with Jack. I'm glad, because as interesting as I find a mobile phone that's mobile all by itself, this permanence–transience idea has me magnetized.

"We have bodies that are deteriorating and moving toward death, and we don't want to think about that, so we create the idea that our spirits live forever, immortal spirits in physical bodies," Katherine says. "That translates psychologically into our push-me-pull-you relationship with permanence and change. Change makes us feel alive but permanence makes us feel safe, so we're constantly moving back and forth between those two." It reminds me of the romantic ricochet I do, from sweet but stifling relationships to exciting but flimsy ones.

I ask her if she thinks women stay with dangerous men because that sense of permanence, even if it's a scary one, makes them feel secure.

"There's no generalization you can make. Sometimes women have nowhere else to go, or they're so used to abuse from growing up with it that they don't see how it can be different. Perhaps they don't feel good about themselves so they don't see any point in trying to leave." And sometimes they have kids or they're scared to leave because they'll get killed. There are too many possibilities for one answer.

"It seems that there are so many instances of no-one-answer to these things," I say.

Katherine turns an analytical eye on me. She says, "Why do we want that one answer, do you think?"

"Security," I reply. If I know how to do it, I won't screw it up ever again. "But there really is no security," I acknowledge, wistfully.

As an explanation for ceaselessly confusing love lives, the tag team of permanence and transience is a very satisfying one. It even helps explains the baffling extremes people come to in love, like being enamored of the dead, the imprisoned, or the dangerous. Being married to a murderer might feel scary, but if he's safely in prison, well, there's your shaky bridge and your security balance all in one. Mad love is better for some people. After all, there's plenty of time for peace and serenity when you're dead.

Unless, of course, someone sticks a phone line in your tomb.

CHAPTER 10

Spiritual Love

DIVINE MADNESS

One day, browsing in a Christian bookstore, I found a diet book titled *Slim for Him*. I was riveted by this idea. No deity has, to my knowledge, ever judged people on their looks; in fact it's one of the only things they *don't* judge you on. Could God really be the sort who had a "No Fat Chicks" bumper sticker on his car, as my brother did when I was in college?

The human body is just a vehicle, like a rental car, something to tote you around while you're in town. Sure, you want to keep it nice, but where you take it is more important than how it looks, isn't it? Greed and gluttony are deadly sins, but those are issues of character; the title *Slim for Him* smacked of appearance. There were several diet books on the shelf, which suggested to me that God might not like a girl who had (as one eloquent wordsmith I know put it) "too much bun for his hot dog."

Slim for Him is actually about using Bible verses to help you practice moderation and offers guidance for staying on track. Admittedly I just skimmed it, but author Patricia Kreml asks God directly for help in passages like this: "I know that through your strength I can be victorious, so teach me to reach for you, not the lemon pie, because you are sweeter by far and can surely satisfy all my desires."[1] Fair enough. In fact, there's something appealing about the God-tastes-better-than-pie approach. And the title invokes the religious devotion with which some people throw themselves into love, make sacrifices, or try to impress the object of their affection, just as others try to impress their gods in the hopes of gaining access to the heaven of their presence.

This is my favorite phase of love, the "smitten" phase, when the person you love is the thing your mind always returns to, when dressing up for them is still a two-hour affair, when, like a religious devotee, life is easy for you because there's only one person to please, and it isn't you— and you *want* to do it. Slavish devotion can be very freeing and sex can be intensely spiritual; combine them and they take you to a plane that's impossible to capture in words. That's why all the parental flapping about "waiting till you find the right person" falls on deaf ears. There *is* no explaining that feeling of "right" until you experience it. It's so elusive it can seem nonexistent, but when it happens it's the only thing that's real.

This intimacy can be terrifying. It can be overwhelming to connect so fully to someone else. And then it's really awkward to have to tell someone with whom you've shared sublime ecstasy to pick up some toilet paper on the way home, even weirder to start talking about things like life insurance and lawn care. What the hell happened? How does something so grand it defies language degenerate into squabbles that end with lines like "She's your mother, *you* take her to Aquarobics."

Cristina Nehring is an American author who lives in France and who made me feel indescribably better about my own discomfort with the transference of romance to mundane life. Her book *A Vindication of Love* is about how 21st-century timidity has broken and domesticated romantic love and made it something tepid, rather than the wild, passionate, erotic, spiritual experience we crave. In her review of the book in the *New York Times*, Katie Roiphe writes, "There is a romanticism here that could look, depending on where you stand, either pure or puerile, either bracing or silly, but it is, either way, an original view, one not generally taken and defended, one most of us could probably use a little more of."[2]

Nehring writes: "We inhabit a world in which every aspect of romance from meeting to mating has been streamlined, safety-checked and emptied of spiritual consequence. The result is that we imagine we live in an erotic culture of unprecedented opportunity when, in fact, we live in an erotic culture that is almost unendurably bland. …Romance in our day is a poor and shrunken thing. To some it remains an explicit embarrassment, a discredited myth, the deceptive sugar that once coated the pill of women's servility. To others, romance has become a recreational sport. Stripped of big meanings it has become another innocuous pastime. It has become "safe sex," harmless fun, a good-natured grasping for physical pleasure with a convenient companion—or indeed with an object."[3]

Not that anyone's necessarily knocking vibrators here (at least I hope not), but I think Nehring is saying that the romantic part of romantic love has become tamed by cynicism and rules. We believe love is successful only if it occurs within social parameters—and only if it lasts.

This idea of manicured, cultivated, and spiritually empty human life is echoed in *Sex at Dawn*. In the transition from foraging to agriculture, the bliss of Adam and Eve in the uncultivated Eden gives way to the misery of tending fields: "Human nature has been landscaped, replanted, weeded, fertilized, fenced off, seeded and irrigated as intensively as any garden or seaside golf course. Human beings have been under cultivation longer than we've been cultivating anything else. Agriculture, one might say, has involved the domestication of the human being as much as of any plant or other animal."[4]

In *The Soul of Sex: Cultivating Life as an Act of Love,* Thomas Moore talks about how anxieties of sexuality keep us from having a richer life: "We have more interest in making our children data managers than in handing on any wisdom we may have acquired from our follies. We are attached to our moralisms because they protect us from the rich possibilities of life. Fundamentally, we don't trust our sexuality. We feel compelled by its allure but wish it didn't complicate life and interfere with our plans."[5]

I found Cristina Nehring via a writer friend who recommended her as a source of good insight for a story I was working on, so I emailed her at her home in France and sent a few questions her way. I found her answers to be surprisingly poetic, especially since, these days, "k" passes for an affirmative response in text messages. (That's "k," short for "OK," as if anyone you or I know is disarming bombs or performing emergency heart surgery, leaving them too pressed for time to type an "o".)

Finally I got her book, a symphonic, exhaustively researched work about how so many philosophical, literary, and feminist icons gave themselves to love with abandon and spiritual passion. This is something Nehring does not see in an age that devalues inspired madness. As a result, what has happened to communication ("k") has, in her estimation, also happened to love. We've edited the soul out of romance.

The vilification of intellectual women who fall for

imperfect matches seems to rankle Nehring the most: "If she felt deeply she cannot, we seem to assume, have *thought* deeply," she writes of the female intellectual.[6] Mary Wollstonecraft, who wrote the first feminist text, *A Vindication of the Rights of Woman,* in 1792 (from which Nehring got her title), was a brilliant author and adventuress and was so smitten with a married American businessman that she tried to kill herself for him. Wollstonecraft was picked apart even by her supporters after her death, and her work was dismissed because she led with her heart. This—and Cristina offers compelling evidence for it—does not happen to male artists. (Wollstonecraft died giving birth to her daughter, Mary, who would grow up to wed the poet Percy Shelley and write the novel *Frankenstein.)*

Nehring also holds up some exemplars of '70s feminism who treated romantic love as the enemy. "It was in the '70s that the antiromantic chorus really swelled: from Germaine Greer and Kate Millett to Shulamith Firestone and Andrea Dworkin, articulate, energetic and often best-selling writers declared sex a glorified form of rape and romance a patriarchal ploy to enslave women. Such voices created a climate in which women who loved were often regarded as dupes."

The sex-positive feminism that followed in the forward-thinking 1990s changed that (or so I think—I might be living proof of it). Yet for all the advantages women have now that we didn't have then, the assumption that we'll want a conventional, safe, domestic love—happy, hetero, and hitched—hasn't changed that much.

NOT ALL BLISS IS DOMESTIC

"My inspiration for *Vindication* was at once the intensity and ferocity of love I witnessed and experienced around me, and the lukewarm timidity with which I saw it discussed every day in the media," Cristina wrote from her home in France in the summer of 2010. "It was the fact that I'd review books about women (like Mary Wollstonecraft, like Margaret Fuller) who had been lovers as well as thinkers and I'd see these women saluted for their ideas and dragged through the mud for their amorous practices. As though the boldness of ideas and the boldness of amorous enterprise weren't closely linked—even inseparable."[7]

Is this domestication and diminution of love a uniquely American phenomenon, or something she sees happening in Europe as well?

"I'm afraid the Europeans will tag along behind the Americans eventually—they too often do—but, for now, the sanitization of love and the fetishism of erotic safety does seem to be an especially American phenomenon. In France people still honor a messy romance, complete with secret trysts, inappropriate partners, and intergenerational love triangles. (Just look at the respective amorous lives of Carla Bruni and Nicolas Sarkozy.) In Germany, there's still a vein of deep romanticism where the notion of "safe sex"—of girding yourself against the very partner with whom you're aiming to fuse—is highly suspect. Only in America are we so proud of being so self-protective and dull in our personal relations."

To champion the madness of Marianne Dashwood in *Sense and Sensibility* over the reserve of the practical, long-suffering Eleanor might seem a little nutsy-cuckoo to some, but this is just what makes it attractive to the romantic spirit:

a) It's more fun.
b) Pain is better than boredom.
c) It's a quest.

In that struggle between permanence and transience someone who gets claustrophobic with permanence (like myself) and is always on the lookout for a well-timed dopamine rush is going to be drawn to this epic, uncertain, literary type of love—or at least to staying for more of a reason than that it's what one is supposed to do. Not all bliss is domestic.

And not all bliss is even blissful. Look back at the Shaky Bridge Theory: "Adrenaline makes the heart grow fonder," Dr. Ian Kerner said.

One of the richest stories that Cristina details is that of Heloise and Abelard, who both suffered agonies beyond imagination for their romance. Nine hundred years after it happened their romance still stirs the imagination of anybody who has one.

Abelard was a French intellectual, handsome, brilliant, and, at the age of 36, chaste until he met Heloise, the likewise beautiful and brilliant daughter of a noble French house. Seeking lower rent payments, Abelard went to Heloise's uncle and asked for inexpensive board in exchange for tutoring the young lady. With that, Cristina writes, "the affair of the twelfth century began." Their erotic passion and adoration consumed them; everyone knew about it and Abelard's promising career started to wobble due to inattention. The uncle found out and insisted they marry, but—get this—*Heloise* was having none of it. She believed only in love freely given and was inconsolable when she had to consent to her uncle's demand that they wed. "We shall both be destroyed," she said.

And they were. Heloise's uncle was still being a pest, so Abelard smuggled her off to a convent where their liaisons continued. By now they had a child, whom Abelard placed with his family. The uncle found out, suspected Abelard was only trying to get rid of Heloise, and had him hunted down and castrated. Heloise spent the rest of her life in convents, Abelard the rest of his in monasteries. They both rose in rank. Abelard barely spoke to Heloise for the first 12 years, and she never contacted him, though she was, Cristina writes, "starving for his thoughts." When Abelard wrote of his suffering it was to his fellow monks, who had been trying to kill him. These writings got into Heloise's hands and she was finally alarmed and pissed off enough to open her mouth—or pick up her pen. She wrote to him for the first time and asked why he wasted his words on murderous monks when she still loved him. And Heloise admitted, Cristina writes, what was a suicidal blasphemy at the time: that her religious service was a sham. She didn't do it for God. She did it for Abelard.

After further correspondence in which Abelard comes off as surprisingly unfeeling, it becomes clear that he really *has* undergone a conversion—and after all, he has been castrated. Castration causes the production of testosterone mostly to cease, so Abelard couldn't feel all the passion his intact wife could. He also had to find a way to live with being butchered and to view it as the path to salvation—or maybe he had genuinely changed. Whichever it was, he still credits Heloise with saving his soul: "Come, my insep-arable companion ... and join me in thanksgiving ... See then how with the dragnets of mercy the Lord has fished us up from the depth of a dangerous sea."

Heloise realizes that Abelard does not have the capacity even to speak of passionate love in the way she would like. So, in an act of compassion for someone who can't show compassion to her, she speaks instead about religious doctrine, which is all he can talk about; and in that act she binds them forever. Heloise spawns what has been called the most important body of work on women's place in religious life written in the middle ages, when religious life was everything. Abelard writes to her tirelessly, composing over 200 hymns for her and eventually requesting he be buried with her and not in the grandeur of his monastery. Almost a thousand years later their passion is alive in the mind of anyone who reads their story.

If you look at their story from a contemporary perspective, modern social norms would have put the kibosh on their love at every single point, starting with the inappropriate student–teacher relationship and the iffy practice of dating the boss's daughter. Heloise's no-nonsense dissing of marriage isn't something you'll hear from many women in a culture where the wedding ring is still pitched to us as the Holy Grail. As for their 12-year hiatus in communication, no one I know would wait that long for anything. Life is short, right? Ironically, in the Middle Ages, when life was even shorter, Heloise didn't dump Abelard to get on top of her Bucket List while she still had a chance. It seems she had already done what she wanted to do before she died, which was to love him.

Other lovers in Nehring's book don't have quite Heloise's endurance. Mary Wollstonecraft attempted suicide. Living a great love has dramatic appeal, but the idea of living *period* should have an even greater appeal.

Cristina has some advice for those whose love quest doesn't end well: "Lament," she writes in her email, "but do so in a form that has lasting value outside the relationship you're lamenting. If you are a writer, try to write a public poem—not a private letter. If you're a traveler, quit the scene of your injury and 'eat, pray, love.' If you're a painter, throw paint onto that canvas like you're Jackson Pollack. If you're a cook, invite over all the colleagues and contacts, friends and foes you neglected while in the throes of love and make the most memorable meal ever. Amorous pain can be the most creative agent in a life; don't let it escape unexploited. Do something that takes you closer to being the person you want to be—not farther away."

"Remember," Cristina says, "that success is the best revenge."

GO, GAGA, GO

Plenty of now rich and famous people have clearly adopted Cristina Nehring's advice about success, including Alanis Morissette (who made her name with the caustic revenge song "You Oughta Know"), Gloria Gaynor ("I Will Survive" is *still* the anthem of newly single women and gay men everywhere), and Carly Simon ("You're So Vain" was probably her biggest hit). My all-time favorite story of comeuppance, though, was what Lady Gaga told *Cosmo* in its April 2010 issue:

"I had a boyfriend who told me I'd never succeed, never be nominated for a Grammy, never have a hit song and that he hoped I'd fail," she says. "I said to him, 'Someday, when we're not together, you won't be able to order a cup of coffee at the f***ing deli without hearing or seeing me.' "[8]

And let's not forget Florence King: "Old ladies know they can no longer cause erections, so they aim for bleeding ulcers."[9]

When I ask Cristina what she thinks about peering into the brain for the secrets of how love works, she says that the more we unlock the mechanics of love, the more compelling and mystical love becomes—especially (and she has a heck of a point here) since we don't know what unleashes the chemicals.

"To speak of dopamine is not functionally different to me than speaking of Cupid. It's simply a different cultural lingo. To talk about serotonin is not more deflating than to talk of a love potion, *Midsummer Night's Dream* style. I don't think it diminishes the romance; I think it increases the mystery."

She's right about not knowing what unleashes the chemistry—you can't strap someone into an fMRI machine and push them to the beach or to the disco to see exactly what happens the moment their neurotransmitters acquire their target.

And yet chemistry must be the basis for that erotic-romantic-spiritual experience: everything we do starts with a signal from the brain. It tells us to breathe, to reach for a wineglass, to say "I love you." We often think of our physical being as an impediment to the divine—but it is also the conduit through which those transcendent feelings of love come to us, so it must also be a channel to the divine, or the source of what we experience as the divine.

MARK AND PATRICIA

"For us our relationship *is* our spiritual practice," Patricia Johnson says. Mark Michaels and Patricia are teachers and award-winning authors of two books on the subject of Tantra.

"Tantra is an ancient Indian spiritual tradition that recognizes sexual energy as a source of personal and spiritual empowerment," Mark says.[10] This doesn't necessarily mean sex acts, Patricia adds, but rather the vibration occurring between feminine and masculine energies, which is much like Sheri Winston's description of yin and yang energy. "If you think of it on the atomic level, you have these polarities that are in constant movement, and that movement is seen as the sexual energy and the source of all creation."

Contrary to its popular image most Tantric practices don't involve sex, according to Mark. Similarly, the *Kama Sutra* isn't just a manual of sex positions (nor is it a Tantric text), but a guide to life and love. Tantra teaches how to be conscious of that "life force" energy and how to use it.

The roots of the word *Tantra*, Mark says, are "tanoi" and "trayati." *Tanoi* means to stretch out, like the English verb *attenuate*. *Trayati* can be translated as "tool." Thus a good definition of Tantra is "tool for expansion."

"What the Tantra practitioner seeks to expand is consciousness, and the tool for accomplishing that is our physical embodiment," Mark says. "So, unlike most spiritual traditions that divide body and spirit and say that body is bad and spirit is good, Tantra says that the body is the tool that we have for attaining the spiritual."

"So it is the vehicle," Patricia adds. "You need it. There's another definition that means 'web' or 'weaving,' weaving yourself into all of consciousness or all of existence. You're seen as the web."

★ ★ ★

Mark and Patricia have a fluid way of handing the conversational baton to each other. They never step on each other's toes or interrupt, which strikes me as unusual for a long-term couple. (Many such couples bicker so incessantly that you want to jump out of the car when you're with them.) Maybe it comes from teaching, or from being in tune with and mindful of each other's energy.

I ask how they met. "We got together not really to date but to practice sexual Tantra together," Mark says. "Because of that we started doing things like eye-gazing and breathing together—and that for us created a foundation for the relationship." They've been married for 10 years and together for 12.

Eye-gazing is exactly what you might think—looking into each other's eyes in that wonderfully gooey way that comes naturally when you're falling in love. I had no idea it had a name; I just knew it was pretty much my favorite thing I've ever done. In Tantra there are formal practices for eye-gazing that help couples connect or reconnect and breathing practices that, among other things, increase blood flow for heightened arousal.

"That's what we do—in our relationship practice and spiritual practice we're doing things that create an environment through which we can fall in love repeatedly," Patricia says.

"The definition of love is profound interest," Mark says. The definition comes from their Indian guru. Maintaining interest in your partner is paramount in a relationship, but Patricia and Mark prefer not to consider it "work" because of the implications of that word. It requires effort, yes, they say, but by maintaining profound interest in your partner—or in yourself if you are practicing solo—you find a connection to the divine.

"The macrocosmic becomes the microcosmic, and vice versa," Patricia says. You gain a sense of the whole of creation through one person's eyes.

But, as Patricia would like to make clear, eye-gazing is not about "active listening," a popular couples therapy technique for conflict resolution where one partner listens to how the other feels about a problem issue and gives feedback that validates their concerns. Citing the work of acclaimed researcher Dr. John Gottman, who with his wife, Dr. Julie Schwartz Gottman, runs the Gottman Relationship Institute, Patricia says that active listening can actually be distancing: it still puts the complained-at partner on the defensive. As Gottman and Nan Silver put it in *The Seven Principals For Making Marriage Work*, "There are some people who can be magnanimous in the face of such criticism—the Dalai Lama comes to mind."[11] Active listening, Patricia says, "doesn't really lead to empathy in which you really crawl into the skin of your beloved and live where they're living."

The classic Tantric sex ritual can take a really long time, including creating atmosphere, breathing, and grooming. But "what happens when you're in a high state of sexual arousal for an extended period is that you go into an altered state of consciousness, which is why there's all this hype about prolonged lovemaking and Tantra," Mark says. "At the most simple level it's about creating brain chemistry that puts you in an altered state."

The two partners in the ritual might not even know each other; "one facilitates the other to take the other higher and higher, to achieve those mystical states," Mark says. "We think applying this conceptually to long-term relationships is an incredibly valuable approach." In Tantra you're not trying to "get yours" from the other person; you're there to serve them in whatever way you can. Mark and Patricia think this approach is sometimes lost in a culture were relationships largely seem to be about getting one's needs met, about expecting and demanding that from a partner. (Compare this to the "smitten phase," discussed earlier, when you feel as if you were put on this earth to make your partner sigh a certain way, not out of obligation, but for the joy of making them happy.) Through serving and caring for another, we get our needs met more fully, Mark says. Patricia adds that it is also not about anticipating a partner's needs and meeting them but appreciating and being empathetic with who they are *now*.

Western culture has, for many years, separated the body and the spirit as if they were kids who caused too much trouble in the classroom. The body, seat of sexual impulses and other imprudent things, was Eddie Haskell, and the mind and soul, connected with elevated matters of God and learning, was Wally Cleaver. But the brain is part of the body and it's required for understanding anything, including ideas about God and the soul. The Greek physician Galen thought that "psychic neuma" resided in the ventricles of the brain. René Descartes thought the soul was in the pineal gland.[12] In any case, if there is such a thing as spirit we need a brain to understand it, sense it, feel it—unless there is some other way we don't know about yet, just as we didn't know about bacteria before the microscope. (One day, I truly hope, someone will come up with a device for communicating with the spirit world that's more penetrating than the Ouija Board. It has "Parker Brothers" written right on it; it's hard to take a portal to the spirit world seriously when its parent company also made Gnip Gnop and Blockhead.) Maybe one day the equivalent of the microscope for the spirit world will come along.

In the meantime, many people do believe in a spiritual realm, whether it offers us Jesus or Oshun or unnamed energies. Some people think erotic love, indeed all love, can help you get there. So what is the difference between love's chemistry and a divine calling? Is there one? In both we are devoted, we seek union with the other, we are willingly vulnerable. I feel that I've experienced spirituality through erotic love, platonic love, and through nature, but I've never had a vision, seen a ghost, or gotten so much as a birthday card from even a minor deity.

Do You and God Have Any Chemistry?

There is a chemical in the brain that seems to be present in both the experience of love and the experience of spirituality, a tangible conduit to spirit: serotonin. *Psychology Today* reported on a Swedish study that concluded that people with more serotonin receptors have more receptivity to spiritual matters.[13] NPR did a series of stories in 2009 based on the book *Fingerprints of God: The Search for the Science of Spirituality*, by NPR's religion correspondent Barbara Bradley Hagerty, which asks questions like "Is God a delusion created by brain chemistry, or is brain chemistry a necessary conduit for people to reach God?"[14] The series included a discussion about how frontal lobe epilepsy may trigger religious visions; studies on how thinking loving thoughts about a partner at a distance may have a beneficial effect on their brain chemistry; and how peyote and LSD, both of which increase serotonin levels, were used in lab tests to trigger religious experiences. Most of these studies were conducted on subjects who identified themselves as believers. I'd be curious to see if they got the same results on someone who counted himself a "strong atheist" on the theistic belief scale Richard Dawkins wrote about in *The God Delusion*. (Dawkins rates himself a 6 on a scale of 1 to 7, where 1 is certitude that God exists and 7 is certitude that God does not exist. Dawkins says, "I cannot know for certain but I think God is very improbable, and I live my life on the assumption that he is not there.")[15]

NADINE BEGIN: A FUTURE QUEEN IN A PRINCESS HABIT

To get more of an idea of how spiritual and worldly love overlap, I wanted to talk to someone else who has been immersed in both.

Before Robert and Nadine Begin were married in 1974 Robert was a priest and Nadine was a nun. They didn't leave the church to be together, but now that they are the life they've built is the stuff of dreams, the fairy tale ending of two lives that began in a quest not for romance but for God.

"I gave my youth to Jesus Christ and my old age to Bob," Nadine says in a phone interview and her soft maternal voice gives way to a laugh, which it does a lot. She has great deal to be happy about and nobody knows it better than she does.[16]

Nadine was born Patricia Grasinski and grew up on farm in Michigan. Her decision to be a nun wasn't pushed on her in childhood, though the nuns at her Catholic school did encourage it. Patricia admired St. Theresa and wanted to be like her.[17]

"It was a feeling I had as if Jesus called me. There were moments when I would just sink right into his presence," she says, and she knew he wanted her to become a nun.

"Then I went to high school and realized all the things that were against it: I love pretty clothes and I like the boys, I love to dance and I love my family and my mother." But she knew she was going. "I told everybody, 'After high school I'm going to the convent.'"

Being certain didn't make it easy. "Three times I walked into the room and said goodbye to my daddy." But once she heard the convent door close behind her she felt at peace. This was where she belonged. "We couldn't go home for Christmas—I cried ten Christmases before I didn't cry." She eventually earned degrees from Madonna College and Wayne State and became a teacher. The children and the school became her life for 20 years, until she requested a change and her Reverend Mother sent her to the convent hospital to become the food supervisor.

This was the 1970s—nuns were changing. They were allowed to show more hair, wear shorter habits—the clothing was less restrictive. "Since I could sew I made this little princess–style habit," Nadine says. (To picture a princess-style dress, just picture Doris Day—it would be fitted at the waist with a slight flare in the skirt. Nadine's went below the knee line.)

She didn't get the job. The supervisor took one look at her and essentially made up reasons to give her the heave-ho. In her cookbook *Feed My Lambs, Feed My Sheep: The Meals and Memories of a Lifetime* Nadine writes that her friends picked her up from that fiasco saying, "Only you, Nadine, could get fired at seven thirty in the morning."

Talk about something being for the best. With that episode behind her Nadine decided to go into an experimental venture with two of her fellow Felician Sisters to teach in a Detroit inner-city school affiliated with St. Margaret Mary's Church (which just happens to be the name of the church and school I went to as a child in Florida).

"The first time I ever saw Bob, he was this handsome priest walking down the steps and he says, 'How may I help you?' and I wanted to tell him how he could help me!"

The job was still a teaching job, but the entire atmosphere was different for a woman who had been around only nuns and children for 20 years.

"There were religious brothers and married couples and we had to go to mass in the morning. Bob was the pastor and he would say the mass and then everybody would go off and do their job and then maybe come back and have dinner together." She was making friends and meeting the kinds of people she hadn't been around in decades.

Soon the experiment ended and it was time to go back to the convent. By this time the nun who had denied Nadine the job at the hospital had become the Reverend Mother and she was no more pleasant this time around. She told the returning nuns that they either put the habit back on and return to the strictures of convent life wholeheartedly, or beat it.

"There was no way we were going to go back to that. We couldn't. We had a certain amount of freedom, and who would want to go back to somebody who is *that* way." She and three of her colleagues asked Rome for dispensation of their vows and left a year later.

Nadine was 42 years old when she learned to drive and got herself a little apartment. She went on dates but never had a serious love. One day she got an unexpected phone call.

"The voice said, 'Would you like a little company?' So, you know who it was!" She's still got a teenager's giddiness about that phone call. Smitten.

Bob and Nadine started dating. Three years later,

sitting in front of the fireplace after dinner at a steakhouse in Windsor, Canada, he proposed to her in French.

"And I don't know French!" She laughs. "I said, 'Oh, say it in English!'"

They were married on Bob's birthday.

Bob had built up a successful construction company, so they were financially secure. Everything was going well for them except finding success at having a child.

"I was going to an old Irish doctor, and he sent us on a cruise. It rained seven nights and still nothing happened!" Nadine's youngest sister was going through a divorce and trying to get through school, so Nadine and Bob invited her two youngest children to come live with them. Things were going well, and they moved on with life. Then, one night, Nadine couldn't eat and realized something was wrong. She took a pregnancy test and got the call back. At 46, Nadine was pregnant.

"Nadine, like Sarah of old, is with child!" Bob announced to friends. She gave birth to a girl, Marie-Chantal, in March 1978.

"There were many, many satisfactions in my life, like the day we got our black veil and the white veil and became the nuns," Nadine says. "But there was no joy, absolutely no joy in my life, in the convent or before the convent, until the day the doctor put her in my arms. If I talk about it today I cry. Such a gift from heaven—the joy was like a holy joy, a spiritual joy. She's thirty-two now and she's still a joy."

The dream of having a vineyard came true a few years later when the Begins decided to open a three-room bed-and-breakfast. They eventually took out some of the cherry trees that had been on the property and friends and neighbors helped plant grapes. The winery opened in

1993, and in 2003 they expanded the inn to 11 rooms. Chantal studied wine management at Adelaide University in Australia, married, and now works with her husband and her parents at the château that was named for her.

That's the fairy tale, right? I mean, Nadine actually *has* a castle. What little girl who wanted to be Cinderella would ever imagine that the happily-ever-after would begin in a convent?

The intriguing thing is, while so many go questing for love and have a tough time finding it, Nadine didn't start out looking for love—her quest was her spiritual calling. The fact is: she followed it. As in, Follow your bliss, as in, Know thyself. It's a classic bit of advice to figure out who you are first and love will come to you, but it's tough advice to take when you're hungry for romance. Nadine followed her spiritual path; no one could talk her out of it—even *she* couldn't talk herself out of it. And romantic love was at the end of it.

I'm not saying this will definitely happen to you, but it's nice to know that it does happen.

As for the differences and similarities between a religious calling and a romantic one, Nadine says they are exactly alike.

"Of course, it is of a spiritual nature—you can't really separate the two. Love is love. I love Jesus. I love Bob. I love Chantal. And it's a commitment; it's closeness, a dedication. I love going to mass in the morning and praying, going to communion, and I love sitting at the table with Bob and Chantal—to me it's all one love and it's all spiritual.

She speaks of her husband as if she just fell in love yesterday. She still takes care of people as she did in the convent, only now "Queen Nadine" has guests and family instead of nuns and little kids. I can count on one hand the number of people I've ever spoken to who sound as happy and content as Nadine does.

I think Nadine's story is an excellent example of love being the result of dopamine and chance. Her meeting Bob was chance, but when they met she was already doing what was *rewarding* for her, so the dopamine was flowing—it is part of the reward circuitry of our brain. Maybe this is what makes people who are confident and happy on their own so attractive. She followed her bliss—her work as a nun, which was fulfilling to her even when it wasn't easy. Bliss isn't about having a good time; it's about being personally fulfilled, as tends to happen when you give yourself to something you love—dancing, teaching, mechanics, God, or another person, whatever you're called to, whether it's easy or not. You find bliss wherever you have the giddy joy of being a fan, where that joy overrides the difficulties, where you *want* to work, you *want* to get hurt, like Lloyd Dobler (John Cusack) in *Say Anything*. That, I think, is where you find you're OK being alone because you never feel alone with your own vision.

MOORE, MOORE, MOORE

Like Nadine Begin, Thomas Moore was once in the clergy, a Catholic monk, but he departed from that calling to become a husband, father, therapist, philosopher, and author of numerous books. In *The Soul of Sex: Cultivating Life as an Act of Love* he elucidates the connection between sensuality, sexuality, and spirituality in a way that leaves no doubt of their interconnectedness. He tells us that it is possible to live all day, every day, in a world of erotic appreciation that is a conduit to spiritual happiness.

The Soul of Sex is like a dessert bar of ideas, such as how to have a sense of the spiritual by not denying the sensual, or by trivializing it. Such as seeing the erotic in our everyday lives, in good food, a beautiful road (as opposed to an efficient highway). He speaks of the "pure seductiveness" of being absorbed in solitary work and how sexuality and spirituality can be allied if we allow ourselves to explore the meaningful nature of the sensual and sexual worlds rather than treating them with shyness and superficiality.[18]

You Sexy Thing: Objectùm-Sexuality

There's a great bit in the movie *Romy and Michele's High School Reunion* where Janeane Garofalo, who has been seriously pining for a boy named Sandy Frank since high school, sees him at the class reunion and says, "That's Sandy Frank? What the hell was I thinking?" And boom! She's done.

It's a great moment because that is precisely how fast this great, mystical, all-consuming experience can end. You never know what's going to provoke it, but the speed with which Prince Charming can turn into Homer Simpson is astounding. Garofalo once did a stand-up bit where she talked about liking a guy so much so much so much—until she saw him try to moonwalk. You can hear the needle slide off the record as her admiration dies a quick, no-nonsense death. How can something that seems so real just evaporate?

There certainly can be a fine line between love and

its evil siblings infatuation, erotomania, obsession, lust, extreme like, and you'll-be-awesome-till-someone-better-comes-along. David Bowie once sang, "My heart's aflame, I'll love you till Tuesday."

Sometimes we think it's love and realize it was just infatuation; this inevitably happens when the other person first tells you they love you. Sometimes we think we've fallen out of love and then realize we've made a huge mistake and want her back. Feelings change—does that make them less real? As Marlene Zuk asked about animals, how do we know it's love?

This makes a particularly fascinating kind of love even more fascinating: Objectùm-Sexuality.

Objectùm-Sexuality is the mind-set of being in love with objects. (Please do not make jokes about your sexually inert spouse here: they exhausted that material on *Married with Children*.) According to the website for Objectùm-Sexuality Internationale (OSI), only about 40 people in the world have OS, but they do, indeed, fall into passionate love with objects such as fences or the Golden Gate Bridge, and they feel that the objects love them in return.[19]

I discovered OS via clips of *Married to the Eiffel Tower,* a BBC documentary that features Erika Eiffel, who very candidly and, I think, bravely, talks about her reciprocated love with various objects, including a bow. (She is an internationally competitive archer). Other people in the film have relationships with carnival rides and fences. It sounds so odd, it doesn't seem real, but when you watch the film you can see their demeanor change and the giddy glow of love come over them when they are looking at the thing—literally—that they love.[20] (OSI, according to its website, does not sanction the film.)

At least people with OS never have to worry about objectifying their partner.

In an email interview, Erika informs me that she was 14 when she first noticed that she had the kind of attachment to objects that most of her peers would have for girls or boys. "There is no real moment of discovery that I can pinpoint; it is a gradual progression from just liking someone to *liking* someone," she writes. She's never felt that attachment to a person, and she says when she tried to do so to fit in with convention it just ended up causing pain on both sides.[21]

It seemed to me that more women than men were profiled in the video, and I ask Erika whether women are more prone to OS than men. "There are more men stepping out and identifying as OS but not as much as women," Erika says. "Mars verses Venus, perhaps. Women are more open to talking about sensitive issues such as love and relationships."

Erika suffered sexual abuse and abandonment as a child, but not all survivors of abuse turn to objects. Dr. Amy Marsh noted in *Discover* magazine, having studied people with OS, "What I'm finding is not much history of sexual abuse, and actually not much in the way of psychiatric diagnoses either. I'm finding they're very happy, and they don't want to change. I am also finding out that quite a few of them have a diagnosis of Asperger's syndrome or autism."[22]

When I ask Erika whether she had any experiences that she believes shaped her romantic feelings about objects, she doesn't focus on her personal past, but on why people with OS choose particular objects on which to bestow their affection. "I do often wonder why I have a particular fondness for certain objects, while others in the community vary with theirs. It is possible that my love for bridges stems from a yearning to connect to things I otherwise could not reach. I also find that many of my deepest and longest loves are objects that were disrespected or mistreated. I am very sensitive to objects that need help and love."

Of course I have to ask Erika how a sexual relationship with an object works. Of course—and fairly—she basically says it is none of my beeswax.

"This is indeed a question that is not up for discussion. I tell you why. To share one's intimate details with the world lessens the value of something that is regarded as deeply personal, spiritual, and sacred. This is not a question that would be broached to the mainstream, and it therefore indicates that our intimate relationships are not held in regard other than as mere curiosity.

"We certainly understand why the question is being broached, because it is 'different,' but we hope one day people will let go of the hang-ups and see that the *sexuality* in OS does not imply the act but the inclination.

"Another point that needs to be made is that intimacy is defined by those involved in the relationship, and what is considered sensual for one may not be for another. In other words, with the strong spiritual nature of many OS people, what is considered intimate for us may not be remotely considered so for human relationships. People assume that what makes them happy is what must make others happy, and in turn they lay this definition on others."

I've never been so pleased with the way a question of mine was not answered. Erika views sharing details as lessening their sacredness, and it is a view I heartily agree with. As Oscar Wilde writes in *The Picture of Dorian Gray*, "When I like people immensely, I never tell their names to any one. It is like surrendering a part of them."

As children, we anthropomorphize objects, assigning

them human qualities and feelings, and even as adults we anthropomorphize our pets, dressing the dog in a tutu because "he likes it" when in fact he likes no such thing. (Back to Marlene's Zuk's observation about how much harder it is to humanize a bug.) We can't actually know whether the dog enjoys looking like a fool, or whether our dolls can actually hear us when we speak to them. I ask Erika how can you tell if an object loves you back, whether she thinks all objects have consciousness, and how they communicate.

"There is a book in this reply," she says, "so I will do my best to condense this answer from my point of view." For her, "What these relationships grow within me and how they propel my life in a forward direction demonstrates the clearest example of reciprocity." Or, as I would interpret it: if it helps, it must be love, it must be working.

There are two schools of thought in the OS community on the question of consciousness, Erika writes. First there is the animist OS, who is captivated by the spiritual nature of the object and who usually has a functioning social life that would be upset by the revelation of his or her relationship with objects. The other group consists of those who have Asperger's syndrome or high-functioning autism. "These Asperger's OS connect to very particular objects, creating a comfort zone which they are averse to changing. From this group comes more willingness to speak openly, as there is a strong obsessive compulsion to anything relating to their object of interest."

Erika is an animist and senses energy in objects. "Not all," she writes, "but ones in particular that I seem to resonate with. We all have antennas but we clearly do not pick up the same channels. It is a case of wiring. Most do not need to hear objects because your antennas are tuned for people. Objects simply serve their purpose and you see them merely in this light."

I'd be an awful hypocrite to tease anyone about anthropomorphizing objects, since I own three decks of tarot cards but I only use one to read for other people because, I'm fond of saying, those cards are "more sensitive" or "they relate better." People assign physical objects all kinds of powers: the power to protect us, connect us, bring us good energy. Your lucky socks, your crucifix or gris-gris bag, your old teddy bear—just objects, right? Not so much.

Being involved with an object seems like an excellent way of avoiding pain because you will always be the one in control. Are you? I ask Erika if she has ever been disappointed by an object that she loves. Can she feel their energy change?

"Absolutely! Quite sadly, this does exist and I have certainly felt rejected from object loves in the past. Our energy collided and there was not enough synergy to either start the relationship or to maintain a longer relationship."

I think it would be so interesting to get someone with OS into an fMRI machine to see if their brain scans are similar to those of people who are smitten with other people. Of course, they might have a little chemistry with the scanner, and then good luck getting them out.

Epilogue

I cried a lot when I wrote this book. It's OK. J.K. Rowling cried when she wrote *Harry Potter* and now she uses $500 bills as Kleenex. It could happen to me.

You'd have to be as hard and cold as a diamond not to cry over love sometimes, your own or someone else's, its beauty or its seeming meanness. Consider this poem Helen Fisher quotes in *Why We Love* about the pain of rejection:

> No doubt this way is best,
> No doubt in time I'd learn
> To hate you like the rest
> I had once loved.

That made me cry. Thank God the poet's name was Snodgrass or I'd never have stopped. I started out being curious about why people (myself included) do what they do in love, things that seem crazy and against our own self-interest, and why we can't wait to do it again. What I discovered was, counting brain chemistry, psychology, fashion, zeitgeist, personal nature, and lifelong changes of circumstance, there are numerous ways to pinpoint how you or someone else came to love a certain way, none of which include your being a romantic defective who should throw in the towel. With neuroscience, psychology, and other disciplines giving us more insight into our behavior and our world every day, we should be better able to respond to our problems in love with grace and to treat the feelings of others with respect. If you think grace and respect are namby-pamby, try chaos and dismissiveness for a while.

Dr. Robert Epstein, whom I interviewed in chapter 8, told me he didn't understand why it matters that love has been viewed in a brain scan. "All that shows you is correlation. It just shows you that this part of the brain lights up when this happens. That doesn't tell you the activity in that part of the brain is causing anything to happen." Genes and environment produce the brain, the behavior, and the emotions you have, he says, and the brain is just part of that system: the effect, not the cause. We knew years ago that different parts of the brain specialize, so it's not really news. So how does knowing what's lighting up in the brain in love give you new insight about love?

How it helps is perspective. It lets me see my own feelings in the abstract, not as factory imperfections but as mutable states. We all have moments where we think our feelings are forever—otherwise there would be no wedding industry. When you are miserable in love you need to know that feelings of inadequacy, failure, and rejection can end, because you often don't believe they can. This knowledge can be the light at the end of the dangerous darkness Nina Paley described so well. It won't help everyone, but it helped me, and I'm not so unique as to think I'm the only one.

It helps to consider how my brain is processing things and what I can do to encourage it to higher ground. Doing something new to get a little high-quality dopamine rush can change my whole outlook. When I feel powerless, doing one little thing I *can* control, like paying a bill or going for a walk, makes my temper vanish. Doing something for the pure bliss of it even if it's not easy—like learning to moonwalk—changes the energy of my whole day. The little lessons culled from the stories and studies in this book, judiciously and personally applied, work. They may not work every time, but my cell phone doesn't work 100 percent of the time either and I'm keeping it.

The stories of people I talked to in this book helped as well—people like Nina, who showed that even when one person doesn't appreciate you the rest of the world just might.

The notion of love as a function of the brain will, I think, make many people who are uncomfortable with emotion more agreeable to dealing with it. People who see prolonged heartbreak as wussiness, weakness, or something they should "just get over" (which is how I used to feel) and who would never talk about it might find it more approachable as a matter of mechanics than as mush. Simply pointing out, "Dude, it's chemical, like a weak vodka tonic," might help someone address the stress before it becomes a heart attack or road rage. Every time something really tragic happens involving a person who has snapped over a lost love, people act shocked and talk about how no one saw it coming, how it could have been prevented, how this or that person or project slipped through the cracks.

People who are in trouble in love often let themselves fall through the cracks by not taking their confusion about love seriously. Many of us go into love woefully unprepared, like riding a Big Wheel into a demolition derby. Everyone is going to fall in love, and the more education we get—not just about the mechanics of sex but about the emotions and relationships that often accompany it—the better. You know what they wasted our time on in high school? Archery. I had to take PE, so I took archery. The only person I wanted to shoot in archery was whoever made me take PE. Most of us would have benefited more from learning about emotional intelligence than from playing yet another game of kickball. But there is no President's Council on Mental Fitness.

Adults need all the help they can get, too. Mental health should be the growth industry of the 2010s, as coffee was in the 1990s and tech was in the 2000s. Therapy salons should be as prevalent as Starbucks. In fact, there should be therapists *in* Starbucks, and in every mall, highway rest area, and airport in the world. The former astronaut whose lovesickness drove her to pursue a romantic rival from Houston to Orlando and assault her in the airport parking lot might have been known for her impressive career instead of the rumor that she wore a diaper on her drive if she'd gassed up at a rest area with a mental health storefront called Screw Loose La Trek. If you can get your eyes, your weight, and your general health checked in a strip mall, why not your head? A diet counseling session at a national franchise takes about 20 minutes; imagine how much it would help you to be able to pop in for a 20-minute tune-up with a love counselor. Yes, the help would be short-term. Yes, some people might need long-term cognitive or drug therapy. But it's better to patch the roof until you can properly fix it than to let it rain on the TV.

An October 2010 story on Pysch Central detailed a Michigan Health Care System study wherein patients who got a simple phone call follow-up from their doctor's office were more likely to stay well for extended periods.[1] It's a bit more complicated than just getting a call, but the point is that *anything* helps more than just holding it in. Imagine what air travel would be like if there were a counseling booth—or a meditation room or an ongoing exercise class—in the airport terminal about 1,000 feet after the security screener, where right now there is nothing but a bar and a Burger King?

People sometimes just need to hear that they are OK. It clears our heads and makes us function better. Feeling that we are safe materially (*I have food and shelter*) is our most basic need, but next in importance after that is feeling that we're safe emotionally (*Someone cares about me*). We need someone to trade oxytocin with.

This is especially true in love, which is our greatest prize and therefore our most vulnerable emotional point. If thinking about love from the perspective of brain chemistry, the Shaky Bridge, or any other insights in this book is helpful to you, or if you have learned from any of the stories of the people in this book, then I'm glad to pass it on. I know just how it feels to think you're clueless about the best thing in life, and I'm glad that others like the people described in this book have had a hand in making me feel better.

And you have to feel better about it so you can do as Maude told Harold: "Go and love some more."

About the Author

 LIZ LANGLEY's writing has appeared in AlterNet, Salon, Jezebel, Details.com, *Glamour* and *Bust*. A popular blogger and columnist for *SexIs Magazine*, she has won awards from the Society of Professional Journalists, Florida Press Association, and the Association of Alternative Newsweeklies. She lives in Orlando, Florida.

Photo by www.miriphoto.com.

Endnotes

PREFACE

1 "Agatha Christie," http://christie.mysterynet.com/.

2 Rachael Rettner, " 'Romantic Love Is an Addiction,' Researchers Say," citing quotes and study by Dr. Helen Fisher, http://www. livescience.com/culture/romantic-rejection-brain-100706. html.

3 Interview with Dr. Amy Marsh, October 4, 2010.

CHAPTER 1

1 Brain anatomy, AtlantaBrainandSpine.com, http://www.atlanta-brainandspine.com/subject.php?pn=brain-anatomy-066.

2 Telephone conversation with Dr. Joseph Shrand, October 28, 2010.

3 Emily Sohn, *Mommy Brain: It's Not What You Think*, Discover. com, October 22, 2010, http://news.discovery.com/human/ mommy-brain-maternal-changes.html.

4 John Storey, *Cultural Theory and Popular Culture* (University of Georgia Press, 2006), 72.

5 MedicineNet.com, Medical Dictionary, http://www.medterms. com/script/main/art.asp?articlekey=7785.

6 MedicineNet.com, Medical Dictionary, http://www.medterms. com/script/main/art.asp?articlekey=9973.

7 MedicineNet.com, Medical Dictionary, http://www.medicinenet. com/script/main/art.asp?articlekey=184.

8 Andrew Koob, *The Root of Thought: Unlocking Glia—the Brain Cell That Will Help Us Sharpen Our Wits, Heal Injury, and Treat Brain Disease* (FT Press, 2009).

9 *Zoom*, episode one, intro, http://www.youtube.com/ watch?v=F7gzHLKT5g4.

10 Kay Moeller, "Music Boosts Dopamine for a Natural High, Says New Study," Gather, http://technology.gather.com/view-Article.action?articleId=281474978896027.

11 Sandra Blakeslee, "Cells That Read Minds," *New York Times*, January 10, 2006, http://www.nytimes.com/2006/01/10/ science/10mirr.html?pagewanted=print.

12 "VS Ramachandran: The Neurons That Shaped Civilization," http://www.youtube.com/watch?v=t0pwKzTRG5E.

13 Helen Fisher, *Why We Love: The Nature and Chemistry of Romantic*

Love (Henry Holt, 2004), 181.

14 BodiesTheExhibition.com,http://www.bodiestheexhibition.com/.

15 Fisher, *Why We Love*, 69.

16 Ibid., 71.

17 Telephone conversation with Dr. Joseph Shrand, October 28, 2010.

18 Michael Haderle, "The Best Fiscal Stimulus: Trust," Miller-McCune, August 9, 2010, http://www.miller-mccune.com/business-economics/the-best-fiscal-stimulus-trust-20005/.

19 Fisher, *Why We Love*, 89.

20 David J. Ley PhD, "Can Infidelity Cure Depression?" Pubsub.com, October 10, 2010, http://pubsub.com/Can-Infidelity-Cure-Depression_Psychology-Relationships-adultery-4Dfz57gknEL,2RSgb0cuXMxE, originally published in *Psychology Today* Blogs.

21 Daniel Amen, *Sex on the Brain: 12 Lessons to Enhance Your Love Life* (Random House, 2007), 52–72.

22 Fisher, *Why We Love*, 162.

23 Ibid., 163.

24 Ibid., 170.

25 Helen E. Fisher, Lucy L. Brown, Arthur Aron, Greg Strong, and Debra Mashek, "Reward, Addiction, and Emotion Regulation Systems Associated With Rejection in Love," Journal of Neurophysiology.com, May 1, 2010, http://jn.physiology.org/content/104/1/51.full.

26 Ibid.

27 Cristen Conger and Molly Edmonds, "This is Your Brain on a Breakup," HowStuffWorks.com, *Stuff Mom Never Told You* (podcast), August 23, 2010, http://itunes.apple.com/us/podcast/this-is-your-brain-on-a-breakup/id304531053?i=86412828.

28 Fisher et al, "Reward, Addiction, and Emotion Regulation Systems."

29 Tara Parker-Pope, "Love and Pain Relief," *New York Times*, October 13, 2010, http://well.blogs.nytimes.com/2010/10/13/love-and-pain-relief/.

30 Lewis Carroll, *Alice's Adventures in Wonderland* and *Through The Looking Glass and What Alice Found There* (Random House, 2002), 225.

31 Cristina Nehring, *A Vindication of Love: Reclaiming Romance for the Twenty-First Century* (HarperCollins, 2009), 263.

32 "Falling In Love Only Takes About a Fifth of a Second, Research Reveals," ScienceDaily.com, October 25, 2010, http://www.

sciencedaily.com/releases/2010/10/101022184957.htm, adapted from "Falling in love is 'more scientific than you think,' according to new study by SU professor," Syracuse University News, October 18, 2010, http://www.syr.edu/news/articles/2010/ortigue-neuroimaging-of-love-10–10.html.

33 Malcolm Gladwell, *Blink*, http://www.gladwell.com/blink/index.html.

34 National Museum of Crime & Punishment, http://www.crimemuseum.org/Crimes_of_Passion.

35 "Daniel Sickles trial: 1859—Lafayette Park Killing," http://law.jrank.org/pages/2550/Daniel-Sickles-Trial-1859-Lafayefte-Park-Killing.html.

36 Dan Collins, "Mercedes Murderess Gets 20 Years," CBS News, Feb. 14, 2003, http://www.cbsnews.com/stories/2003/02/21/national/main541423.shtml.

37 Telephone conversation with Marlene Zuk, July 16, 2010.

38 Helen Fisher, *Why Him? Why Her? Finding Real Love by Understanding Your Personality Type* (Henry Holt, 2009).

39 Telephone conversation with Helen Fisher, May 24, 2010.

CHAPTER 2

1 Marlene Zuk, *Riddled with Life: Friendly Worms, Ladybug Sex, and the Parasites That Make Us Who We Are* (Houghton Mifflin Harcourt, 2007), 157.

2 Christopher Ryan and Cacilda Jethá, *Sex at Dawn: The Prehistoric Origins of Modern Sexuality* (HarperCollins, 2010), 92.

3 Marlene Zuk, "The Truth About Misassigned Paternity," *Los Angeles Times*, June 20, 2010, http://articles.latimes.com/2010/jun/20/opinion/la-oe-zuk-paternity-20100620.

4 Koko's First Interspecies Web Chat (transcript), http://www.koko.org/world/talk_aol.html.

5 Amina Khan, "Chimpanzees mourn their dead like humans do, research finds," *Los Angeles Times*, April 27, 2010, http://articles.latimes.com/2010/apr/27/science/la-sci-chimps-death-20100427.

6 "Echo: An Elephant to Remember," Elephant Emotions, PBS, http://www.pbs.org/wnet/nature/episodes/unforgettable-elephants/elephant-emotions/4489/.

7 Tracy V. Wilson, "How Kissing Works," http://people.howstuffworks.com/kissing.htm.

8 Betsy Mason, "Scientists Agree: It's In His Kiss," Wired Science, February 13, 2009, http://www.wired.com/wired-

science/2009/02/kissingscience/.

CHAPTER 3

1 Daniel Amen, *Sex on the Brain: 12 Lessons to Enhance Your Love Life* (Random House, 2007), 52–72.

2 Sebnem Arsu, "The Oldest Line in the World," *New York Times*, Feb. 14, 2006, http://travel2.nytimes.com/2006/02/14/international/europe/14poem.html.

3 Sheri Winston, *Women's Anatomy of Arousal: Secret Maps to Buried Pleasure* (Mango Garden Press, 2010).

4 Telephone conversation with Sheri Winston, Oct. 11, 2010.

5 "Flavor Flav," TMZ.com, http://www.tmz.com/person/flavor-flav/2/.

6 F. Bryant Furlow, *The Smell of Love*, reviewed in *Psychology Today*, August 13, 2010, http://www.psychologytoday.com/articles/200910/the-smell-love?page=2.

7 "Smell the Love," University of Cambridge, August 4, 2010, http://www.admin.cam.ac.uk/news/dp/2010080301.

8 "What an Ovulating Girl Wants: Manly Men," Livescience, MSNBC.MSN.com, April 12, 2007.

9 "The Laws of Attraction," Oprah.com, April 3, 2009, http://www.oprah.com/relationships/The-Science-of-Sex-Appeal/print/1.

10 Eric Bland, "Women's Natural Scent More Seductive Than Perfume," Discovery News, February 10, 2010, http://news.discovery.com/human/women-perfume-natural-scent.html.

11 Rebecca Skloot, "Lap-Dance Science," *New York Times*, Dec. 9. 2007, http://www.nytimes.com/2007/12/09/magazine/09lapdance.html?ex=1354856400&en=348764b6b1728e69&ei=5090&partner=rssuserland&emc=rss.

12 Ryan and Jethá, *Sex at Dawn*, 85.

13 Ibid., 62.

14 Liz Langley, "Monkey See, Monkey Screw," *Orlando Weekly*, June 11, 1998, http://www2.orlandoweekly.com/columns/story.asp?id=743.

15 Frans B. M. de Waal, "Bonobo Sex and Society," http://www.primates.com/bonobos/bonobosexsoc.html, originally published in *Scientific American*, March 1995, 82–88.

16 Helen Fisher, *Why Him? Why Her? Finding Real Love by Understanding Your Personality Type* (Henry Holt, 2009), 100.

17 Conversation with Ward Hall, April 29, 2010.

18 Foundation for Ichthyosis and Related Skin Types, http://www.firstskinfoundation.org/.

19 "3 Rules for Office Romance," CBS Moneywatch, July 13, 2010, http://moneywatch.bnet.com/career-advice/article/office-romance-3-rules-for-a-workplace-relationship/443526/.

20 Joe Nickell, *Secrets of the Sideshows* (University of Kentucky Press, 2005), 148.

21 "Causative gene for human 'lobster claw' syndrome identified," May 21, 2002, http://www.innovations-report.de/html/berichte/biowissenschaften_chemie/bericht-10041.html.

22 Joshua Foer, "The 'Ostrich-Footed' Vadoma of Zimbabwe," Boing-Boing.Net, June 22, 2009, http://boingboing.net/2009/06/22/the-ostrich-footed-v.html; "Vadoma Tribe—The Ostrich People of Zimbabwe," http://www.youtube.com/watch?v=3-fvz3TtD0c.

23 Stuart B. McIver, *Murder in the Tropics* (Pineapple Press, 1995), 148.

24 "Grady Stiles (1937–1992)," Find a Grave Memorial, http://www.findagrave.com/cgi-bin/fg.cgi?page=gr&GRid=8301721.

25 Nickell, *Secrets of the Sideshows*, 150.

26 "Lobster Boy's Stepson Gets Life Sentence," *Milwaukee Journal*, August 10, 1994, http://news.google.com/newspapers?nid=1499&dat=19940810&id=IkwcAAAAIBAJ&sjid=JH8EAAAAIBAJ&pg=5414,894005.

27 Article: Addenda, *Washington Post*, October 15, 1994, http://www.highbeam.com/doc/1P2–914337.html.

28 Francine Hornberger, *Carny Folk: The World's Weirdest Sideshow Acts* (Citadel Press, 2005), 164.

29 Nickell, *Secrets of the Sideshows*, 150.

CHAPTER 4

1 *Crazy Love*, documentary film, dir. Dan Klores (Shoot the Moon Productions, 2007).

2 Amy Turner, "Burt and Linda Pugach: The Story behind Crazy Love," *Times* (UK), June 29, 2008, http://entertainment.timesonline.co.uk/tol/arts_and_entertainment/film/article4212049.ece.

3 Marianne MacDonald, "Meet the Pugachs," *Observer* (UK), August 5, 2007, http://www.guardian.co.uk/lifeandstyle/2007/aug/05/familyandrelationships3.

4 Ibid.

5 Norimitsu Onishi, "Jury Clears Man, 70, of Abuse Charges," *New York Times*, May 1, 1997, http://www.nytimes.com/1997/05/01/nyregion/jury-clears-man-70-of-abuse-charges.html.

6 Conversation with Burt Pugach, May 17, 2010.

7   "Crazy Love-er Burt Pugach Sues HBO, Dan Klores," Radar Online, http://www.radaronline.com/exclusives/2008/07/crazy-love-burt-pugach-sues-dan-klores-hbo.php.

8   Robert B. Ward, *New York State Government* (Rockefeller Institute Press, 2006), 467, http://books.google.com/books?id=DnXSo_XPgWIC&pg=PA467&lpg=PA467&dq=attica+reform+mail+phone&source=bl&ots=dbaslIkXaN&sig=YjgvXZKyK11LkRi-Ms1Nr2ZF2t8&hl=en&ei=N1d3TK2BJYOdlge68vDrCw&sa=X&oi=book_result&ct=result&resnum=8&ved=0CD8Q6AEwBw#v=onepage&q=mail&f=false.

9   "The More You Ruv Someone," *Avenue Q*, Lyrics on Demand, http://www.lyricsondemand.com/soundtracks/a/avenueqlyrics/themoreyouruvsomeonelyrics.html.

10 William Shakespeare, *Othello, The Moor of Venice*, Act 5, Scene 2, http://shakespeare.mit.edu/othello/othello.5.2.html; David Byrne, "Everyone's in Love with You," http://www.nomore-lyrics.net/david_byrne-lyrics/287200-everyones_in_love_with_you-lyrics.html; Oscar Wilde, *The Ballad of Reading Gaol*, http://www.poetry-online.org/wilde_the_ballad_of_reading_goal.htm.

11 Fisher, *Why We Love*, 164.

12 Telephone conversation with Helen Fisher, May 24, 2010.

13 Matthew Busse, "Amygdala and Cortisol," Livestrong.com, http://www.livestrong.com/article/146203-amygdala-and-cortisol/; Ronald T. Potter-Efron, *Rage: A Step-by-Step Guide to Overcoming Explosive Anger* (New Harbinger Publications, 2007), 83.

14 Leonard Berkowitz, *Frustration–Aggression Hypothesis: Examination and Reformulation* (American Psychological Association, 1989), http://www.radford.edu/~jaspelme/_private/gradsoc_articles/aggression/frustration percent20aggression.pdf.

15 Richard Alleyne, *Political views 'hard-wired' into your brain*, Telegraph (UK), Dec 28, 2010, http://www.telegraph.co.uk/science/science-news/8228192/Political-views-hard-wired-into-your-brain.html.

16 "Brain Location for Fear of Losing Money Pinpointed—The Amygdala," Science Daily, Feb. 9, 2010, http://www.science-daily.com/releases/2010/02/100208154645.htm.

17 Catherine Donaldson-Evans, "Brain Size Tied to Richer Social Lives," AOL Health, Dec 27, 2010, http://www.aolhealth.com/2010/12/27/brain-size-social-lives/.

18 Mark Lisheron, "Trove of Police Evidence to be Made Public Dec. 18 Reveals Charles Whitman's Malevolent Yet Mundane

Psyche," *Statesman*, Dec. 9, 2001, http://www.statesman.com/specialreports/content/specialreports/whitman/index.html; "Charles Whitman, 1/5" from Investigation Discovery, http://www.youtube.com/watch?v=__4bYWS91I0&feature=related.

19 Rhwan Joseph, PhD, "Charles Whitman: The Amygdala & Mass Murder," Brain-Mind.com, http://brainmind.com/Case5.html.

20 Jordana Scheiver, "Woman sets husband's penis alight to stop him cheating, court told," *Courier-Mail* (Australia), Sept. 28, 2010, http://www.couriermail.com.rau/news/national/woman-sets-husbands-penis-alight-to-stop-him-cheating-court-told/story-e6freooo-1225930546506.

21 Sean Fewster, "Slain father Satish Narayan 'beat, bullied kids' " Adelaide Now, *Courier-Mail* (Australia), November 24, 2010, http://www.couriermail.com.au/news/national/slain-father-beat-bullied-kids/story-e6freooo-1225960121790.

22 Telephone conversation with Dr. Ian Kerner, October 6, 2010.

23 Cindy M. Meston and Penny F. Frohlich, "Love at First Fright: Partner Salience Moderates Roller-Coaster-Induced Excitation Transfer," *Archives of Sexual Behavior*, December 2003, http://homepage.psy.utexas.edu/homepage/group/MestonLAB/Publications/rollercoaster.pdf.

24 Donald G. Dutton and Arthur P. Aron, "Some Evidence for Heightened Sexual Attraction Under Conditions of High Anxiety," *Journal of Personality and Social Psychology*, 30:4 (1974), http://www.fpce.uc.pt/niips/novoplano/ps1/documentos/dutton percent26aron1974.pdf.

25 *Who's Afraid of Virginia Woolf?* 1966—Memorable Quotes, http://www.imdb.com/title/tt0061184/quotes.

26 Bun E. Carlos, Rick Nielsen, Tom Petersson, Julian Raymond, Robin Zander, "Closer, The Ballad of Burt and Lynda," http://www.metrolyrics.com/closer-the-ballad-of-burt-and-linda-lyrics-cheap-trick.html.

CHAPTER 5

1 Chuck Shepherd, "News of The Weird," October 18, 2009, http://groups.google.com/group/newsoftheweird/browse_thread/thread/3d15bb5bb9961273/1bc6c318ba6ce8b4?show_docid=1bc6c318ba6ce8b4.

2 Thomas Hargrove and Guido H. Stempel III, "Poll probes Americans' belief in UFOs, life on other planets," Scripps Howard News Service, July 15, 2008, http://www.scrippsnews.com/

node/34758.

3 Telephone conversations with Lynette Horn, June 12 and August 17, 2010.

4 Arthur David Horn, *Humanity's Extraterrestrial Origins* (A & L Horn, 1994), xxiii.

5 Horn, *Humanity's Extraterrestrial Origins*.

6 "Asperger Symptoms in Adults," Asperger-Advice.com, http://www.asperger-advice.com/asperger-symptoms-in-adults.html; communication with Dr. Amy Marsh, February 28, 2011.

7 Dr. Amy Marsh, "The Intimate Aspie," http://www.dramymarsh-sexologist.com/theintimateaspie/index.html.

8 Telephone conversation with Dr. Amy Marsh, October 5, 2010.

9 Tony Attwood, *The Complete Guide to Asperger's Syndrome* Jessica Kingsley Publishers, 2008).

10 Emine Saner, "Soul Survivor," *Guardian* (UK), September 17, 2007, http://www.guardian.co.uk/film/2007/sep/19/1.

11 Quoted in Andrew Buncombe, "Asperger's Syndrome: The ballad of Nikki Bacharach," *Independent* (UK), January 8, 2007, http://www.independent.co.uk/news/world/americas/aspergers-syndrome-the-ballad-of-nikki-bacharach-431201.html.

12 Dr. Mandy Roy, Dr. Wolfgang Dillo, Dr. Hinderk M. Emrich, and Dr. Martin D. Ohlmeier, "Asperger's Syndrome in Adulthood," *Deutsches Ärtzeblatt International*, January 2009, http://www.ncbi.nlm.nih.gov/pmc/articles/PMC2695286/.

13 Quoted in Andrew Buncombe, "Asperger's Syndrome: The ballad of Nikki Bacharach," *Independent* (UK), January 8, 2007, http://www.independent.co.uk/news/world/americas/aspergers-syndrome-the-ballad-of-nikki-bacharach-431201.html.

14 Lady Hellion, "The Christian FemDomme," Christians & BDSM, 2004, http://www.christiansandbdsm.com/femdomme.html.

15 Telephone conversation with Lynette Horn, June 12, 2010.

16 Quoted in Deepak Chopra, *Muhammad: A Story of the Last Prophet* (HarperOne, 2010), 265.

CHAPTER 6

1 David Sheff, *All We Are Saying: The Last Major Interview with John and Yoko* (MacMillan, 1981), 102.

2 Richard, Buskin, "John Lennon," HowStuffWorks, http://entertainment.howstuffworks.com/john-lennon30.htm.

3 "Virginia Eliza Clemm Poe," Find a Grave Memorial, http://www.findagrave.com/cgi-bin/fg.cgi?page=gr&GRid=33076902.

4 "Edgar Allan Poe's Tamerlane Sets Record at NY auction," *Tele-*

graph (UK), Dec. 4, 2009, http://www.telegraph.co.uk/culture/books/6730153/Edgar-Allan-Poes-Tamerlane-sets-record-at-NY-auction.html.

5 Edgar Allan Poe, *Eleonora,* http://poestories.com/read/eleonora.

6 Edgar Allan Poe, *Berenice,* http://poestories.com/read/berenice.

7 Edgar Allan Poe, *Annabel Lee,* http://www.eapoe.org/works/poems/annabela.htm.

8 The Edgar Allan Poe Society of Baltimore, http://www.eapoe.org/index.htm.

9 "Edgar Allan Poe to Mrs. Maria Clemm and Miss Virginia Clemm" (excerpt), *August 29, 1835,* http://www.eapoe.org/works/letters/p3508290.htm.

10 Richard P. Benton, "Friends and Enemies: Women in the Life of Edgar Allan Poe," http://www.eapoe.org/papers/psbbooks/pb19871c.htm.

11 "Edgar Allan Poe to Elizabeth R. Tutt," http://www.eapoe.org/works/letters/p4207070.htm.

12 Benton, "Friends and Enemies."

13 Ibid.

14 Ryan and Jethá, *Sex at Dawn,* 31.

15 "Cousin Marriage Laws Outdated, Expert Argues," ScienceDaily.com, Dec. 25, 2008, http://www.sciencedaily.com/releases/2008/12/081222221535.htm; Steve Connor, "There's Nothing Wrong With Cousins Getting Married, Scientists Say," *Independent* (UK), Dec. 24, 2008, http://emilie.hermit.net/content/cousin-marriage-ok-theres-nothing-wrong-cousins-getting-married-scientists-say.

16 Anna North, "Mackenzie Phillips Incest Puts 'Genetic Sexual Attraction' in the Spotlight," Jezebel, September 29, 2009, http://m.jezebel.com/5370344/mackenzie-phillips-incest-puts-genetic-sexual-attraction-in-the-spotlight.

17 Valerie Hanley, "Couple discover they are siblings: Child courts blamed after strangers fall in love, have a son—and then find out they are half-brother and sister," *Daily Mail* (UK), May 30, 2010, http://www.dailymail.co.uk/news/article-1282575/Couple-discover-siblings-Child-courts-blamed-strangers-fall-love-son—half-brother-sister.html#ixzz0pTdZ2kuY.

18 Aida Edemariam and Kate Connolly, "Blood Ties," *Guardian* (UK), February 28, 2007, http://www.guardian.co.uk/world/2007/feb/28/germany.familyandrelationships.

19 Telephone conversation with Joe Soll, June 22, 2010.

20 Telephone conversation with Barbara Gonyo, February 22, 2011.

21 "Mom Jailed Over Sex With 14-year-old son," MSNBC, July 13, 2010, http://www.msnbc.msn.com/id/38217476/; Caroline Black, "Aimee L. Sword Gets up to 30 Years for Sex with Biological Son," CBS News, July 13, 2010, http://www.cbsnews.com/8301–504083_162–20010375–504083.html.

22 Helen Fisher, *Why We Love,* 164.

23 Allan Hall, "Switzerland Considers Repealing Incest Laws," *Telegraph* (UK), Dec. 13, 2010, http://www.telegraph.co.uk/news/worldnews/europe/switzerland/8198917/Switzerland-considers-repealing-incest-laws.html.

24 "Australia's Adoption Rate Plummets," *Brisbane Times,* February 21, 2008, http://www.brisbanetimes.com.au/news/national/australias-adoption-rate-plummets/2008/02/21/1203467220788.html.

25 Telephone conversation with Charles Martin, July 3, 2010.

CHAPTER 7

1 *Sita Sings the Blues,* http://www.sitasingstheblues.com/watch.html; Nina Paley's blog, http://blog.ninapaley.com/.

2 Roger Ebert, Roger Ebert's Film Festival: *Sita Sings the Blues,* http://www.ebertfest.com/eleven/frame_sitasingstheblues.html.

3 Conversations with Nina Paley, April 2010 and May 13, 2010.

4 Alternatives to Marriage Project, http://www.unmarried.org/.

5 Alissa Meagher, "SU Study Finds Effects of Love, Drugs Alike," *Daily Orange,* October 11, 2010, http://www.dailyorange.com/feature/su-study-finds-effects-of-love-drugs-alike-1.1676223.

6 Rick Nauert PhD, "Brain Imaging Shows Brain Changes in Depression," Psych Central News, September 2, 2010, http://psychcentral.com/news/2010/09/02/brain-imaging-shows-brain-changes-in-depression/17541.html.

7 "The Numbers Count: Mental Disorders in America," National Institute of Mental Health, http://www.nimh.nih.gov/health/publications/the-numbers-count-mental-disorders-in-america/index.shtml#ConwellSuiAging.

8 Telephone conversation with Helen Fisher, May 24, 2010.

CHAPTER 8

1 *Snapped*: *Nikki Reynolds,* Oxygen Network, http://www.hulu.com/watch/100084/snapped-nikki-reynolds.

2 Conversation with Nikki Reynolds, Gadsden Correctional Facility, Quincy, Florida, June 14, 2010.

3 "Psychiatric Disorders: Borderline Personality Disorder," AllPsych Onine, http://allpsych.com/disorders/personality/borderline.html.

4 Florida Laws: 775.027, Insanity Defense, http://law.onecle.com/florida/crimes/775.027.html.

5 T.J. Holmes, "Walk in My Shoes: Inside the Teen Brain," CNN American Morning, December 17. 2009, http://amfix.blogs.cnn.com/2009/12/17/walk-in-my-shoes-inside-the-teen-brain/.

6 *Frontline: Inside the Teenage Brain*, PBS, http://www.pbs.org/wgbh/pages/frontline/shows/teenbrain/.

7 Robert Epstein PhD, *Teen 2.0: Saving Our Children and Families from the Torment of Adolescence* (Quill Driver Books, 2010); http://drrobertepstein.com/.

8 Telephone conversation with Dr. Robert Epstein, October 29, 2010.

9 Robert Epstein, "The Myth of the Teen Brain," *Scientific American Mind*, April/May 2007, 59.

10 Telephone conversation with Dr. Joseph Shrand, October 28, 2010.

CHAPTER 9

1 "A Brief History of the Conch Republic," http://www.conchrepublic.com/history.htm.

2 Richard Arthur Norton, "Carl Tanzler Von Cosel (1877–1952) of Florida," http://boards.ancestry.com/surnames.tanzler/1/mb.ashx.

3 Katherine Ramsland, "A Macabre Love Story," http://www.trutv.com/library/crime/serial_killers/notorious/necrophiles/story_6.html.

4 Ben Harrison, *Undying Love: The True Story of a Passion That Defied Death* (MacMillan, 2001).

5 Aliyah Shahid, "Pennsylvania widow Jean Stevens, 91, lived with corpses of husband, twin," *New York Daily News*, July 6, 2010, http://www.nydailynews.com/news/national/2010/07/06/2010–07–06_pennsylvania_widow_jean_stevens_91_lived_with_corpses_of_husband_twin.html.

6 "Le Van, the man who sleeps with death," Look at Vietnam, Dec. 2, 2009, http://www.lookatvietnam.com/2009/12/le-van-the-man-who-sleeps-with-death.html.

7 *Twin Peaks*: "The Funeral of Laura Palmer," http://www.youtube.com/watch?v=H5J_ahUvqto.

8   *Ponette* (9/10), http://www.youtube.com/watch?v=XYxiOisUtxA
&feature=related.

9   David Brown and Helen Nugent, " 'Together forever' couple,
Sir Edward and Joan Downes, raise new suicide fears," *Times*
(UK), July 15, 2009; Charlotte Higgins and Owen Bowcott,
"Sir Edward Downes and Lady Downes arrange natural finale,"
Guardian (UK), July 14, 2009, http://www.guardian.co.uk/
society/2009/jul/14/edward-downes-assisted-suicide-law.

10 Henry Brodaty and Adrienne Withall, "Suicide after Bereave-
ment—an Overlooked Problem," August 29, 2008, http://
www.medscape.com/viewarticle/578535.

11 S. Zisook and S.R. Shuchter, "Depression through the first year after
the death of a spouse," *American Journal of Psychiatry, 1991,* http://
ajp.psychiatryonline.org/cgi/content/abstract/148/10/1346.

12 Corey Kilgannon, "Making it Work: Tracking Gertrude Tredwell's
Ghost," *New York Times*, October 25, 1998, http://www.
nytimes.com/1998/10/25/nyregion/making-it-work-tracking-
gertrude-treadwell-s-ghost.html.

13 Andrew Groen, "The Psychology of Fanboyism," August 3,
2010, http://www.gamepro.com/article/features/216012/the-
psychology-of-fanboyism/.

14 Katherine Ramsland, *Cemetery Stories: Haunted Graveyards,
Embalming Secrets, and the Life of a Corpse After Death* (Harper-
Collins, 2001); Westgate: The Azrael Project Online, www.
westgatenecromantic.com.

15 Conversation with Katherine Ramsland, May 8, 2010.

16 Adam Parfrey, ed., *Apocalypse Culture* (Feral House, 1990); Jim
Morton, "The Unrepentant Necrophile: An Interview with
Karen   Greenlee,"   http://www.nokilli.com/sacto/karen-
greenlee.htm.

17 Katherine Ramsland, "Women Who Kill: Black Widows II,"
http://www.trutv.com/library/crime/notorious_murders/
women/women_killers2/6b.html; Joseph Geringer, "Black
Widows: Veiled in Their Own Web of Darkness," http://
www.trutv.com/library/crime/criminal_mind/psychology/
widows/5.html.

18 Erich Fromm, *The Anatomy of Human Destructiveness* (Macmillan,
1992) 369.

19 Erich Fromm, "Creators and Destroyers," *Saturday Review,* January
4, 1964, 22–25, http://www.erich-fromm.de/data/pdf/1964f-
e.pdf.

20 Marlene Zuk, *Sexual Selections: What We Can and Can't Learn about*

Sex from Animals (University of California Press, 2002), 3.

21 Jason Chen, "iPhone App Lets Someone Propose to Your Future Wife For You," Gizmodo.com, Feb 23, 2009.

22 Fromm, *Creators and Destroyers.*

23 Katherine Ramsland, "Love and Death: The Sunset Strip Killers," http://www.trutv.com/library/crime/serial_killers/partners/cbundy/index_1.html.

24 Katherine Ramsland and Patrick Norman McGrain, *Inside the Minds of Sexual Predators* (Praeger/ABC-CLIO, 2010), 80.

25 Telephone conversation with Dr. Anandhi Narasimhan, June 10, 2010.

26 "An Underlying Cause for Psychopathic Behavior?" Science Daily, May 27, 2010, http://www.sciencedaily.com/releases/2010/04/100427091723.htm.

27 Sheila Isenberg, *Women Who Love Men Who Kill* (Dell Publishing, 1991), 136.

28 Ibid.

29 "Study: PET Imaging Shows Fewer Dopamine Receptors in Drug Addicts," Health Imaging, April 28, 2010, http://www.healthimaging.com/index.php?option=com_articles&article=21931.

30 Conversation with Katherine Ramsland, May 8, 2010.

31 "The Androygyne," http://www.reconnections.net/androgyny.htm.

CHAPTER 10

1 Patricia Kreml, *Slim for Him: Biblical Devotions on Diet* (Logos International, 1978), 4.

2 Katie Roiphe, "Feverish Liaisons," *New York Times*, June 19, 2009, http://www.nytimes.com/2009/06/21/books/review/Roiphe-t.html?_r=1.

3 Cristina Nehring, *A Vindication of Love: Reclaiming Romance for the Twenty-First Century* (HarperCollins, 2009), 7.

4 Ryan and Jethá, *Sex at Dawn*, 82–83.

5 Thomas Moore, *The Soul of Sex: Cultivating Life as an Act of Love* (HarperCollins, 1998), 235.

6 Nehring, *Vindication of Love*, 3.

7 Email interview with Cristina Nehring, July 26, 2010.

8 "Lady Gaga: My Ex Said I'd 'Never Succeed' " *Us*, February 25, 2010, http://www.usmagazine.com/celebritynews/news/pic-lady-gaga-poses-in-lingerie-looks-normal-2010252.

9 Florence King, *Southern Ladies and Gentlemen* (Macmillan, 1993), 179.

10 Telephone conversation with Mark Michaels and Patricia Johnson, October 19, 2010.

11 John Gottman and Nan Silver, *The Seven Principles for Making Marriage Work: A Practical Guide from the Country's Foremost Relationship Expert* (Three Rivers Press, 2000), 11.

12 "Descartes and the Pineal Gland," Stanford Encyclopedia of Philosophy, rev. November 5, 2008, http://plato.stanford.edu/entries/pineal-gland/.

13 "Of Serotonin and Spirituality," *Psychology Today*, July 8, 2008, http://www.psychologytoday.com/articles/200402/serotonin-and-spirituality.

14 "Is This Your Brain on God?" NPR, http://www.npr.org/templates/story/story.php?storyId=110997741.

15 Jim Holt, "Beyond Belief," review of *The God Delusion*, by Richard Dawkins, *New York Times*, October 22, 2006, http://www.nytimes.com/2006/10/22/books/review/Holt.t.html.

16 Conversation with Nadine Begin, August 12, 2010.

17 Nadine Begin, *Feed My Lambs, Feed My Sheep: The Meals and Memories of a Lifetime* (Prism Publications, 2009).

18 Thomas Moore, *The Soul of Sex: Cultivating Life as an Act of Love* (HarperCollins, 1998).

19 Objectùm-Sexuality Internationale, http://www.objectum-sexuality.org/.

20 *Strange Love: Married to the Eiffel Tower,* http://www.youtube.com/watch?v=yXlaS_jYBFQ&feature=related.

21 Email conversation with Erika Eiffel, July 21, 2010.

22 "The End of Divorce? Growing Numbers of People Marrying Inanimate Objects," *Discover*, April 13, 2009, http://blogs.discovermagazine.com/discoblog/2009/04/13/the-end-of-divorce-growing-numbers-of-people-marrying-inanimate-objects/.

EPILOGUE

1 Rick Nauert PhD, "Phone Reinforcement Improves Depression Care," PsychCentral, October 27, 2010, http://psychcentral.com/news/2010/10/27/phone-reinforcement-improves-depression-care/20201.html.